SERVING LATINO COMMUNITIES

A How-To-Do-It Manual for Librarians

Camila Alire
Orlando Archibeque

HOW-TO-DO-IT MANUALS
FOR LIBRARIANS

NUMBER 80

NEAL-SCHUMAN PUBLISHERS, INC.
New York, London

Published by Neal-Schuman Publishers, Inc.
100 Varick Street
New York, NY 10013

Printed and bound in the United States of America.

Library of Congress Cataloging-in-Publication Data

Alire, Camila A.
    Serving Latino communities : a how-to-do-it manual for librarians /
by Camila Alire and Orlando Archibeque.
        p.   cm.—(How-to-do-it manuals for librarians ; no. 80)
    Includes bibliographical references and index.
    ISBN 1-55570-276-7
    1. Hispanic Americans and libraries. 2. School libraries—United States.
3. Public libraries—Services to Hispanic Americans. I. Archibeque,
Orlando. II. Title. III. Series: How-to-do-it manuals for libraries ; no. 80.
Z711.8.A375   1998
027.6.'3—dc21   97–49203
                                                       CIP

CONTENTS

LIST OF FIGURES

PREFACE

The idea for writing *Serving Latino Communities: A How-To-Do-It Manual for Librarians* grew out of the desperation of a regional library system director in Colorado. Like many states, Colorado has regional library systems strategically located throughout the state. These systems are instrumental in providing consultative services to libraries in many rural, remote, and urban areas of Colorado.

The Southwest Regional Library System serves the portion of Colorado bordering northern New Mexico that is rich with Latino and Native American populations and cultural influences. The director of the system called to ask if we would develop a workshop for her system members addressing the need for library services to Latinos in the area. Not surprisingly, the Latino population in southwest Colorado definitely comprised the majority of the system's underserved population.

This director was very concerned that the libraries in her system develop services that address Latino information needs and that they reach out to the underserved Latino people in their communities. She explained that service was not necessarily lacking because the library staff refused to serve this underserved group, but because they had no idea how to initiate services for Latinos. Many times well-intentioned library staff have their hearts in the right place but are very insecure about developing services and programs for people who are culturally, ethnically, and racially different.

We jumped at the chance to develop such a workshop. It started in that system and has since been presented to five of Colorado's seven regional library systems. It also has been presented at the annual joint conference of the Colorado Library Association/ Mountain Plains Library Association.

Later on, we adapted the workshop to fit the concerns of school library media centers and presented it at the annual conference of the Colorado Educational Media Association. Word quickly spread about our workshops; we were invited to do out-of-state presentations at the 1994 national conference of the Public Library Association (PLA) and at the 1994 tri-conference of the Kansas Library Association, Kansas Association of School Librarians, and the Kansas Association for Educational Communications and Technology. It was at the PLA conference that we were encouraged by colleagues and publishers to share our workshop with other library staff in the country through the printed word. Voilà, this book!

Our research and information on library services for the Latino community have been augmented with visits to various libraries throughout the country that are noted for their integrated services to their Latino populations. We interviewed librarians in various libraries in New York City, Queens, Newark, Chicago, El Paso, Tucson, and various communities in California—Chula Vista, San Diego, San Ysidro, Fullerton, Santa Ana, Santa Monica, East Los Angeles, Oxnard, and Santa Barbara. Many practical ideas and program materials from these libraries are incorporated in this book. They have proven to be successful in attracting and keeping members of the Latino community as strong users of the library.

There is definitely a need to assist libraries contemplating reaching out to the underserved Latinos in their communities. The purpose of *Serving Latino Communities* is to expand the information we have gathered and share it with the rest of the country. This book provides a systematic, step-by-step process for library staff to use in their development of library services to underserved Latinos.

This manual is designed primarily for those public libraries that are serious about reaching all of their community residents. It is also intended for those small and medium-sized public libraries that are thinking about or beginning to plan services to Latinos. Much of the information contained in this book can also readily be adapted for school library media center personnel who are interested in this topic. More importantly, much of the book can be adapted for those public libraries and school library media centers wishing to provide services to their underserved minority communities—no matter their race or ethnicity.

Serving Latino Communities is organized to allow library staff to approach serving their underserved community systematically. Chapter 1 centers on introducing you to the Latino culture—it explains ethnic terminology used to describe this group and presents the Latino culture in the broadest sense.

Chapter 2 focuses primarily on the changing demographics of our nation's Latino population. This chapter begins to build an understanding of the Latino population that libraries will need in order to develop services to their underserved Latino population.

Chapter 3 explores the need for presenting various levels of decision-makers—boards of trustees, city councils, county commissioners, and the like—with a sound rationale for providing services to the Latino community. The rationale will also help when talking with library staff and other library users. It focuses on the use of local demographic data to support the library's position to expand its services to its underserved community. In addition, this chapter examines the use of other rationale—economic, political, children as users, and social responsibility—to support the library's efforts. The chapter covers the need for a library services paradigm shift and the importance of library policy statements on services to minorities.

Because the Latino community has traditionally fallen into the nonuser category, Chapter 4 discusses the need to know the Latino community. It centers on how to assess Latino information needs using such techniques as community surveys, interviews, and focus groups.

So what services and programs does a library consider offering to attract its underserved Latino population? Chapter 5 is one of the creative parts of this book. This chapter examines library services and programs that can be offered, focusing on examples of successful programs from libraries throughout the country.

The next obvious question is "How do we pay for new programs/services?" In Chapter 6 we examine the issues of internal funding and budgeting for proposed services to Latinos. We focus on external funding possibilities; we include some funding success stories, discuss grant writing, and present a sample proposal format. We also share innovative grant proposal ideas that have been successfully funded.

Chapter 7 addresses a related concern—staffing—which is problematic for many libraries. We discuss the realities libraries may face, such as an all-white staff and training that staff to be sensitive to ethnic and cultural differences. In addition, we address the recruitment of Latino professionals, paraprofessionals, volunteers, and trustees.

Chapter 8 can easily be summarized as partnerships, partnerships, and partnerships. This chapter explores the need for and the exciting possibilities of networking with external agencies and organizations, such as social services agencies, religious and church groups, and service clubs.

Chapter 9 provides guidance on starting a Latino collection. It offers practical advice for selectors and addresses some management issues, such as reviewing and revising collection development policies and practices. Additionally, it provides some ideas on how to improve access to the collection.

Everything else in place, how does a library attract its underserved Latino population to its facility? Outreach is absolutely critical, and in Chapter 10 we discuss the need for effective outreach and marketing/public relations. The chapter includes tips and examples of successful promotional materials from other libraries.

Because we wanted to provide as much assistance as possible,

Chapter 11 includes many resources we and others have found extremely helpful in efforts to provide library services to Latinos. This chapter includes our specific recommendations for publications, organizations, and Internet resources.

Real life will dictate that any library preparing for or beginning to offer library services to Latinos will meet challenges from all sides. With each chapter, we present possible challenges that a library must be prepared for when undertaking this venture. We would be remiss if we did not prepare the reader for these potential challenges.

Use this manual. It will help lessen the frustrations you might experience when embarking on your efforts to reach a vital, underserved population in your community. There are enough hints, tips, and examples to assist you in initiating this extremely important effort. The bottom line is to remember that what you are preparing to do is what our wonderful profession is all about—providing equal information access to all, regardless of ethnicity or race. This process includes reaching out to the underserved Latinos in your community.

ACKNOWLEDGMENTS

We want to thank Christina Fredrich, Andra Crull, and Mary Dodge for their assistance on this project. We give another round of thanks to all the dedicated librarians who were more than willing to share their expertise and successes. A special acknowledgement goes to our families (Janet, Alan, and our parents, Molly and J. R. Archibeque, and Mary and the late Joe Alire) for their continual support and understanding of our efforts and commitment.

1 THE LATINO COMMUNITY: A GROWING CLIENTELE

CHALLENGE

Martha: *I'm a little bit nervous about the first adult program I'm offering this week for our Latino community. We have 35 people signed up, which is more than we ever expected!*

Ivonne: *That's exciting, but why are you nervous?*

Martha: *Well, I know their culture is different than mine, and I don't want to say or do something that could possibly offend anyone attending.*

For the most part, library and information services have been geared to persons who felt more comfortable in utilizing them, who approached them with a background of education and literacy, and who were, for the most part, book-oriented members of the middle and upper class. By contrast, members of society who lack an adequate education, who are the "informationally-deprived," and who consist of a fair number of cultural minorities, frequently have been unaware of the services available to them at their local library or unconvinced that such services would be of any benefit to them. For whatever reason, they have not been a part of the library's clientele.[1]

Because Latinos have not traditionally been a part of the public library's clientele, we want to introduce you to our community. It is important that you know the basic elements of this underserved community. Learning these elements is no different from learning about any new, nontraditional clientele. For example, if a large senior residential complex was built in your service area, it would have a significant impact on your community's population and tax base, and you would have to prepare your library to attract and serve those senior residents.

Serving this new senior clientele with a different outlook and tradition, varying socioeconomic backgrounds, and special information needs would be a challenge for your library. You and your staff would be busy learning all you could learn about the senior citizen culture in general—values, attitudes, needs, and so forth. The same process applies to your discovering the Latino community.

Since much confusion can result from the many terms used when referring to this cultural group, we thought it necessary to discuss ethnic terminology in this chapter. We also provide a general flavor for the Latino culture and traditions.

TERMINOLOGY

The single most important lesson to learn in this section is that no universally accepted term describes the incredibly diverse population that is the focus of this book. For the overall population, the most popular terms currently in use are Latinos, Hispanics, Hispanic-Americans and Spanish-speaking. As you will see later, each smaller cultural group within the larger umbrella group has its own terms to describe itself.

For libraries and other service-oriented organizations, the variety of terms can be problematic. As employees of successful service-oriented organizations that strive to be responsible, helpful, culturally sensitive, and responsive to users, librarians don't want to offend someone unintentionally by using the wrong term. So naturally, we, as caring individuals, take cues about the right words to use from the minority group members themselves. The problem is that there is little agreement as to terminology within the Latino community. In this section we will describe the most popular terms and indicate our own personal preferences and the reasons for our choices.

Why are there so many terms for this group? Why can't there be just one universally accepted term that everyone can use? In answering this question, it may help to remember that this is not a new phenomenon. For example, we saw (and continue to see) a variety of terms used in the black community; many of the terms came about during the civil rights movement when feelings of black pride changed the way many African Americans thought and felt about themselves. New terms like Afro-Americans, blacks, African Americans, and so forth, came into existence as individuals in black communities redefined their identities based on the new realities or expanded visions of their lives. Accordingly, some terms came into vogue, some remained, some changed meaning, some were adopted by certain members, and some terms that were originally imposed from outside the black population were totally rejected by others. No one term could encompass all the variations in life experience. Because the life experience for blacks in this country has changed so dramatically since the civil rights movement, so too have the terms used to describe this population.

Because people's lives are always changing and because language is always evolving, many terms may be used at any one time. Ethnic terminology is in a constant state of flux because of individual self-examination, group identification, and personal preference. The term that a person of color uses to refer to himself or herself is a very personal, intimate choice. This term may change several times during the person's lifetime as this individual examines and reexamines his or her own identity.

This pattern is currently taking place within the Latino community. As individuals reexamine and redefine their identities based on new realities or hoped-for possibilities, new words and phrases are on their way in. They coexist with other more established terms that may be on the way out. Terms that may have been *imposed* from the outside may give way to terms of choice. From the title of our book, it is apparent that we prefer to use Latino to describe the population that is the focus of this book. What follows is a brief explanation of this term and our rationale for choosing it.

Hispanic and Latino are the two most prevalent ethnic terms in use today. They are similar in that both terms refer to the composite group that includes individuals from a wide variety of culturally related, though distinct, groups. Both terms are broadly interpreted to include individuals with Spanish-language or Spanish-heritage backgrounds from the Americas (American Southwest, Mexico, and Central and South America); the Caribbean areas with Spanish influence (primarily the Dominican Republic, Puerto Rico, and Cuba); and Spain.

While both terms are attempts to describe the same population, the terms can be, but are not necessarily, quite different in attitude. One obvious and major difference is that Hispanic is obviously an English word while Latino is a Spanish word meaning Latin, as in Latin America. Another major difference between the terms has to do with the issue of acculturation. Very generally speaking, Hispanic tends to connote acceptance of majority cultural values, integration into the majority culture, and political traditionalism; while Latino tends to connote the acceptance, preservation, and promotion of a unique cultural heritage, and political activism. A third major difference is that the terms emphasize different racial and cultural backgrounds. Individuals who use Hispanic generally are emphasizing European Spanish heritage, while those who use Latino are acknowledging and celebrating indigenous or mestizo (mixed European and Indian) backgrounds.

The tendencies noted here are just that—very broad generalizations. There are always exceptions. To complicate matters a bit, there are regional differences in the choice of terms: Latino seems to be gaining popularity on the east and west coasts and in major urban centers, while Hispanic (or the Spanish *Hispano*) tends to be the preferred term in many areas of the American Southwest.

There are also generational differences to consider. Most young adults, for example, may prefer the term Latino. As an example, the music that is increasing in popularity today is referred to as Latino music, never Hispanic music. Generally speaking, older generations may not be comfortable with the term Latino. Thus, within the same family there can be a variety of terms used with parents and grandparents using Spanish or Hispanic and adolescents using Latino.

One other term, Spanish-speaking, seems to be on its way out. This term was popular during the late 1960s and early 1970s, and many organizations created then used it in their official names. An example in the library field is the national organization REFORMA, founded in 1971, and originally referred to as the National Association of Spanish-Speaking Librarians in the United States. Its subtitle was changed in 1984 to National Association to Promote Library Services to the Spanish-Speaking. It would not be surprising if, at some time in the future, REFORMA would change its subtitle to reflect more popular terminology.

Up to this point, we have only addressed the multiplicity of pan-ethnic terms that attempt to describe a very large, composite group. In addition to these terms, other terms refer to specific cultural groups within this larger population. Among Latinos, there are three major cultural groups: Mexican Americans, Cuban Americans, and Puerto Ricans. However, in addition to these three cultures, the United States has recently experienced a large number of immigrants (both documented and undocumented) from Central America, South America, and the Caribbean. Individuals from each of these many cultural groups can and do use a number of different terms to refer to themselves. It is not necessary for us to provide all the terms here for all the various Latino cultural groups.

We can illustrate this multiplicity of terms within a cultural group by examining the terminology used by one such group, those with a Mexican heritage. One finds a variety of terms to describe this population: Chicano, Mexicano, Mexican American, and Hispano, to name the most popular ones. There is no one universally accepted term. Usage may vary from one region to another, from one generation to another, and from one income class to another. As previously mentioned, there may even be variation within the same family. The same is true for each of the cultural groups noted above; there will always be a number of terms for each distinct group.

For both practical and philosophical reasons, when referring to the overall larger population group, we use the term Latino. For practical reasons, it would be too difficult to refer to Latinos/Hispanics/Spanish-speaking/Hispanic Americans; so we decided to settle on one term. We also have philosophical reasons for choosing this term. It is a self-chosen term that is gaining in popularity, especially along both coasts and in larger urban centers, and it is increasingly being used by youth and by those who acknowledge and emphasize their indigenous and mestizo backgrounds. Occasionally we may have to use the term Hispanic, because of its use in official census publications. When referring to the current majority population in this country, we use the term white.

To summarize, there are two broad categories of terms with which you should be familiar. First, several ethnic terms are used when referring to the entire Latino population. Second, other terms are used when referring to specific cultural groups within the Latino population. None of these terms enjoys universal acceptance among people within the Latino community. The usage of a specific term reflects a personal choice that may change over one's lifetime. Our choice, for both practical and philosophical reasons, is to use the term Latino.

There is one challenge for any person who is sensitive to and respects the differences of others. That difficult challenge is trying not to offend others. In the case of ethnic terminology, the potential problem lies in using a different term from the one used by a Latino individual. We want to offer you a few hints on how to handle this.

First of all, if you are unsure about the terminology to use for the Latino group you have in your community, we recommend that you ask one of your formal or informal Latino leaders. If you have Latino friends or acquaintances, ask them what they prefer being called.

Also, check the media. If you have a local or area newspaper or radio station, pay attention to the ethnic terminology they use. You can bet that if they use the wrong term, someone will set them straight.

If you have several Latino subgroups, we suggest you do the same. Let's say you know that your community has residents who are second- and third-generation Mexican American. Most recently, your community has also experienced an influx of Salvadoran and Guatemalan immigrants. It is important to ask representatives from each Latino subgroup what ethnic term they prefer. More than likely, they will use either Latino or Hispanic, or they will choose a term that applies only to their specific cultural background.

Second, we must accept that we all make mistakes. If you or a staff member uses the wrong term, and someone informs you that he or she is not Hispanic, Latino, or whatever, then apologize and ask the individual what he or she prefers being called.

Third, inform your staff about the terminology preferred by your Latino residents and *why*. Our suggestions are not necessarily to make you politically correct but to ensure that your Latino customers will return to the library.

We offer one last piece of advice for you and your staff. Body language and tone of voice are very important when addressing anyone. Consequently, remember two points. You basically want your underserved Latinos to enter a new and different establishment—your library—which is perceived as a traditionally white institution. Understand that they will come with some apprehension. Also, you want your new Latino users to be return customers. So how your library personnel treat them and interact with them will be important.

THE LATINO CULTURAL AND SOCIAL FRAMEWORK

> Latino culture is a lens through which the hardships and contradictions of our long journey from Latin America and the Caribbean ought to be pondered. We come with a set bag of archetypes, a difficult view of our collective past and a hopeful sense of the future.[2]

Having discussed the complexity of terminology in the previous section, we find it equally challenging to describe the Latino cultural and social framework. The Latino culture consists of that bag of collective prototypes, each belonging to a specific subculture. For example, the Mexican American subculture is somewhat different from the subculture of Latinos of Puerto Rican descent which is different from the Guatemalan subculture, and so forth. There are cultural differences in food, dance, some music, and/or Spanish-language colloquialisms. For example, Spanglish—the combination of Spanish and English words to form new words or expressions—is probably more dominant in the Mexican and Mexican American culture.

The similarities among the Latino subgroups are greater than the differences. What are the similarities within the Latino subgroups? It is important for you to understand the overall Latino culture. The Spanish language is one commonality. Even if a Latino in this country grows up monolingual in English, that does not deny the historical and cultural importance of the Spanish language for that person.

Another commonality is the role of religion in Latino culture. Not all Latinos are Catholics, but many have either been raised Catholic or come from families that have a historical affiliation with Catholicism. Regardless of religious affiliation, Latinos tend to have a strong religious background.

From a social perspective, you need to know about other common elements among Latinos. First of all, *la familia* (the family) is a very important social institution. The nuclear family—husband, wife, children, grandparents—is responsible for childrearing, in general. There is also an extended family that includes all the other relatives who provide an important economic and social support system. Consequently, you may find different members of the family, not always the mother, bringing Latino children into your library.

Latino families, generally, are hierarchical, with the male being the dominant and authoritarian figure and the female maintaining the major role of childrearing and being the more nurturing parent. Even among today's generation of Latinos where the female may work outside the home, the hierarchical structure prevails.

Because many two-parent Latino families have both parents working, the patriarchal role of the father is now considered more of a value and/or belief. That is, in the past, the respect of the Latino father was based more on his being the breadwinner and protector. However, with the Latino mother working today, the matriarchal role, in reality, has increased in everyday life. She not only maintains the role of childrearing but also has become one of the two breadwinners.

With the Latino male traditionally being the authority, don't be surprised if Latino family members act differently when they visit the library with the father than when they are in the library without him. When the entire family visits the library, respect demonstrated to the father will go a long way toward making the family feel welcomed and valued.

Another important trait in the Latino culture is *machismo*. Although many Latinos would consider the macho Latino to be more stereotypical than real, machismo is still prevalent today much to the chagrin of some more-liberated Latinas. Latino males are stereotypically depicted as demonstrating excessive aggression and sexual vigor, and having little regard for some women.[3] However, machismo also historically and traditionally connotes bravery, courage, and protection of and respect for family. This goes hand in hand with the male as the dominant figure.

Also within the Latino culture is the practice of *compadrazgo*, which literally means a strong co-parent; what it really means is a social practice where very close family friends, *compadres,* are considered to be important members of the Latino family. Compadres generally can have a socioeconomic influence on the family, such as childrearing, finances, and religion. Additionally, *compadre* is a term of endearment.

CONCLUSION

We have provided you with a flavor of the cultural and social characteristics of Latinos, along with ethnic terminology considerations. This succinct cultural portrait of Latinos lays the foundation for the rest of the book. If you didn't know much about Latinos, you now have a basic head start in understanding the vibrant Latino culture.

We strongly recommend that you learn more about the Latinos in your community. Since Latinos come from such diverse backgrounds, you need to determine which subcultures are in your community. For example, the New Americans Project at the Queens Public Library probably serves almost every Latino subgroup (and its respective subculture) that arrives in this country. That is definitely a challenge! Even the small community in Kansas, which is experiencing an influx of Latino immigrants from more than one Latin American country, has its challenge.

NOTES

1. National Commission on Library and Information Services, *Report of the Task Force on Library and Information Services to Cultural Minorities* (Washington, D.C.: U.S. Government Printing Office, 1983), 1.
2. Ilan Stavans, *The Hispanic Condition: Reflections of Culture and Identity in America* (New York: Harper Collins, 1995), 190.
3. Stavans, *The Hispanic Condition*, 109.

2 WHY LIBRARY SERVICES TO LATINOS?

CHALLENGE

Ed: *We have such a large Latino population in our community; I wonder why they don't use our library. Shouldn't we think about developing some programs or services for them?*

Susan: *Why should we bother developing anything when they don't use the library anyway?*

John: *Maybe Ed has a good point. I was just reviewing the new census data for our city and county. Did you know that in the last ten years the Latino population alone increased by 23 percent? My daughter mentioned the other day that many Latino kids in her class primarily speak Spanish.*

Here is a prime example of "what comes first, the chicken or the egg?" Why should you try to attract and serve Latinos or any underserved minority in your community? You know they are not library users.

One of the great tenets of our profession is that libraries should provide equal access to information for all people. We can serve as a role model for other institutions by trying to reach all people with our services.

As important, the demographics of this country are quickly changing, revealing a very diverse population. Businesses, government agencies, and nonprofit organizations rely on this country's demographic data to analyze trends and to help them make strategic decisions concerning the development of products and services for customers of the future. Libraries should be no different.

According to Webster's, demography is defined as the "statistical study of populations." Demographers use statistics or data to ascertain the characteristics of a population. When doing this, they look for any patterns of change within that population and then make future projections based on those changes.

As information professionals, we need to look at Latino demographic data to search for patterns of change that affect our libraries and the services we will provide in the future. The demographic information in this chapter will assist you in understanding why libraries with a service area that includes the Latino community should proactively develop outreach services to raise the status of the underserved Latino community from information-poor to information-rich.

LATINO DEMOGRAPHICS

The major demographic and socioeconomic statistics that provide an overview of Latinos in the United States are highlighted in this section. The data presented here come primarily from the 1990 census and from recent projections provided by the U.S. Bureau of the Census.[1]

A few words about terminology are in order. Since the Census Bureau used the term Hispanic for the 1990 census (and will continue to do so for the 2000 census), the term Latino does not appear anywhere in any official census publications. Consequently, there are no official government statistics on Latinos. In keeping with our preferred terminology, we will substitute the Latino term for the United States government's officially accepted Hispanic term. We should state up front that demographers would probably cringe at such a substitution. Fortunately, our purpose here is not to be 100% in line with government terms, but to highlight demographic and socioeconomic factors and trends that impact delivery of library services, programs, and materials to Latinos.

THE GROWING LATINO POPULATION

Latinos are already a large segment of the American population with rapid growth projected to continue well into the 21st century. The 1990 census showed that there were 22.4 million Latinos in the United States, totaling approximately 9% of the American population. This means that nearly one of 11 United States residents is of Latino background. Population growth rates in recent years have been very high. Between 1980 and 1990, the number of Latinos grew by an amazing 53%, which is approximately seven times the growth rate for the general population! The Census Bureau recently estimated that in 1995, the number of Latinos increased to 26.9 million, which translates to a 20.1% increase between the years 1990 and 1995.

The Bureau of the Census periodically issues a number of forecasts for various racial and ethnic groups. If the Bureau's mid-range projections are correct, there will be approximately 31.3 million Latinos in the year 2000. Latinos will become the largest minority group in the United States by the year 2010, outnumbering the African American population 41 million to 40.1 million. By the year 2030 there will be 65 million Latinos, growing to 96 million by mid-century. By 2050 Latinos will make up 25.7% of the total United States population. This fast-growing segment of the population is already having and will continue to have a dramatic impact on libraries and other service agencies providing services to Latinos.

When you combine this large and growing Latino population with the very high population growth rate among the Asian/Pacific Islanders (which experienced a 50% increase between the years 1980 and 1990), the already large African American population (12.3% of the total United States resident population in 1990), and a significant number of Native Americans, it is easy to see why the word minority is quickly becoming outdated and being replaced by the term emerging majority. It is estimated that people of color will make up the majority of the American population sometime around the middle of the 21st century.

DISTINCT LATINO SUBGROUPS

Latinos come from culturally related but distinct groups. The cultural diversity within this population is astounding, sometimes even bewildering to Latinos themselves.

Figure 2–1 shows that three cultural groups (Mexican, Puerto Rican, and Cuban) make up nearly 80% of the total Latino population. A little over 61% of Latinos are from Mexican backgrounds. Puerto Ricans and Cubans are the second and third largest groups, making up 12.1% and 4.8% of Latinos, respectively. Dominicans are another major cultural group, accounting for 2.4% of all Latinos.

Six percent of Latinos are from Central American backgrounds. This Central American category includes Salvadorans, Guatemalans, Nicaraguans, Hondurans, Panamanians, and Costa Ricans.

South Americans make up 4.7% of Latinos. This South American category includes Colombians, Ecuadorians, Peruvians, Argentinians, and Chileans.

Planning library services for Latinos who may come from quite different cultural backgrounds will be a significant challenge. It will be particularly challenging to public libraries in the medium-sized to large urban centers, where Latino populations are more likely to be heterogeneous.

THE YOUNG LATINO POPULATION

Latinos are younger than the general population. The 1990 census shows that the Latino population has a higher proportion of young adults and children than the general population. Nearly 40% of Latinos are under 20, compared with 28% for the general population. Recently released Census Bureau figures indicate that Latino preschoolers (those under five years of age) now outnumber their African American counterparts. Clearly, children's services librarians, school library media specialists, and young-adult (YA) librarians will need to respond creatively to this large and rapidly growing segment of the Latino population.

Figure 2–1. Latino Populations

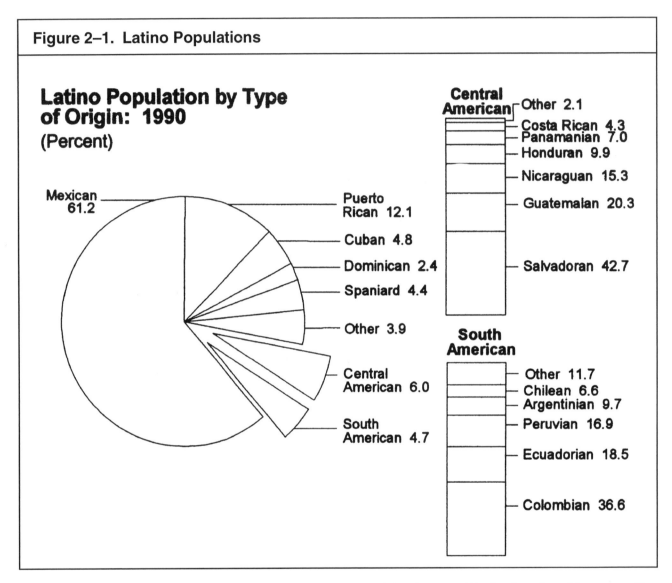

Latino Population by Type of Origin: 1990
(Percent)

Mexican 61.2

Puerto Rican 12.1

Cuban 4.8

Dominican 2.4

Spaniard 4.4

Other 3.9

Central American 6.0

South American 4.7

Central American

Other 2.1
Costa Rican 4.3
Panamanian 7.0
Honduran 9.9
Nicaraguan 15.3
Guatemalan 20.3
Salvadoran 42.7

South American

Other 11.7
Chilean 6.6
Argentinian 9.7
Peruvian 16.9
Ecuadorian 18.5
Colombian 36.6

Source: Adapted from a chart that appears in: U.S. Bureau of the Census, *We the American Hispanics*. Prepared by the Ethnic and Hispanic Statistics Branch, Population Division, Bureau of the Census. Washington, D.C., 1993, 4.

LATINO EDUCATIONAL ATTAINMENT

The educational attainment of Latinos lags behind that of the general population. While Latinos have made great strides in educational attainment over the last 20-odd years, there is still much progress to be made. As evidence of improvement, in 1970 less than one-third of Latinos ages 25 years and over completed at least four years of high school; the 1990 census shows that about half of those Latinos 25 and over at least completed high school. Further evidence of improvements can be seen in the awarding of college degrees to Latinos. The 1990 census shows that 9.2% of Latinos ages 25 years and over completed four years or more of college. Though still low when compared to non-Latinos (21.2% completed four or more years of college), this is a significant improvement from 1970, when only 4.5% of Latinos 25 years and over completed four years or more of college. Though educational attainment levels among Latinos are improving, there are still significant and disturbing differences in educational attainment between Latinos and non-Latinos. Nearly half (49.8%) of Latinos in 1990 had at least a high school diploma, compared with 77.2% of the non-Latino population.

LATINO POVERTY STATUS

Poverty is a fact of life for a significant number of Latino families. One million Latino families (22.3% of all Latino families) were living in poverty in 1990. This rate is more than double the poverty rate for non-Latino families (less than 10%). Eighteen percent of Latino children (under 18) lived in poverty in 1990. Latino women and the elderly have disturbingly high poverty rates when compared with the population in general. In 1990 27% of Latino women lived in poverty compared with 13% of non-Latinos. Elderly Latinos (24%) are twice as likely as non-Latinos (12%) to live in poverty.

The 1990 statistics on median income (using 1989 dollars) also show a disturbing picture. The median income for all American families in 1990 was $35,225. For Latino families the median income was $25,064. For Latino families headed by a female with no husband present (approximately 22% of all Latino families), the median income plummeted to $12,406.

Since the poverty levels are so high and the income levels are so low for Latinos, it should come as no surprise that employment patterns vary significantly between Latinos and non-Latinos. Here are but a few statistics from 1990 to illustrate these labor force disparities:

- 28% of Latino adult males work as operators, fabricators, and laborers, compared with 19% of non-Latino males.
- 24% of Latino adult females are employed in service occupations, compared with 17% of non-Latino females.

- Only 17% of Latino adult females are employed in managerial or professional positions, compared with 25% of non-Latino females.
- Only 12% of Latino males held management and professional jobs, while 27% of non-Latino adult males held such positions.

NATIVE-BORN LATINOS

A majority of Latinos are native-born. The 1990 census indicates that a very large majority (64%) of Latinos are born in the United States. An additional 10% of Latinos are foreign-born, naturalized citizens. The remaining 26% of Latinos are foreign-born, noncitizens.

THE CHANGING LATINO MOSAIC

Why is there such a large percentage of foreign-born, noncitizens (26%)? This fact is due partly to undocumented immigration, and partly to the relatively recent and large numbers of Latino immigrants—many of these recent arrivals have not had time to go through the normal naturalization process. Almost four million foreign-born Latinos (or half of all 7.8 million foreign-born Latinos) arrived in the United States between the years 1980 and 1990. There were approximately 1.6 million immigrants from Mexico and 160,000 from Cuba during this decade. It was also during this time that large numbers of Dominicans and Central and South Americans began to immigrate to the United States. Although immigrants came from these regions in previous decades, the numbers have dramatically increased since 1980.

By 1990 there were 565,000 Salvadorans, 500,000 Dominicans, nearly 400,000 Colombians, 260,000 Guatemalans, 200,000 Nicaraguans, 190,000 Ecuadorians, 175,000 Peruvians, 131,000 Hondurans, and 100,000 Argentinians residing in this country. When combined with the already large and still growing numbers of Latinos of Mexican, Puerto Rican, and Cuban origin, these new arrivals helped to create a true Latino mosaic in this country.

USE OF SPANISH AND ENGLISH LANGUAGES

The 1990 census shows that about 78% of Latinos speak Spanish at home. But this statistic presents only part of the language picture. Half of all Latinos that speak Spanish at home report that they speak English very well. Consequently, a fairly large number of Latinos are bilingual, which presents some challenges (and some opportunities!) for libraries providing services and collections for this population.

CONCLUSION

The national data presented in this chapter present a very complex portrait of Latinos in the United States. This rapidly growing segment of the population is made up of a variety of culturally related, though distinct groups. When compared to the general population, Latinos are significantly younger, are disproportionately represented in lower income groups, have a relatively high level of bilingualism, and lag behind the general population with respect to educational attainment. The complex portrait presented here is certainly quite a challenge for public libraries involved in developing services and collections for Latinos.

A word of advice—when you look at data like these, it is tempting to simplify things by focusing solely on the population segment that is highlighted instead of examining the full range of the entire Latino community's needs. For example, we have seen that the Latino population is generally younger than the population as a whole, so a seemingly rational strategy for public libraries would be to funnel huge amounts of resources into children's services and collections. However, to do so would neglect the needs of Latino youths and adults. Similarly, since 78% of Latinos speak Spanish at home, it might be tempting to put all of a library's resources into Spanish-language materials, but this approach would neglect the needs of a very large number of individuals seeking bilingual or English-language materials. As is the case with most things in life, balance is the key!

NOTES

1.   U.S. Bureau of the Census, *Census of Population: Persons of Hispanic Origin in the United States*, prepared by the Economics and Statistics Administration, Department of Commerce (Washington, D.C.: U.S. Government Printing Office, 1993); U.S. Bureau of the Census, *Current Population Reports: Population Projections of the United States by Age, Sex, Race, and Hispanic Origin: 1995 to 2050*, prepared by the Economics and Statistics Administration, Department of Commerce (Washington, D.C.: U.S. Government Printing Office, 1996); U.S. Bureau of the Census, *We the American Hispanics*, prepared by Ethnic and Hispanic Statistics Branch, Population Division, Bureau of the Census (Washington, D.C.: U.S. Government Printing Office, 1993).

3 A PLACE TO START: BUILDING YOUR RATIONALE

CHALLENGE

Shirley:	*Since we proposed developing some services to attract Latinos in our community, I've met with some opposition from others concerning the library not having enough resources to support those services. Some people think the library's doing just fine to meet the needs of our regular users from the community. They just don't understand the need to reach out to Latino residents, most of whom they say don't even live near the library.*
Maria:	*I think we need to be proactive and be prepared to respond to those concerns. We need to develop a sound rationale based not on emotional reasoning but on philosophical and intellectual reasoning. I know we can convince our staff and the board of trustees if we do our homework and prepare some good, solid reasons for developing and extending these services to our Latino residents.*

It is important to recognize that providing library services and collections tailored to the needs of Hispanic residents is not a supplemental service, but part of the natural function of any library serving a multicultural community.[1]

This statement seems like common sense, but the reality of trying to provide services to the underserved Latinos in your community demonstrates that it is easier said than done. Most of you have already determined that something has to be done to provide library services for Latinos in your community. Having realized that is the first step in meeting the challenge ahead of you. The bigger challenge is convincing your library staff, board of trustees, government officials, and sometimes the general public that library resources—human, time, and financial—need to be expended to reach out and serve your Latino community. For most, this will not be an easy task. It is our purpose in this chapter to provide a framework to help you defend your position of service. Using the tips provided, you will need to add the necessary local information that best supports and complements your position. We also provide a framework for organizing your presentation.

We have already presented in Chapter 2 some national demographic data about Latinos. Obtaining and using more pertinent local data coupled with presenting a strong rationale is the place to start. Since attitudes will not change overnight and because you are committed to serving your entire community, you will find yourself repeating your data and rationale over and over. It will become second nature to present and/or defend to any audience your position to serve Latinos in your community. Good for you!

DEMOGRAPHICS AND YOUR RATIONALE

As a planner of library services, you already know how important demographic data are. In this section, we will give you step-by-step instructions on how and where to obtain local Latino demographic data easily from the U.S. Census Bureau. Of course, obtaining all the data in the world will not help much if the data just sit on the shelf. But if it is relatively easy to obtain the data, you should have more time to analyze and understand what you find, and you will benefit in a number of ways:

- You will gain a better understanding of your target Latino audience.
- You will be better prepared to identify and define your goals.
- You will be better prepared to develop strategies to meet Latino user needs.
- Most important, you will be able to demonstrate to others (staff, the community in general, and funding authorities) that there is a need for your library to initiate or improve library services to Latinos.

If we were limited to recommending only one Census Bureau series of publications, we would recommend the *Social and Economic Characteristics* series.[2] In this series (also known as the CP-2 series) you will find a summary volume for the United States as a whole, and separate volumes for each state, the District of Columbia, Puerto Rico, and the Virgin Islands. We highly recommend this series because it contains the most useful information in one place; it is very well known to reference librarians; and, most likely, it is already in your local collection. Small public libraries will probably have only the volume covering their state. However, larger public libraries should have many volumes covering other states, and regional depository libraries will have the entire collection. If you do not have the appropriate volumes covering your geographic area, we strongly recommend that you order them because they provide very detailed and useful demographic information.

For the 1990 census, most households received a short questionnaire asking for basic information, such as age, race, marital status, and housing value (or rent). Since there is a need for much more detailed demographic and socioeconomic information, the Census Bureau developed a method to ascertain more information. A much smaller number of households (nearly one out of every six households) received a detailed questionnaire with additional questions about income, occupation, and housing costs. Some of the data published in this *Social and Economic Characteristics* series are based not on the 100% count but rather on this smaller sample of households. Therefore, some of the data presented are subject to the usual sampling variability errors. Fortunately, our purpose here is not to be 100% accurate; we are primarily interested in the highlights.

Before we get into the specifics, a quick word about terminology is appropriate. The Bureau of the Census uses the term Hispanic. When referring to a specific table title within this Bureau of the Census publication, we will also use this term. However, in keeping with our chosen terminology, we will use the term Latino in all other instances.

We also need to clarify some Census Bureau terminology pertaining to race and origin. Question number 4 of the 1990 census questionnaire asked respondents to choose one of five racial backgrounds: White, Black or Negro, American Indian or Eskimo or Aleut, Asian or Pacific Islander (with ten suboptions), and Other Race. Since Latino was not an option, each Latino respondent had to choose the option that seemed to be the best match. Reflecting the diversity within the Latino community, the 1990 census revealed that there were Latinos in each of these five racial categories.

Since Latinos can be of any race, and since the Census Bureau needed a way to capture data on Latinos (which the Bureau refers to as of "Spanish/Hispanic origin"), there was an additional question on the census questionnaire pertaining to origin. Each respondent was asked if he or she was of "Spanish/Hispanic origin."

With these two race and origin questions on the questionnaire, the Census Bureau was able to report census data for the different races, for "Hispanic origin," and for each race minus "Hispanic origin."

What does this all mean? Mostly it means that the Census Bureau has many difficulties when it comes to collecting and reporting data broken down by race. It also means that you have to exercise caution when examining such data.

A typical census table that provides data broken down by race or origin will have many different race/origin categories such as "White", "Hispanic", "White, Not of Hispanic Origin", "Black", "Black, Not of Hispanic Origin", "Asian or Pacific Islander", "Asian or Pacific Islander, Not of Hispanic Origin", et cetera. Good examples of this categorization appear in Figures 3–1 and 3–2 which we will discuss later.

In 1990 census publications "White" refers to all individuals (including Latinos) who chose "White" as their race. The Census Bureau term for whites who are not of Latino origin (or who would typically be called white by the average person) is "White, Not of Hispanic Origin."

It's a bit confusing, but if you remember that Latinos can be of any race, you'll soon be a master at understanding census data broken down by race or origin.

SPECIFIC AND USEFUL CENSUS TABLES

Each volume in the *Social and Economic Characteristics* series is divided into some 234 individual tables, which obviously can be intimidating to novice users. Fortunately, only a few of these tables provide data on Latinos, so we can concentrate our efforts only on those that are most appropriate.

Once you have the appropriate state (or district or territory) volume in hand, the rest is relatively easy. We are providing a step-by-step guide for obtaining the most useful data, using data extracted from selected tables to illustrate. Appendix A at the end of this chapter presents a demographics worksheet that can be photocopied and later filled in with the appropriate data from your service area.

Step 1: Obtain data on the size of the Latino population, relative to other groups in your service area.

Use the following tables that provide the data

For a county:	Table 6
For a city:	Table 7

Each of these tables is called "Race and Hispanic Origin: 1990." Tables 6 and 7, covering counties and places/county subdivisions, respectively, are especially important tables regarding Latinos. Each table is divided into six individually titled segments. The segments titled "Race and Hispanic Origin," "Percent Distribution by Race," and "Percent Distribution by Hispanic Origin," will provide the data you need.

Figure 3–1 provides data from Table 6 for Pueblo County, Colorado. The table shows that 35.7% of Pueblo's total population is of Hispanic origin, that is, Latino. Since this figure is well above the national average of 9%, it is a strong

Figure 3-1. Census Data on Population By Race

Table 6.   Race and Hispanic Origin: 1990

Pueblo County, Colorado

RACE AND HISPANIC ORIGIN

All persons	123,051
White	104,312
Hispanic origin	28,740
Not of Hispanic Origin	75,572
Black	2,111
Hispanic origin	178
Not of Hispanic Origin	1,933
American Indian, Eskimo, Aleut	1,044
Hispanic origin	356
Not of Hispanic Origin	688
Asian or Pacific Islander	839
Hispanic origin	93
Not of Hispanic Origin	746
Other Race	14,745
Hispanic origin	14,600
Not of Hispanic Origin	145

PERCENT DISTRIBUTION BY RACE

All persons	100.0
White	84.8
Black	1.7
American Indian, Eskimo, Aleut	.8
American Indian	.8
Asian or Pacific Islander	.7
Asian	.6
Pacific Islander	.1
Other Race	12.0

PERCENT DISTRIBUTION BY HISPANIC ORIGIN

All persons	100.0
Hispanic origin (of any race)	35.7
Mexican	23.7
Puerto Rican	.3
Cuban	——
Other Hispanic	11.7
Not of Hispanic origin	64.3

Source: U.S. Bureau of the Census. 1990 Census of Population, Social and Economic Characteristics: Colorado.
Prepared by Economics and Statistics Administration, Department of Commerce, Washington, D.C., 1993.

indicator that Latinos in Pueblo should be provided specialized collections and services. Also, notice in this table that there are Latinos in all five racial categories. The "Other Race" category is particularly interesting because it shows that nearly everyone (14,600 out of 14,745) who selected this option is Latino.

Step 2: **Obtain specific information on the origin of individuals within the Latino community.**

Use the following tables that provide the data

For a county:	Table 6
For a city:	Table 7

As we saw in the previous chapter, the Latino community is a heterogeneous group. Use Table 6 or Table 7 again, but this time use the segment titled "Hispanic Origin." This segment of the table provides population figures for the individual subcultures within the Latino community in your service area. Figure 3–2 is a sample illustration from Table 7, providing data for the city of Miramar, Florida. Although Miramar is a small community (40,663), its Latino community is quite diverse. In fact, there are 16 Latino subgroups in Miramar, Florida! Libraries that serve such diverse Latino communities need to develop programs and collections to serve all the Latino subcultures in their service areas.

For example, the library could celebrate some of the national holidays celebrated by the immigrants from different Latin American and Caribbean regions. A list and description of those national holidays is included in Chapter 5, Appendix A.

Step 3: **Obtain data on the age distribution within the Latino community in your service area.**

Use the following tables that provide the data

For a county:	Table 151
For a place of 10,000 or more:	Table 180

As a planner of library services, you understand the usefulness of knowing the age distribution within your service area. Use Table 151 (for counties) or Table 180 (for larger communities) to find specific data on the number of Latinos in your service area that fall into each of the 17 cohorts ranging from "Under 3 years" to "75 years and over." To find such data for smaller communities (2,500–9,999), consult the appropriate state volume from a companion census se-

Figure 3-2. Census Data on Latino Subcultures

Table 7.   Race and Hispanic Origin: 1990

Miramar, Florida

ALL PERSONS	40,663
Hispanic origin (of any race)	6,712
Mexican	266
Puerto Rican	2,163
Cuban	1,745
Other Hispanic	2,538
Dominican (Domincan Republic)	414
Central American	414
Costa Rican	37
Guatemalan	4
Honduran	60
Nicaraguan	31
Panamanian	264
Salvadoran	4
Other Central American	14
South American	1,345
Argentinean	10
Chilean	31
Colombian	630
Ecuadorian	293
Peruvian	238
Venezuelan	37
Other South American	106
All other Hispanic	365
Not of Hispanic origin	33,951

Source: U.S. Bureau of the Census. 1990 Census of Population, Social and Economic Characteristics: Florida. Prepared by Economics and Statistics Administration, Department of Commerce, Washington, D.C., 1993.

ries called the *1990 Census of Population: General Population Characteristics*;[3] Table 68 ("Age and Sex by Race and Hispanic Origin") provides the needed data.

For example, Figure 3–3 shows data extracted from Table 180 for Dodge City, Kansas, a community of 21,129. Note the large number of Latinos under the age of five. In communities like these, libraries can support the Latino community by developing a wide range of children's and parenting programs.

Figure 3-3. Census Data on Age Distribution

Table 180. Age, Fertility, and Household and Family Composition by Race and Hispanic Origin: 1990

Dodge City, Kansas

Age	Hispanic Origin (of any race)
All Persons	4,007
Under 3 years	328
3 and 4 years	301
5 to 9 years	481
10 to 14 years	259
15 to 17 years	119
18 and 19 years	238
20 to 24 years	689
25 to 29 years	467
30 to 34 years	327
35 to 39 years	134
40 to 44 years	187
45 to 49 years	117
50 to 54 years	56
55 to 59 years	68
60 to 64 years	108
65 to 74 years	95
75 years and over	33
Median age	22.0

Source: U.S. Bureau of the Census. 1990 Census of Population, Social and Economic Characteristics: Kansas. Prepared by Economics and Statistics Administration, Department of Commerce, Washington, D.C., 1993.

Step 4: Obtain information about the percentage of foreign-born Latinos in your service area.

Use Table 12 to locate these data. Table 12 is a summary table, providing data for all counties and cities. Its title is "Summary of Social and Economic Characteristics for Hispanic Origin Persons and for Households and Families with an Hispanic Origin Householder."

As you learned in the previous chapter, you cannot assume that all Latinos are very recent immigrants to the United States. Table 12 will give you a basic understanding of how many Latinos in your service area are foreign-born.

As an example, Figure 3–4 shows county-level data for all the counties in New Jersey. Note that the counties vary widely in the percentage of foreign-born Latinos. In Cumberland County, for example, only 5.3% of Latinos are foreign-born, whereas the corresponding figure for Union County is 56%. Libraries with high percentages of foreign-born Latinos will most likely be developing specialized services for relatively new immigrants.

Step 5: Obtain data on language spoken in the home and on English language ability.

Use the following tables that provide the data

For a county:	Table 152
For a place of over 10,000:	Table 181
For a place of 2,500–9,999:	Table 205

You cannot assume that all Latinos in your service area are monolingual Spanish-speakers. Library planners will need to gather information on language usage within the Latino community. The tables listed above will provide useful information in understanding language abilities in your service area.

Tables 152 and 181 are called "Age, Sex, Ability to Speak English, and Disability by Race and Hispanic Origin"; Table 211 is called "Social Characteristics for Selected Hispanic Origin Groups." These three tables provide age-level data (ages 5–17, 18–64, 65–74, 75 and over) on the ability to speak a language other than English; and of these other-language speakers, you can find age-level data on the number who report they speak English "very well." It is unfortunate that the age categories are rather large (particularly the 18–64 age group), but these are the best census data available on this subject.

Figure 3–5, as an example, shows language ability data for Pecos County, Texas. The data, extracted from Table 152, show that of Pecos County's 7,438 Latinos, ages five years and over, 2,930 report that they do not speak English very well. Among other things, the data can be used to support the idea of developing a variety of Spanish-language materials, services, and programming in the library.

Step 6: Obtain data on educational attainment levels for the Latino community in your service area.

Use the following tables that provide the data

Figure 3-4. Census Data on Foreign-Born Latinos

Table 12.   Summary of Social and Economic Characteristics for Hispanic Origin Persons and for Households and Families with an Hispanic Origin Householder: 1990

New Jersey Counties	All Hispanic Origin Persons Total	Percent Foreign- Born
Atlantic County	15,438	13.9
Bergen County	48,912	50.9
Burlington County	12,980	15.0
Camden County	33,180	8.7
Cape May County	1,995	11.2
Cumberland County	17,349	5.3
Essex County	93,210	34.8
Gloucester County	3,494	14.3
Hudson County	181,222	54.3
Hunterdon County	1,812	26.3
Mercer County	18,723	23.8
Middlesex County	58,021	35.0
Monmouth County	21,834	26.2
Morris County	19,480	43.9
Ocean County	13,785	18.2
Passaic County	96,182	42.7
Salem County	1,243	9.4
Somerset County	10,188	45.1
Sussex County	2,725	17.2
Union County	66,885	56.0
Warren County	1,686	24.5

Source: U.S. Bureau of the Census. 1990 Census of Population, Social and Economic Characteristics: New Jersey. Prepared by Economics and Statistics Administration, Department of Commerce, Washington, D.C., 1993.

For a county:	Table 152
For a place of over 10,000:	Table 181
For a place of 2,500–9,999:	Table 205

You used these same tables to get the information in Step 5. These three tables also provide detailed information on educational attainment. For individuals in the 18–24 years age category, you can obtain data on the number of high school graduates, the number of those who have attended

Figure 3-5. Census Data on Ability to Speak English

Table 152. Education, Ability to Speak English, and Disability by Race and Hispanic Origin: 1990

Pecos County, Texas

Ability to Speak English	White	Hispanic Origin (of any race)	White, not of Hispanic Origin
Persons 5 years and over	8,761	7,438	5,828
Speak a language other than English	2,883	6,649	385
5 to 17 years	718	2,038	95
18 to 64 years	1,847	4,058	244
65 to 74 years	201	339	44
75 years and over	117	214	2
Do not speak English very well	1,310	2,930	86
5 to 17 years	311	680	40
18 to 64 years	763	1,795	46
65 to 74 years	127	263	——
75 years and over	109	192	——

Source: U.S. Bureau of the Census. 1990 Census of Population, Social and Economic Characteristics: Texas. Prepared by Economics and Statistics Administration, Department of Commerce, Washington, D.C., 1993.

some college, and the number of bachelor's degree (or higher) recipients. For those in the 25 years and over age category, you can determine the number of Latinos in different educational attainment levels ranging from less than fifth grade to graduate/professional degree.

For example, Figure 3–6 shows educational attainment level data for Latinos in Joliet, Illinois, extracted from Table 181. The data show that a significant number of Latinos, ages 25 years and over, do not have a high school diploma. This fact is certainly not unique to Joliet, a community of 76,836 which is 12.3% Latino. Among the many things libraries can do to improve Latino educational attainment levels is to develop strong Graduate Equivalency Diploma (GED) collections and work with other agencies to provide GED classes.

Figure 3-6. Census Data on Educational Attainment

Table 181. Education, Ability to Speak English, and Disability by Race and Hispanic Origin: 1990

Joliet, Illinois

Educational Attainment	White	Hispanic Origin (of any race)
Persons 18 to 24 years	5,194	1,594
High school graduate (includes equivalency)	1,705	422
Some college or associate degree	2,125	397
Bachelor's degree or higher	433	30
Persons 25 years and over	36,108	4,147
Less than 5th grade	439	669
5th to 8th grade	2,833	998
9th to 12th grade, no diploma	5,550	980
High school graduate (includes equivalency)	11,761	879
Some college, no degree	7,059	391
Associate degree, occupational program	1,042	37
Associate degree, academic program	1,251	60
Bachelor's degree	3,869	107
Graduate or professional degree	2,304	26
Persons 25 years and over	36,108	4,147
Percent less than 5th grade	1.2	16.1
Percent high school graduate or higher	75.6	36.2
Percent some college or higher	43.0	15.0
Percent bachelor's degree or higher	17.1	3.2

Source: U.S. Bureau of the Census. 1990 Census of Population, Social and Economic Characteristics: Illinois. Prepared by Economics and Statistics Administration, Department of Commerce, Washington, D.C., 1993.

Step 7: Obtain data about the income levels of Latinos in your service area.

Use the following tables that provide the data

For summary information:	Table 12
For a county:	Table 157
For a place of over 10,000:	Table 186
For a place of 2,500–9,999:	Table 207

Table 12 is a summary table providing valuable information on the median income of Latino households and families, per capita income, and the percentage of Latino persons and households below the poverty level for counties and cities.

For example, Figure 3–7 shows income data, extracted from Table 12, for Latinos in several counties in Colorado. Note the very low ($5,828) per capita income in 1989 for Latinos in Conejos County, one of the poorest counties in the country.

The other three tables (157, 186, and 207) cover counties, larger places, and smaller places, respectively. These tables can be used for a variety of data needs. Here you can find the number of Latino households that fall into nine income categories, ranging from "Less than $5,000" to "$100,000 or more." You will also find very detailed data on family median income, family mean income, per capita income, and the number and percentage of Latinos in your service area who are under the poverty level. This census information is very useful when developing your economic rationale for providing services to Latinos in your community.

Figure 3–8, as an example, shows detailed income data, extracted from Table 157, for Conejos County, Colorado. Libraries in such poor areas as Conejos County often develop partnerships with other agencies in the area to develop programs and collections because they lack the resources to do these things on their own.

Step 8: Obtain labor force and unemployment data for Latinos in your service area.

Use the following tables that provide the data

For general information:	Table 12
For a county:	Table 156
For a place over 10,000:	Table 185
For a place of 2,500–9,999:	Table 206

Figure 3-7. Census Data on Income and Poverty

Table 152. Summary of Social and Economic Characteristics for Hispanic Origin Persons and for Households and Families with an Hispanic Origin Householder: 1990

Selected counties in Colorado	Median income in 1989 (dollars)		Per capita income in 1989 (dollars)	Income in 1989 below poverty level	
				Percent of persons for whom poverty status is determined	Percent of families
	Households	Families			
Adams County	28,532	29,979	9,334	16.2	15.1
Alamosa County	16,074	18,154	6,973	31.8	29.1
Arapahoe County	32,562	37,354	11,902	11.0	9.4
Archuleta County	16,638	17,414	7,165	31.2	28.5
Bent County	17,356	17,300	6,394	29.1	24.3
Boulder County	23,134	25,241	8,913	22.8	21.8
Chaffee County	14,688	24,531	7,587	21.7	19.5
Conejos County	12,202	13,932	5,828	39.5	34.0

Source: U.S. Bureau of the Census. 1990 Census of Population, Social and Economic Characteristics: Colorado. Prepared by Economics and Statistics Administration, Department of Commerce, Washington, D.C., 1993.

Table 12 provides summary information for all cities and counties in your state. For your service area, you can find the percentage of Latinos ages 16 years and over who are in the labor force, and you can find their unemployment rate. In addition, the table gives the percentage of Latinos who are employed in managerial and professional specialty occupations.

For example, Figure 3–9 shows the summary labor force data, extracted from Table 12, for several places and county subdivisions in New York. Note the double-digit unemployment rates for Latinos in Newburgh, North Bellport, and New York City. As you know, unemployment can vary markedly from one quarter to another, so you cannot make too many generalizations from this 1990 data. If your library is in an area with high unemployment rates for Latinos, you can develop bilingual programs and collections around a va-

Figure 3-8. Census Data on Income Brackets

Table 157. Income in 1989 of Households, Families, and Persons by Race and Hispanic Origin: 1990

Conejos County, Colorado

Income in 1989	White	Hispanic Origin (of any race)	White, not of Hispanic Origin
Households	**2,162**	**1,572**	**949**
Less than $5,000	293	209	130
$5,000 to $9,999	408	355	130
$10,000 to $14,999	380	368	123
$15,000 to $24,999	464	344	185
$25,000 to $34,999	281	148	172
$35,000 to $49,999	190	83	126
$50,000 to $74,999	117	55	64
$75,000 to $99,999	22	10	12
$100,000 or more	7	—	7
Median (dollars)	15,000	12,202	19,041
Mean (dollars)	20,104	16,556	24,054
Families	**1,679**	**1,228**	**731**
Less than $5,000	166	125	56
$5,000 to $9,999	223	208	67
$10,000 to $14,999	326	325	101
$15,000 to $24,999	400	291	165
$25,000 to $34,999	247	133	150
$35,000 to $49,999	177	83	113
$50,000 to $74,999	111	53	60
$75,000 to $99,999	22	10	12
$100,000 or more	7	—	7
Median (dollars)	18,014	13,932	22,902
Mean (dollars)	22,725	18,518	27,523

Source: U.S. Bureau of the Census. 1990 Census of Population, Social and Economic Characteristics: Colorado. Prepared by Economics and Statistics Administration, Department of Commerce, Washington, D.C., 1993.

Figure 3-9. Census Data on Labor and Employment

Table 12. Summary of Social and Economic Characteristics for Hispanic Origin Persons and for Households and Families with an Hispanic Origin Householder: 1990

Selected Places and County Subdivisions in New York	Total Hispanic Origin	Persons 16 years and over Percent in labor force	Civilian labor force- Percent unemployed	Employed persons 16 years and over Percent in Managerial and professional specialty occupations
Newburgh city	6,025	70.9	8.6	5.6
Newburgh town	1,400	80.6	10.0	23.8
New Cassel CDP	1,904	82.6	4.2	4.6
New City CDP	1,228	70.9	4.7	39.4
New Rochelle city	7,044	75.8	5.9	13.2
New Windsor town	1,294	77.5	8.1	13.5
New York City	1,737,927	59.1	13.4	15.3
North Bay Shore CDP	4,693	68.0	5.1	7.6
North Bellport CDP	1,315	75.8	12.1	9.2
North Hempstead town	12,373	77.5	6.1	16.4

Source: U.S. Bureau of the Census. 1990 Census of Population, Social and Economic Characteristics: New York. Prepared by Economics and Statistics Administration, Department of Commerce, Washington, D.C., 1993.

riety of themes, such as job improvement skills, resumé writing, and starting a new business.

The other three tables (156, 185, and 206) cover counties, larger places, and smaller places, respectively. Tables 156 and 185 are entitled "Occupation of Employed Persons by Race and Hispanic Origin: 1990"; Table 206 is entitled "Labor Force Characteristics by Race and Hispanic Origin: 1990." Of particular interest in these tables are the segments of the tables concerning the number of Latinos employed in each of six occupational levels ranging from "Operators, fabricators, and laborers" to "Managerial and professional specialty occupations" and the number of Latinos employed in each of 13 very broad industry classifications (for example, mining, construction, and transportation).

As an example, Figure 3–10 gives a sample illustration of Latino labor force data for the city of Newburg, New York. Looking at this table, you could surmise that since the largest number of Latino employees are blue-collar workers (service workers and laborers), Latino library programming could include employee rights, tenant rights, income tax advice, and the like. Also, self-help, coping skills, and recreational library materials would be popular.

By following these eight steps, you can obtain a useful demographic profile of Latinos in your community, at a very low cost.

As mentioned earlier, Appendix A includes a Latino demographics worksheet that you can complete with data obtained from the appropriate tables covering your service area. You can use the completed worksheet to develop part of your rationale for providing services to Latinos.

PRESENTATION OF A SOUND RATIONALE

There are other reasons for providing services to Latinos besides the changing demographics of your area. Much of what we will share is just common sense, but you have to be prepared to approach your rationale systematically. The rest of this chapter focuses on the main points to consider for your rationale, including the development of Latino human potential from an economic perspective; the development of Latino children as library users; the development of a future political base; and the development of a social responsibility perspective.

Additionally, we will discuss the need to make a paradigm shift from aiming library services predominantly to your white majority users to integrating library services for Latinos in your community. You will also need to consider developing a library policy statement that reflects services to your minority community. This statement can be part of your library's mission statement, or it can be a statement attached to your mission statement.

Last but not least, we recommend that you consider using several documents relating to equality of access that have been endorsed by the American Library Association (ALA); these documents will help build and support your rationale.

Figure 3-10. Census Data on Occupation

Table 185. Occupation of Employed Persons by Race and Hispanic Origin: 1990

Newburgh, New York

Employed persons 16 years and over	White 5,856	Black 3,073	Hispanic Origin (of any race) 2,535	White, not of Hispanic origin 4,975
Managerial and professional specialty occupations	1,331	526	143	1,310
Executive, administrative, and managerial occupations	618	230	42	602
Officials and administrators, public administration	25	10	—	25
Management and related occupations	126	51	9	126
Professional specialty occupations	713	296	101	708
Engineers and natural scientists	79	36	17	79
Engineers	14	36	—	14
Health diagnosing occupations	13	26	—	13
Health assessment and treating occupations	134	52	—	134
Teachers, librarians, and counselors	328	109	71	323
Teachers, elementary and secondary schools	185	98	43	185
Technical, sales, and administrative support occupations	1,760	670	467	1,569
Health technologists and technicians	58	32	—	58
Technologists and technicians, except health	163	70	6	157
Sales occupations	618	144	156	537
Supervisors and proprietors, sales occupations	128	12	53	104
Sales representatives, commodities and finance	120	54	5	115
Other sales occupations	370	78	98	318
Cashiers	154	51	43	128
Administrative support occupations, including clerical	921	424	305	817
Computer equipment operators	52	32	7	52
Secretaries, stenographers, and typists	230	79	71	214
Financial records processing occupations	101	15	32	89
Mail and message distributing occupations	60	10	10	54
Service occupations	1,082	877	694	869
Private household occupations	17	54	16	17
Protective service occupations	107	131	45	94
Police and firefighters	30	47	—	30
Service occupations except protective and household	958	692	633	758
Food service operations	331	172	232	282
Cleaning and building service occupations	305	150	292	175
Farming, forestry, and fishing occupations	61	33	49	37
Farm operators and managers	—	9	—	—
Farm workers and related occupations	49	24	37	37
Precision production, craft and repair occupations	598	207	223	508
Mechanics and repairers	104	55	33	95
Construction trades	321	59	83	274
Precision production occupations	173	93	107	139
Operators, fabricators, and laborers	1,024	760	959	682
Machine operators and tenders, except precision	294	220	510	123
Fabricators, assemblers, inspectors, and samplers	225	161	207	154
Transportation occupations	122	94	30	109
Motor vehicle operators	122	64	30	109
Material moving equipment operators	21	50	—	21
Handlers, equipment cleaners, helpers, and laborers	362	235	212	275
Construction laborers	49	30	—	49
Freight, stock, and material handlers	141	78	71	124

Source: U.S. Bureau of the Census. 1990 Census of Population, Social and Economic Characteristics: Colorado. Prepared by Economics and Statistics Administration, Department of Commerce, Washington, D.C., 1993.

ECONOMIC RATIONALE

One of the most effective ways to convince a group of people, no matter their socioeconomic background, of the importance of a service is to tell them how it will affect their wallets. Without fail, this method gets everybody's attention.

If you were to record all the services, programs, and materials—along with the rationale for each item—that your library currently provides that could develop any individual's potential, you could come up with a long list. If you were to try making the same list of services or potential services for Latinos in your community, you would probably find that the reasons are basically the same.

Like other groups, Latinos want to improve their economic well-being and the well-being of their families. We like to think of it as developing human potential. One way Latinos can do that is to be able to compete for higher-paying jobs. What role can the library play here? Providing bilingual materials on job search strategies such as resumé writing and providing bilingual programming on the same subject are just two ideas. The more informed Latinos are, the better they will be at preparing for, applying for, and interviewing for jobs.

Libraries already successfully serving their Latino communities maintain that the more popular materials for Latino adults are self-help materials. Materials on resumé writing and other job search strategies are very popular. Decision-makers will listen when you tell them that outreach to Latinos in your community has the potential to make those residents even more economically productive in the community. Latinos, like all other residents, already contribute to your community's economy. Latinos pay taxes—sales, income, and/or property—which in turn support public services such as police, fire, and library.

If you have any anecdotal information that could support any of the rationales we are mentioning, note and share them with your audience. Telling a real-life story that illustrates your point is an effective persuasion technique. For example, let us say that a Latino middle-aged gentleman, who was just laid off from his job, came into your library for the first time as a referral and requested help in getting information on job search strategies and preparing a resumé. Your librarian was able to assist in meeting his information needs. Several weeks later, the gentleman returned to thank the librarian and let the librarian know that he got a job right away and was told that his resumé was the best resumé submitted to the employer. That is good, solid anecdotal information you can use to your advantage.

Literacy Programs as Part of the Economic Rationale

A more fundamental role that librarians can play in developing Latinos' human potential is addressing literacy. Whether or not a library is directly involved in offering a literacy program is not the issue. The important point is that libraries are in the position to tie literacy with libraries and with the economic success of the community's residents.

Libraries can position themselves with their decision-makers and others by becoming involved in literacy development efforts. If developing a literacy program as an outreach effort not only to the Latino community but to the community as a whole is not a possibility, then the library needs to position itself as an effective partner with already-established literacy programs. Libraries are in the best position to link literacy programs with relevant library services and library programming.

Illiteracy is more predominant in lower socioeconomic groups. Most national and state data will show that illiteracy is most prevalent among minority groups. Figure 3–11 on page 38 provides general literacy fast facts that you can use in your presentation.

There are no direct illiteracy data available at the local level; such information is often inferred from other data such as educational attainment data. However, a recent government publication, *Adult Literacy in America*,[4] presents information on the various dimensions of illiteracy gathered through a national survey. This research project gave functional literacy tests to a large nationwide sample. Data from that study can be used to present a national picture of illiteracy.

The most common way to determine illiteracy rates is based on the percentage of adults, ages 18 and over or ages 25 and over, who do not *start* or do not *finish* high school. Researchers working on the national adult literacy survey (NALS) have reconfirmed that people who do not start or finish high school score very low on functional literacy tests. You can determine your local illiteracy rates by using educational attainment data for your community.

You can get data on high school dropout rates for adults, ages 18 years and over or 25 years and over, in your community or county; these educational attainment data will help strengthen your argument.[5] The point is, the more literate Latinos in your community become, the more economically productive they can be.

By involving Latino parents in literacy and reading, public libraries can indirectly affect Latino student achievement in schools. Once Latino parents learn to read, they will also understand the importance of reading often to their children. Public library programs that promote parents reading to children can become "extremely helpful tools in developing literacy by involving parents and the community in the schooling process and creating a link between home and school."[6]

Remember that bridging library services for Latinos with developing their human potential and providing opportunities for them to improve their economic status in the community is a strong rationale. All of this, in turn, contributes to the community's economy. Remember to use whatever demographic data are available and to include anecdotal information that supports your points. Also, if you can incorporate any visual aids (charts, posters, graphics) to *show* your point, you will improve your presentation.

Last but not least, we want to make sure we don't leave you with the wrong impression about Latinos and their contributions to the economy. Here are some data on the economic success of Latinos in the United States. For example, Latinos have the highest labor force participation rate (78.2%) in the country. They doubled their middle-class status from 1980 to 1990. In 1980, 19.2% of the Latinos in America were earning $25,000 or over; whereas in 1990 that figure more than doubled to 48.2%. They spend over $200 billion each year in the United States, which is twice the gross domestic product (GDP) for Argentina and Austria. This consumer spending total is almost the size of the entire Mexican economy.[7]

Such information can also be used to help dispel the stereotype some people have of Latinos being lazy and on welfare. The bottom line is that the more informed your Latino residents become, the more they will be able to make good economic decisions throughout their lifetime.

LATINO CHILDREN AS LIBRARY USERS RATIONALE

> It is not an exaggeration to say that the future of our society is at stake if we don't address the problems of our young people today. Our economic survival as a nation depends on our ability to offer a literate, competitive workforce for the future.[8]

Another strong rationale to provide library services to Latinos in your community is to contribute to the educational, social, and personal development of Latino children. Your library can have a tremendous impact on this age group which has such a strong potential to succeed. The economic rationale applies to this group, as well as to adults.

Everyone agrees that, in general, children are our future. This future will affect many babyboomers who already find themselves holding onto and protecting their wallets more and more. How we adults assist in the development of the full potential of our children is vitally important and does not rest solely with the educational system. Libraries also should play a significant role in developing our children and young adults regardless of their color. Because Latino children have the same *potential* (but not necessarily the same opportunities) as other children to become productive members of our society, our profession has an important role in developing that potential.

Most children, including Latino children, will eventually contribute financially to your decision-makers' retirements. Let them know

---

Figure 3-11. National Literacy Fast Facts

Did you know that...

➤ 27 million Americans cannot read or write.

➤ An additional 47 million are only marginally literate.

➤ A 1985 test conducted by the National Assessment of Progress indicated that 80% of young adults in the U.S. (21–35 years of age) could not read a bus schedule, 73% could not interpret a newspaper story, 63% could not follow written directions.

➤ It is estimated that 56% of Latinos in this country and 44% of African Americans (compared to 16% of whites) are thought to be functionally illiterate.

➤ Approximately 60% of all persons incarcerated in U.S. prisons are illiterate.

➤ Approximately 85% of all juvenile offenders have problems reading.

➤ Up to 87% of non-English speakers who are illiterate in English are also illiterate in their native language.[9]

---

that! It makes sense to support any effort that will allow children to achieve their potential. The benefit of this investment—providing library services to Latino children—would far outweigh the initial cost of these services in their formative years. The future economic success of Latino children will affect everyone's future economic well-being.

We cannot say enough about how important libraries can be in developing the human potential in children, and in this case Latino children. Children are our future small-business owners, government officials, artists, corporate executives, military personnel, public safety employees, politicians, teachers, and other white- and blue-collar workers. You will need to convince your decision-makers that everyone in the community has a personal stake in the success of Latino children.

It is never too early to start involving preschool Latino children in libraries. This involvement is the critical first phase in combatting illiteracy in children and young adults. Again, you can use data in your rationale comparing high school dropout rates of whites to dropout rates of Latinos.

One other message about Latino children as library users that can be made and is further elaborated in the next section deals with the children as a future political base in the community. These children are the voters of the future. Of course, that is assuming that they will be literate enough to vote and will have learned the importance of voting. Libraries can play a major role in achieving these goals.

The important point to remember and to share with decision-makers is that if we provide library services to Latino children, they will be better able to utilize the library as an important information resource in their lifelong learning process. The library will always be available to help them make well-informed decisions.

Shape the rationale in the preceding paragraphs to fit your local situation. Again, if you can think of any local anecdotes to illustrate and support your Latino children rationale, incorporate them into your presentation.

FUTURE POLITICAL BASE RATIONALE

Once you have demonstrated a solid rationale for Latino children's services, you need to present another rationale. It deals with the development of another future political base for the library. This rationale is most effective with your library staff, your board of trustees, and other library users.

Basically, this rationale employs the same reasoning used by libraries for the development of Latino human potential. That is, how can Latino library users assist the library in the future? By serving a segment of the community that has never been served before—the Latino community—the library is indirectly developing another strong political base.

Libraries should always be cognizant of the potential effect their users can have on their future fiscal well-being. Latinos who use their public library to meet their information needs—personal, professional and recreational—will be the same folks who will learn the importance of registering to vote, and they will learn how to find the necessary information to help them decide how to vote.

A satisfied customer is an ardent supporter. By serving a segment of the community that has never been served before, the library is developing an additional support group that can possibly make the voting difference on a mill levy or a bond issue. This same informed Latino community can lobby its local city officials, state legislature, and national congressional representatives on issues that affect community library services. Again, this is a rationale hard to argue against.

When visiting public libraries around the country that were noted for serving their Latino communities, we inevitably found that these libraries were also able to develop some of their Latino users into overall library advocates—board of trustees members, Friends of the Library members, employees, and/or volunteers. It's that advocacy we are talking about. Most libraries usually do not underestimate the role of white library users as advocates; but many do not think of Latinos (and other minorities) as potential advocates, only because Latinos are traditionally not part of their library user base.

This advocacy potential is available to public libraries once they develop their Latino library user base. For example, the East Los Angeles County Library was able to develop a strong and active Friends of the Library group consisting of local Latino library users and local Latino celebrities. This Friends group has been very active in fund-raising and supporting library programs that the library was unable to support financially. In fact, because of their political action, this Latino group applied the necessary pressure to restore many of the library's eliminated hours.

Using this rationale of developing the library's political base is most effective with library staff. The challenge many libraries face is convincing staff members that library services must be extended to serve another nonuser group in the community—Latinos. When you explain that expanding services to the Latino community affects them in the long run, the staff is more willing to listen and support changes in services. Developing another political base of support affects their library jobs because the Latino community can help pass bond issues for a new building or mill levies to increase materials, services, and salaries.

SOCIAL RESPONSIBILITY RATIONALE

The fourth rationale to develop library services to the Latino community deals with social responsibility. Recently, within the library profession, there seems to be a backlash against the role of librarians and libraries in dealing with social issues, because many of these issues supposedly have nothing to do with libraries and library services. However, there should be no misunderstanding about the issue of providing library services to your Latino community.

Regina Minudri, city librarian for years in Berkeley, California, said at a conference that public libraries' efforts reaching out to serve their minority community "was just the right thing to do."[10] That is, libraries have a social responsibility to serve the chronically disenfranchised, and, in this case, the Latino population.

If libraries assume the role of serving a culturally diverse society, then they are fostering a climate for racial harmony among all groups within their communities. People tend to fear the unknown; consequently, we all have a tendency to fear those who may not look, speak, or live as we do.

Libraries can play an important role in developing healthy race relationships between people who are different ethnically and socially. How do they do this? They can purchase materials and promote programming that can educate and enlighten their majority users. Knowledge and understanding of and respect for the Latino culture will help reduce that fear.[11]

We will caution you that this rationale could probably be the least effective of all the rationales you present. This one is more philosophically based than it is pragmatic. Nonetheless, it is still a very usable rationale. Again, build your rationale around your local environment and use any anecdotes or examples that will support your rationale.

LIBRARY SERVICES PARADIGM SHIFT

We quoted the Chicago Public Library Hispanic Services Committee at the beginning of this chapter about the importance of meeting the library and information needs of your Latino residents, not as supplemental services, but as part of the natural function of any library serving a multicultural community. This is an ideal. We totally agree with this position statement; and it is definitely something for which we want to strive. However, the realities of your local situation might suggest that your local decision-makers may not recognize their community as a multicultural community relative to library services or any other public services offered by the local government.

You need to develop and present a shift in your library services paradigm. Such a shift incorporates library services for Latinos as an integral part of your library's existing services. It isn't that all services are necessarily new. The new Latino library user will drive the shift in how public libraries deliver services to them and other potential Latino users. The sooner you can do this in your efforts to serve Latinos in your community, the better. This approach will help lay to rest the funding opposition from others as mentioned in our challenge at the beginning of this chapter.

It isn't the Latino communities' fault that libraries have chosen not to reach out to and provide services for them as they have for their white populations. Providing services to Latinos should not be viewed as a funding issue. That is, finding the funds to tailor services to attract Latinos to the library should not be more important than serving them. Remember to point out to your audience that the Latinos in your community pay taxes—sales, property, and/or income. Their taxes *already* support the library and other public services. If Latinos have not benefitted from your library services, then it may be because they have not been aggressively pursued as users; they may not have been assertive in demanding services; or their needs may not have been known or met in the past.

It is important to remember that Latino information needs are as important as the needs of others but they will probably also differ from your non-minority current users' needs. What is offered to your current clientele will not necessarily work for serving a Latino clientele. Other people may not understand this difference, and that is why advocating for the development of such services will be an issue. You need to anticipate this potential opposition and be prepared to address or respond to those issues.

LIBRARY POLICY STATEMENT

One way to initiate this change in services to Latinos is through a library policy statement. A library policy statement describes a service your library provides or a position it holds. It is important for you to remember that once a statement is included as policy, it becomes policy. Policy statements provide the teeth behind your library's services and procedures. That is why it is necessary that your policies address the importance of and need for your library to develop and provide library services to your minority community (in this case, Latinos).

Earlier, when writing about the paradigm shift in library services, we mentioned how important it is to integrate library services for Latinos into existing services. Christine Talbot suggests that this integration be reflected in your library's overall policy statements.[12] Depending on your governing structure, you may need your board's approval for any policy statements. Even if you do not need board approval, we suggest you inform your board of this new policy statement and thus remind them of the library's responsibility to meet the needs of all members of the community.

Some policy statements are short and to the point; others are long and full of detail. The following is an example of a brief library policy statement regarding services to people of color in the community: "The library should ensure that all of its services reflect the cultural and ethnic make-up and particular needs of the community it serves."[13] Figures 3–12 and 3–13 are examples of longer policy statements.

USEFUL AMERICAN LIBRARY ASSOCIATION DOCUMENTS

Three documents endorsed by the American Library Association (ALA) can help you with your rationale. You may want to refer to any or all of them; you may want to make any or all of them available to your audience. Together, these three documents express our profession's highest principles as they relate to the provision of equal access to library and information services for everyone in the community.

Adopted in 1988 by the Reference and Adult Services Division (RASD, now known as the Reference and User Services Association) of the ALA, the "RASD Guidelines for Library Services to Hispanics" is a policy statement issued by a nationally recognized library organization that affirms the responsibilities of libraries to provide library services to Latinos in every community. For your convenience, the text appears in Appendix B at the end of this chapter.

The "Library Bill of Rights" was originally adopted by the ALA in 1948, and has been amended several times since then. This document is one of the cornerstones of our profession, affirming that all libraries should provide resources for the interest, information, and enlightenment of all people in the community. The text of this document is

---

Figure 3-12. Sample Library Policy Statement

The Morris Public Library believes that all people in the community should be encouraged to use the public library and that the library should be prepared to meet their needs. The library also believes that all people in our community need to understand and appreciate the varying and diverse cultures of the people who live in our service area and the state.

Consequently:

The Morris Public Library will recruit, hire, place, and advance ethnic minority employees, volunteers and trustees to reflect the ethnic make-up of our community. The Morris Public Library will treat members of ethnic groups with sensitivity, courtesy and respect.

The library will offer services designed with the ethnic populations community in mind.

The library will have a collection that contains a wide variety of materials by, about, and in the language of the ethnic population of our service area and the state.

The Morris Public Library will celebrate the heritage and culture of the various populations in our community and in Colorado.

The library will develop partnerships with community groups in order to better serve ethnic populations.

Permission to reprint granted by Nancy Bolt, Colorado State Library

included in Appendix C. A Spanish translation is included in Appendix D.

The "Freedom to Read" statement was originally adopted in 1953 by the ALA and the American Book Publishers Council, which later consolidated with the American Educational Publishers Institute to become the Association of American Publishers. The "Freedom to Read" statement has subsequently been endorsed by many national organizations supporting the freedom to read. The statement affirms the proposition that it is in society's best interest for publishers and librarians to make available a diversity of opinion and thought, including materials that may not be popular with the majority. If the presence of Spanish books in your library is challenged, you can use this document to support Latinos and their freedom to read. The text of this document is included in Appendix E.

Figure 3-13. Sample Library Policy Statement

The Morris Public Library is committed to a policy of equal opportunity for all people of our service area, regardless of race, color, ancestry, religion, sex, national origin, marital status, sexual preference, physical or mental disability, political preference, or age.

Our policy is to ensure balance in our workforce, staff, volunteers and trustees in a manner that mirrors the demographics of our service area and that each member of the Morris Library team demonstrate sensitivity to and respect for all other staff in a manner based on the spirit as well as the letter of equity.

Our employees and trustees are expected to make every reasonable effort to act in a spirit of assuring that service to patrons is reflective of the demographics of our service area.

Permission to reprint granted by Nancy Bolt, Colorado State Library

PRESENTATION OF RATIONALE

We will leave you with a simple framework to organize your presentation—the five "W's" (who, what, why, when, where) and one "H" (how). Do not forget to include whatever demographic data you have collected to support your rationale when you use this framework. The six questions need not necessarily be used in the same order; place them in the order that will most benefit you in your presentation.

1. WHO is involved in this library proposal?
(a) Your public library (name); and (b) Latinos in your community.
2. WHAT is involved in this proposal?
Providing library services for Latinos in your community. Use some general demographic data for your service area or city/county area to support your rationale. Start with getting your board to adopt a policy statement regarding library services to your multicultural community and then proceed from there.
3. WHY is it important for the library to be involved?
Design and build your rationale here using the topical areas presented earlier. Remember to gather and use any local and relevant anecdotal information.
4. HOW will the library be involved?
Explain what services you plan to offer; how you plan to provide those services (methodology); what costs are involved (optional); and what you plan for outreach efforts. Also, you may need to design an implementation plan with a phase-in component.

5. WHEN does the library propose implementing these actions? Offer a timeline that reflects all of the above.
6. WHERE will the library provide these services for Latinos? This information is dependent on where your Latino community is located in your library service area. You may only have one main library, which would make this section easy; or, if you have several branches with Latino residents in their service areas, you may want to start in one of the branches and then phase the others in. Again, your decision will depend on your local service area and funding situations.

CONCLUSION

It was our intent that, after reading this chapter, you would have a solid foundation from which to start. Try to adapt the rationale concepts to fit your local situation and determine what demographic data will be helpful. You may even come up with additional lines of reasoning specific to your situation. Remember that if you use national data, you need also to use local data to make your rationale more relevant to your audience. In addition, anecdotal material draws the picture for your audience and will help clarify and strengthen your rationale.

For some of you, building a rationale may not be so important because you already have a solid base of support from staff and governing bodies. Others may need to plan carefully what is in your rationale, what supporting materials are needed to sustain it, and how you are going to present it—because you may have the challenge of the century.

Remember that you can use different lines of reasoning depending on your audience. For example, you may use all of them when addressing your staff or board of trustees or funding body. On the other hand, you may just want to concentrate on some of them when addressing a group of educators. As with any presentation, knowing your audience is as important as delivering your message. Remember that your goal is to convince your audience—supporters, neutral folks, and your opposition—that providing library services to your Latino community must happen.

NOTES

1. Hispanic Services Committee, *Hispanic Services: A Practical Manual for the Public Librarian* (Chicago: Chicago Public Library, 1990), 1.
2. U.S. Bureau of the Census, *Census of Population: Social and Economic Characteristics*, 1990, Series CP-2, prepared by the Economics and Statistics Administration, Department of Commerce (Washington, D.C.: U.S. Government Printing Office, 1993).
3. U.S. Bureau of the Census, *Census of Population: General Population Characteristics*, 1990, Series CP-1, prepared by the Economics and Statistics Administration, Department of Commerce (Washington, D.C.: U.S. Government Printing Office, 1992).
4. Irwin Kirsch and others, *Adult Literacy in America: A First Look at the Results of the National Adult Literacy Survey*, a special study commissioned at the request of the National Center for Education Statistics (Washington, D.C.: U.S. Government Printing Office, 1993).
5. U.S. Bureau of the Census, *County and City Data Book 1994: A Statistical Abstract Supplement*, 12th edition, prepared by the Economics and Statistics Administration, Department of Commerce (Washington, D.C.: U.S. Government Printing Office, 1994).
6. Rebecca Constantino, "It's Like a Lot of Things in America: Linguistic Minority Parents Use of Libraries," *School Library Media Quarterly* 22 (Winter, 1994): 87.
7. Phillip M. Burgess, "Immigrants Help Golden State Go," *Rocky Mountain News*, 26 March 1996, Commentary sec., 27A.
8. Ramiro Salazar, "The Bottom Line: Saving Youth Means Saving Our Future," in *Library Services for Children and Youth: Dollars and Sense* (New York: Neal-Schuman Publishers, 1994), 34.
9. Data were extracted from a literacy flyer provided by the El Paso Literacy Center, Clardy Fox Branch, El Paso Public Library. The flyer cites the source of information as *Building the New Texas: Humanities Perspectives on the Environment, Health Care, and Literacy in Texas*, Texas Committee for the Humanities.
10. Regina Minudri, "Managing Diversity: Library Directors Speak Out," Speech at Annual Conference of the California Library Association, Oakland, Calif., Nov. 14, 1993.
11. Christine Talbot, "What Is a Multicultural Library Service?" *Library Association Record* 92 (July 1990): 501–503.
12. Talbot, "What Is a Multicultural Library Service?" 503.
13. Talbot, 501.

APPENDIX A
LATINO DEMOGRAPHICS WORKSHEET

1990 Latino Demographics for _____
(city or county)

To complete this chart for your service area, obtain the appropriate state volume in the *Social and Economic Characteristics* series, and consult the tables listed below.

Population Overview (from Table 6 or 7)
    Total population of service area   _____
    Total Latino population   _____
    Latino population as a percentage
        of total population   _____

Latino Subcultural Groups (from Table 6 or 7)

    Total Latinos (of any race)   _____
    Mexican   _____
    Puerto Rican   _____
    Cuban   _____
    Other Latino   _____
        Dominican Republic   _____
        Central American   _____
            Costa Rican   _____
            Guatemalan   _____
            Honduran   _____
            Nicaraguan   _____
            Panamanian   _____
            Salvadoran   _____
            Other Central American   _____
        South American   _____
            Argentinean   _____
            Chilean   _____
            Colombian   _____
            Peruvian   _____
            Venezuelan   _____
            Other South American   _____

Latino Age Distribution (from Table 151 or 180; for smaller communities, use Table 168 of the *General Population Characteristics* series)

Total Latinos   _____

    Under 3 years   _____

    3 and 4 years   _____

    5 to 9 years   _____

    10 to 14 years   _____

    15 to 17 years   _____

    18 and 19 years   _____

    20 to 24 years   _____

    25 to 29 years   _____

    30 to 34 years   _____

    35 to 39 years   _____

    40 to 44 years   _____

    45 to 49 years   _____

    50 to 54 years   _____

    55 to 59 years   _____

    60 to 64 years   _____

    65 to 74 years   _____

    75 years and older   _____

Mean Age   _____

Foreign-Born Latinos (from Table 12)

    Total Number of Latinos   _____

    Percentage of Total Number of Latinos
    who are foreign-born   _____

Language Spoken by Latinos and Ability to Speak English (from Table 152, 181, or 205)

    Number of Latinos 5 years and over   _____

    Speak a language other than English   _____

        5 to 17 years   _____

        18 to 64 years   _____

        65 to 74 years   _____

        75 years and over   _____

    Do not speak English very well   _____

        5 to 17 years   _____

        18 to 64 years   _____

        65 to 74 years   _____

        75 years and over   _____

Latino Educational Attainment (from Table 152, 181, or 205)

    Latinos 18 to 24 years   _____
        High school graduate (includes equivalency)   _____
        Some college or associate degree   _____
        Bachelor's degree or higher   _____

    Latinos 25 years and over   _____
        Less than 5th grade   _____
        5th to 8th grade   _____
        9th to 12th grade, no diploma   _____
        High school graduate (includes equivalency)   _____
        Some college, no degree   _____
        Associate degree, occupational program   _____
        Associate degree, academic program   _____
        Bachelor's degree   _____
        Graduate or professional degree   _____

    Latinos 25 years and over   _____
        Percent less than 5th grade   _____
        Percent high school graduate or higher   _____
        Percent some college or higher   _____
        Percent bachelor's degree or higher   _____

    Latino Males 25 to 34 years   _____
        Percent high school graduate or higher   _____
        Percent bachelor's degree or higher   _____

    Latino Females 25 to 34 years   _____
        Percent high school graduate or higher   _____
        Percent bachelor's degree or higher   _____

Latino Income in 1989 Dollars (from Table 12)

    Household median income   _____
    Family median income   _____
    Per capita income   _____

Latinos Below Poverty Level (from Table 12)

    Percent of Latino families below poverty level   _____

Income Levels in 1989 (from Table 157, 186, or 207)

	White	Latino	White, not of Latino origin
Total Households			
Less than $5,000	_____	_____	_____
$5,000 to $9,999	_____	_____	_____
$10,000 to $14,999	_____	_____	_____
$15,000 to $24,999	_____	_____	_____
$25,000 to $34,999	_____	_____	_____
$35,000 to $49,999	_____	_____	_____
$50,000 to $74,999	_____	_____	_____
$75,000 to $99,999	_____	_____	_____
$100,000 or more	_____	_____	_____
Median (dollars)	_____	_____	_____
Mean (dollars)	_____	_____	_____
Total Families			
Less than $5,000	_____	_____	_____
$5,000 to $9,999	_____	_____	_____
$10,000 to $14,999	_____	_____	_____
$15,000 to $24,999	_____	_____	_____
$25,000 to $34,999	_____	_____	_____
$35,000 to $49,999	_____	_____	_____
$50,000 to $74,999	_____	_____	_____
$75,000 to $99,999	_____	_____	_____
$100,000 or more	_____	_____	_____
Median (dollars)	_____	_____	_____
Mean (dollars)	_____	_____	_____

Latino Labor Force in 1990 (from Table 12)

Latinos 16 years and over, percent in labor force   _____

Latino civilian labor force, percent unemployed   _____

Occupation of Employed Latinos (from Table 156, 185, or 206)

Employed Latinos 16 years and over
  Managerial and professional   _____
  Technical, sales, and administrative support   _____
  Service   _____
  Farming, forestry, and fishing   _____
  Precision production, craft, and repair   _____
  Operators, fabricators, and laborers   _____

APPENDIX B
REFERENCE AND ADULT SERVICES DIVISION GUIDELINES FOR LIBRARY SERVICES TO HISPANICS

Prepared by the Library Services to the Spanish Speaking Committee, Reference and Adult Services Division (RASD), American Library Association. Adopted by the RASD Board of Directors, January 1988, and submitted to the ALA Standards Committee for review.

1. INTRODUCTION

In this document the RASD Committee on Library Services to the Spanish Speaking has reached a goal in the articulation of long-awaited guidelines to reach this important minority community. Provision of library services to Hispanics can prove to be complex: nationality, regional differences, and culture provide myriad combinations for that single community. As an example, there are significant linguistic and cultural differences reflected in the varieties of Spanish spoken by Mexicans, Puerto Ricans, Cubans, and other Hispanic groups. To recognize these differences and to respond correctly to them is a major theme within these guidelines.

REFORMA, the National Association to Promote Library Services to the Spanish-speaking, has taken an active role in the production of this document: one committee member served as liaison to REFORMA, and the organization has given input and has reviewed the final document.

Although these guidelines were written by persons with professional interest in service to Hispanics, they were written consciously for all librarians who only now may need to initiate service to this population. In that sense, the guidelines are a basic beginner's manual intended for a hypothetical librarian serving as an administrator of a medium-to-small institution having become aware of the needs of a Hispanic community within its service area. As with any guidelines, these are designed to aid in the development of that service and to remind readers of professional concerns regarding the target population and of the staff who work with that population.

Although the division is aware of numerous terms for this target population, it has chosen the word "Hispanic" as the term has been used in the 1980 Census (see Appendix A).

2. COLLECTION AND SELECTION OF MATERIALS

Persons in the Hispanic communities in the United States do not all speak and read only Spanish; they do not all speak and read only English, nor are they all bilingual. The members of these communities have diverse needs and are entitled to access to materials diverse enough to meet those needs. There are standard criteria to aid in the selection of these library materials.

2.1 RELEVANCY.

The selection of library materials for Hispanics should meet the educational and recreational needs of the community by providing relevant and culturally sensitive materials. Stereotypes should be avoided.

2.2 LANGUAGE.

The collection should contain materials in Spanish, materials in English, and bilingual materials. Materials selected should reflect the particular linguistic characteristics of the community served. They should also include standard Spanish language titles from Spain and other Hispanic cultures.

2.3 PHYSICAL ACCESS.

If a separate collection of materials for Hispanics is maintained by the library, it should be visible and accessible to the community. In libraries that do not separate these materials, adherence to 2.4 is strongly recommended.

2.4 BIBLIOGRAPHIC ACCESS.

Bibliographic access to the library's collection should include Spanish-language subject headings in the public catalog when appropriate for the population served. Locally produced access and identification aids, including lists, bibliographies, and point-of-use bibliographic instructional materials, should be in Spanish when appropriate.

2.5 FORMATS.

Print and nonprint materials, whether educational or recreational, should be included.

3. PROGRAMS, SERVICES, AND COMMUNITY RELATIONS

Programming, both traditional and nontraditional, is an effective vehicle to attract and meet the needs of the members of the Hispanic community. This is particularly true for those who have recently immigrated and who are unfamiliar with the library services available in the United States. As a result of the potentially limited resources available for service to Hispanics within any given institution, cooperation among all libraries serving the target population is encouraged. Such cooperation may manifest itself in the sharing of program costs, cooperative acquisitions, or joint borrowing privileges, to name but a few.

3.1 DIVERSITY OF CULTURE.

Because the population served may comprise several different Hispanic cultures, each specific culture must be considered in the development of programming and should be accurately reflected in its content.

3.2 OUTREACH SERVICES.

In order to aid in the planning and delivery of library services to meet community needs, there should be an ongoing process of community analysis and assessment. To further these aims:
(1) the library should participate in the work of local community organizations of Hispanics; and
(2) the library should work with such organizations in the development and presentation of library programs and services.

3.3 INTERCULTURAL UNDERSTANDING.

As part of its activities in working with local populations in which a multiplicity of cultures is represented, the library should actively promote intercultural communication and cooperation among them.

3.4 SERVICE TO NONUSERS.

Attention should be paid to the library non-user. Programs, literature, and publicity should be used in nontraditional ways and in settings designed to attract those for whom libraries are not part of the experience of life.

3.5 BIBLIOGRAPHIC INSTRUCTION.

Bibliographic instruction should be offered in Spanish when necessary.

3.6 LANGUAGE.

In keeping with the ALA policy in support of multilingual services, the language used for programming and services (Spanish, English, bilingual or monolingual) as well as vocabulary, accent, and nuance must be carefully selected. Choices should be based upon the characteristics of the local community.

4. PERSONNEL

Librarians serving Hispanic communities should be actively recruited. Contact should be made with Hispanic graduates of library education programs accredited by the American Library Association, and extensive use should be made of hotlines, minority recruiting services, and services provided by Hispanic library organizations. Professional staff should be recruited from library education programs accredited by the American Library Association. Written personnel procedures and affirmative action programs should be established and fully implemented. See the *ALA Policy Manual* for amplification of these.

4.1 QUALIFICATION—PROFESSIONAL AND SUPPORT STAFF.

(1) In addition to the required standards for librarians and support staff, bilingualism and biculturalism are qualities that should be sought; these qualities will ensure sensitivity to the library and information needs of the Hispanic community and enhance service delivery.

(2) Bilingual and bicultural librarians and support staff should be adequately compensated in positions where job specifications or actual conditions require the knowledge of Spanish.

4.2 STAFF DEVELOPMENT.

(1) Librarians and support staff should be provided opportunities to exchange information and ideas as well as to participate in continuing education programs that would enhance the service provided to libraries in Hispanic communities. Examples of programs that could be explored include training in teaching English as a second language, acquisition of Spanish-language materials, citizenship requirements, and community information services.

(2) Opportunities for advancement should be provided and encouraged by the library administration.

5. BUILDINGS

The library building, through its location, architecture, and appearance, should be an attraction, not a barrier, to members of the Hispanic community.

5.1 INTERIOR AND EXTERIOR.

While the structure may not be able to be altered in any significant way, interior and exterior decor can be modified by choosing decorations and graphics to create an ambience suitable to the clientele served. Care must be taken that the alterations made will conform to the culture of the community.

5.2 SIGNAGE.

In any library serving a bilingual community, signs should be bilingual. Attention must be paid to the particular dialect of Spanish used so that the wording, phraseology, and connotation of the language conform to the culture of the community. Signage should be both prominent and visible.

5.3 LOCATION.

When it is possible to control the location of the library within the community to be served, a location should be considered that will induce the target population into the library. When space is allocated within existing structures, it should be both visible and accessible.

APPENDIX A

Persons of Spanish/Hispanic origin or descent are those who reported either Mexican, Puerto Rican, Cuban, or other Spanish/Hispanic origin in question 7. Persons who reported "other Spanish/Hispanic" origin were those whose origins are from Spain or the Spanish-speaking countries of Central or South America, or they are persons identifying their origin or descent as being Spanish, Spanish-American, Hispano, Latino, etc.

Origin or descent can be regarded as the ancestry, nationality group, lineage, or country in which the person or person's parents or ancestors were born before their arrival in the United States. It is important to note that persons of Spanish origin may be of any race. In this report, households and families are classified by the Spanish origin of the householder. (Source: U.S. Dept. of Commerce, Bureau of the Census. *1980 Census of Population,* "General Social and Economic Characteristics: United States Summary," Appendix, p. B-4, B-5). Adopted January 1988. Reprinted with permission of the American Library Association.

APPENDIX C
LIBRARY BILL OF RIGHTS

The American Library Association affirms that all libraries are forums for information and ideas, and that the following basic policies should guide their services:

1. Books and other library resources should be provided for the interest, information, and enlightenment of all people of the community the library serves. Materials should not be excluded because of the origin, background, or views of those contributing to their creation.
2. Libraries should provide materials and information presenting all points of view on current and historical issues. Materials should not be proscribed or removed because of partisan or doctrinal disapproval.
3. Libraries should challenge censorship in the fulfillment of their responsibility to provide information and enlightenment.
4. Libraries should cooperate with all persons and groups concerned with resisting abridgement of free expression and free access to ideas.
5. A person's right to use a library should not be denied or abridged because of origin, age, background, or views.
6. Libraries which make exhibit spaces and meeting rooms available to the public they serve should make such facilities available on an equitable basis, regardless of the beliefs or affiliations of individuals or groups requesting their use.

Adopted June 18, 1948. Amended February 2, 1961; June 27, 1967; and January 23, 1980, by the ALA Council. Reprinted with permission of the American Library Association.

APPENDIX D
DECLARACIÓN DE LOS DERECHOS DE LAS BIBLIOTECAS

La Asociación de Bibliotecas de los Estados Unidos de America (American Library Association) afirma que todas las bibliotecas son foros abiertos para la información y las ideas, y que las siguientes normas basicas deben dirigir sus servicios.

1. Con el fin de satisfacer el interés de sus usuarios y darles acceso a todo tipo de información, toda bibloteca debe poner sus libros y otros recursos a la disposición de todos los integrantes de la comunidad a la cual sirve.

2. Toda biblioteca debe proveer información y materiales que representen todos los puntos de vista sobre temas históricos y de actualidad. Ningun material debe ser prohibido ni retirado de circulación por motivos doctrinarios o partidistas.

3. En su misión de proveer información sin restricciones, toda biblioteca debe enfrentarse a todo acto y tipo de censura.

4. Toda biblioteca debe cooperar con todos los individuos y grupos interesados en oponerse a cualquiera restriccion a la libre expresión y el libre acceso a las ideas.

5. No se le debe negar a ninguna persona el derecho de usar la biblioteca por motivos de origen, edad, antecedentes personales o punto de vista.

6. Toda biblioteca que cuente con espacio disponible para exhibiciones o reuniones publicas, debe ofrecerlo en forma equitativa, sin tener en cuenta la creencia o afiliación de los individuos o grupos que soliciten su uso.

Adoptado el 18 de junio 1948. Enmendad el 2 de febrero de 1961 y el 23 de enero de 1980 por el Consejo de la Asociación de Bibliotecas de los Estados Unidos de America (Council of the American Library Association). Reprinted with permission of the American Library Association.

APPENDIX E
THE FREEDOM TO READ

The freedom to read is essential to our democracy. It is continuously under attack. Private groups and public authorities in various parts of the country are working to remove books from sale, to censor textbooks, to label "controversial" books, to distribute lists of "objectionable" books or authors, and to purge libraries. These actions apparently rise from a view that our national tradition of free expression is no longer valid; that censorship and suppression are needed to avoid the subversion of politics and the corruption of morals. We, as citizens devoted to the use of books and as librarians and publishers responsible for disseminating them, wish to assert the public interest in the preservation of the freedom to read.

We are deeply concerned about these attempts at suppression. Most such attempts rest on a denial of the fundamental premise of democracy: that the ordinary citizen, by exercising critical judgment, will accept the good and reject the bad. The censors, public and private, assume that they should determine what is good and what is bad for their fellow-citizens.

We trust Americans to recognize propaganda, and to reject it. We do not believe they are prepared to sacrifice their heritage of a free press in order to be "protected" against what others think may be bad for them. We believe they still favor free enterprise in ideas and expression.

We are aware, of course, that books are not alone in being subjected to efforts at suppression. We are aware that these efforts are related to a larger pattern of pressures being brought against education, the press, films, radio, and television. The problem is not only one of actual censorship. The shadow of fear cast by these pressures leads, we suspect, to an even larger voluntary curtailment of expression by those who seek to avoid controversy.

Such pressure toward conformity is perhaps natural to a time of uneasy change and pervading fear. Especially when so many of our apprehensions are directed against an ideology, the expression of a dissident idea becomes a thing feared in itself, and we tend to move against it as against a hostile deed, with suppression.

And yet suppression is never more dangerous than in such a time of social tension. Freedom has given the United States the elasticity to endure strain. Freedom keeps open the path of novel and creative solutions, and enables change to come by choice. Every silencing of a heresy, every enforcement of an orthodoxy, diminishes the toughness and resilience of our society and leaves it the less able to deal with stress.

Now as always in our history, books are among our greatest instruments of freedom. They are almost the only means for making generally available ideas or manners of expression that can initially command only a small audience. They are the natural medium for the new idea and the untried voice from which come the original contributions to social growth. They are essential to the extended discussion which serious thought requires, and to the accumulation of knowledge and ideas into organized collections.

We believe that free communication is essential to the preservation of a free society and a creative culture. We believe that these pressures towards conformity present the danger of limiting the range and variety of inquiry and expression on which our democracy and our culture depend. We believe that every American community must jealously guard the freedom to publish and to circulate, in order to preserve its own freedom to read. We believe that publishers and librarians have a profound responsibility to give validity to that freedom to read by making it possible for the readers to choose freely from a variety of offerings.

The freedom to read is guaranteed by the Constitution. Those with faith in free people will stand firm on these constitutional guarantees of essential rights and will exercise the responsibilities that accompany these rights.

We therefore affirm these propositions:

1. It is in the public interest for publishers and librarians to make available the widest diversity of views and expressions, including those which are unorthodox or unpopular with the majority.

   Creative thought is by definition new, and what is new is different. The bearer of every new thought is a rebel until that idea is refined and tested. Totalitarian systems attempt to maintain themselves in power by the ruthless suppression of any concept which challenges the established orthodoxy. The power of a democratic system to adapt to change is vastly strengthened by the freedom of its citizens to choose widely from among conflicting opinions offered freely to them. To stifle every nonconformist idea at birth would mark the end of the democratic process. Furthermore, only through the constant activity of weighing and selecting can the democratic mind attain the strength demanded by times like these. We need to know not only what we believe but why we believe it.

2. Publishers, librarians, and booksellers do not need to endorse every idea or presentation contained in the books they make available. It would conflict with the public interest for them to

establish their own political, moral, or aesthetic views as a standard for determining what books should be published or circulated.

Publishers and librarians serve the educational process by helping to make available knowledge and ideas required for the growth of the mind and the increase of learning. They do not foster education by imposing as mentors the patterns of their own thought. The people should have the freedom to read and consider a broader range of ideas than those that may be held by any single librarian or publisher or government or church. It is wrong that what one can read should be confined to what another thinks proper.

3. It is contrary to the public interest for publishers or librarians to determine the acceptability of a book on the basis of the personal history or political affiliations of the author.

A book should be judged as a book. No art or literature can flourish if it is to be measured by the political views or private lives of its creators. No society of free people can flourish which draws up lists of writers to whom it will not listen, whatever they may have to say.

4. There is no place in our society for the efforts to coerce the taste of others, to confine adults to the reading of matter deemed suitable for adolescents, or to inhibit the efforts of writers to achieve artistic expression.

To some, much of modern literature is shocking. But is not much of life itself shocking? We cut off literature at the source if we prevent writers from dealing with the stuff of life. Parents and teachers have a responsibility to prepare the young to meet the diversity of experiences in life to which they will be exposed, as they have a responsibility to help them learn to think critically for themselves. These are affirmative responsibilities, not to be discharged simply by preventing them from reading works for which they are not yet prepared. In these matters taste differs, and taste cannot be legislated; nor can machinery be devised which will suit the demands of one group without limiting the freedom of others.

5. It is not in the public interest to force a reader to accept with any book the prejudgment of a label characterizing the book or author as subversive or dangerous.

The idea of labeling presupposes the existence of individuals or groups with wisdom to determine by authority what is good or bad for the citizen. It presupposes that individuals must be directed in making up their minds about the ideas they examine. But Americans do not need others to do their thinking for them.

6. It is the responsibility of publishers and librarians, as guardians of the people's freedom to read, to contest encroachments upon that freedom by individuals or groups seeking to impose their own standards or tastes upon the community at large.

It is inevitable in the give and take of the democratic process that the political, the moral, or the aesthetic concepts of an individual or group will occasionally collide with those of another individual or group. In a free society individuals are free to determine for themselves what they wish to read, and each group is free to determine what it will recommend to its freely associated members. But no group has the right to take the law into its own hands, and to impose its own concept of politics or morality upon other members of a democratic society. Freedom is no freedom if it is accorded only to the accepted and the inoffensive.

7. It is the responsibility of publishers and librarians to give full meaning to the freedom to read by providing books that enrich the quality and diversity of thought and expression. By the exercise of this affirmative responsibility, they can demonstrate that the answer to a bad book is a good one, the answer to a bad idea is a good one.

The freedom to read is of little consequence when expended on the trivial; it is frustrated when the reader cannot obtain matter fit for that reader's purpose. What is needed is not only the absence of restraint, but the positive provision of opportunity for the people to read the best that has been thought and said. Books are the major channel by which the intellectual inheritance is handed down, and the principal means of its testing and growth. The defense of their freedom and integrity, and the enlargement of their service to society, requires of all publishers and librarians the utmost of their faculties, and deserves of all citizens the fullest of their support.

We state these propositions neither lightly nor as easy generalizations. We here stake out a lofty claim for the value of books. We do so because we believe that they are good, possessed of enormous variety and usefulness, worthy of cherishing and keeping free. We realize that the application of these propositions may mean the dissemination of ideas and manners of expression that are repugnant to many persons. We do not state these propositions in the comfortable belief that what people read is unimportant. We believe rather that what people read is deeply important; that ideas can be dangerous; but that the suppression of ideas is fatal to a democratic society. Freedom itself is a dangerous way of life, but it is ours.

This statement was originally issued in May 1953 by the Westchester Conference of the American Library Association and the American Book Publishers Council, which in 1970 consolidated with the American Educational Publishers Institute to become the Association of American Publishers (AAP).

Adopted June 25, 1953. Revised January 28, 1972 and January 16, 1991, by the ALA Council and the AAP Freedom to Read Committee.

A joint statement by:

American Library Association
Association of American Publishers

Subsequently endorsed by:

American Booksellers Association
American Booksellers Foundation for Free Expression
American Civil Liberties Union
American Federation of Teachers AFL-CIO
Anti-Defamation League of B'nai B'rith
Association of American University Presses
Children's Book Council
Freedom to Read Foundation
International Reading Association
Thomas Jefferson Center for the Protection of Free Expression
National Association of College Stores
National Council of Teachers of English
P.E.N.—American Center
People for the American Way
Periodical and Book Association of America
Sex Information and Education Council of the U.S.
Society of Professional Journalists
Women's National Book Association
YWCA of the U.S.A.
Reprinted with permission of the American Library Association.

4 KNOW YOUR COMMUNITY

CHALLENGE

Alice: *I've seen the demographics on Latinos in our community, but the data don't tell me anything about their information needs. I want to be helpful and responsible, but I don't really know where to begin. Some libraries buy lots of Spanish books but they just sit on the shelves. I sure don't want that to happen here. I've got to make good use of my limited budget.*

George: *You're right. The demographics help but we need more useful data, especially about what Latinos in our community want in terms of library programs and materials. Remember when we did that community-wide analysis two years ago? We made some significant improvements as a result of that assessment. I think we need something similar, focusing on the Latino community. That should give us some of the information we need.*

In Chapters 2 and 3 you gained some important insights into the demographics of Latinos in the United States, and you learned how to find the important Latino demographics for your local service area. As useful as the 1990 census is in providing demographic information on Latinos in your community, it definitely has some significant limitations:

- The data from the 1990 census may not accurately reflect the current demographics in your service area, especially if your community has experienced a dramatic and very recent influx of Latino immigrants. Fortunately for all of us, the 2000 census is almost upon us, so in just a few years we will have access to newer data.
- It is very likely that the 1990 census significantly undercounted Latinos, as well as other racial/ethnic groups, in many communities. The undercounting of minorities, which can result in reductions in the allocation of federal dollars to local governments, was considered so problematic that a number of U.S. cities filed legal actions against the Bureau of the Census.[1]
- The census questionnaire does not include library-specific questions. Therefore, census data will never be able to provide all the information needed by library planners.

These shortcomings make it necessary for you to supplement your demographic analysis with a community needs assessment which will provide very specific, library-related information about the Latino community. It will be your guide as you begin to develop library services, programs, and collections for Latinos.

In this chapter, we provide some tips on how to analyze the specific information needs of your local Latino residents. Analyzing a community and its information needs is certainly nothing new. Fortunately, there is a well-established, comprehensive, and easily accessible body of literature on the subject. Salvador Güereña has compiled a very useful bibliography that will be of assistance to those who are responsible for doing community analysis and needs assessment of Latino communities.[2]

LATINO COMMUNITY NEEDS ASSESSMENT

Before we get into the specifics of "how" to conduct a Latino needs assessment, it is important that we address the "why." In our interviews with librarians around the country, we found that needs assessment was considered to be an essential element in planning services for Latinos. Most libraries that were successful in developing library services for Latinos systematically collected primary data about the Latino community and used the data to guide the development of services, programs, and collections. Although no two libraries used identical procedures, the important point was that they had conducted a needs assessment at one time or another. As a result of this assessment, each of these libraries was better informed about Latinos in its community and about their unique information needs. Subsequently, each library was able to allocate resources where they were most needed.

Conducting a needs assessment offers your library numerous benefits. You will be better able to determine how well or poorly your library is currently meeting the needs of Latinos. By having a clear picture of where your library is now, you will have a better understanding of where you need to be in the future, and you will gain some insight into the steps you can take to get there. By interacting with and obtaining data about the Latino community, you will gain valuable information about the perceived quality or extent of your existing services, programs, and collections. You will be able to use this information to help you make decisions about how your library can improve. Identifying the information needs and wants of Latinos in your community will enable you to develop new programs, services, and collections that meet Latino customer needs. Finding out what Latinos in your community currently think of your services and collections will help you develop a plan to meet the current and future information needs of Latinos in your community.

As we approach the new millennium, nearly all of us are struggling with flat budgets, and some are dealing with significant budget cuts. If we lived in an ideal world with unlimited library resources, we would not have to be so concerned with such assessments. The real world of financial constraints requires us to use our limited resources wisely. With citizens and politicians calling for smaller government and greater accountability, we have an obligation to get the biggest bang for the buck. The needs assessment will help you decide where best to put your limited human and financial resources in order to maximize results.

Another potential benefit of studying your community is that the needs analysis itself can often serve as a method of marketing your existing library services. Conducting this assessment serves as notice to Latinos and to the general community that your library is serious about developing or strengthening ties between the library and the Latino community.

Finally, the information you obtain may help you convince major constituencies that significant changes in library services or operations are needed. You may be faced with staff, managers, boards of trustees, or vocal users who are reluctant to have the status quo changed. The information you gather will serve as ammunition when you are challenged for advocating significant changes.

Conducting this needs assessment will require a fair amount of interaction between the library and the Latino community. As with any major library initiative that involves significant outside contact with the public, it's best if your governing board hears about this needs assessment project firsthand from you, rather than secondhand from an outside source. Gaining board approval for this project will help ensure your success.

We will discuss several needs assessment techniques: surveys, informal interviews, and focus groups. For each technique we will present a brief overview and offer some helpful tips and advice.

COMMUNITY SURVEYS

In this section we will take you step-by-step through each major phase involved in surveying Latinos in your community, with particular emphasis on the challenges you face if you choose this method.

Step 1: Develop the questionnaire.

Broadly speaking, the questionnaire you develop should ask Latino respondents about their perceptions of library services and collections, and about their information needs and wants. Like other questionnaires you have developed, it should also include demographic questions about the respondent. This information will enable you to link responses to demographic characteristics. Including such questions in your survey enables you to make a statement like "Most Latino young adult respondents say they would go to the library more often if there were more Latino music compact discs and CD players in the library."

Because librarians are familiar with questionnaires, they are often used in library research. As you know, it is easy to construct a questionnaire; it is relatively difficult to construct a good questionnaire that elicits the needed information. If you decide to use this type of assessment, one of the major challenges that awaits you is the development of the questionnaire.

Another major challenge is the Latino population's heterogeneous language usage. For example, in any Latino community, you are likely to find English-Spanish bilingual individuals as well as English-monolingual and Spanish-monolingual individuals. Therefore, your questionnaire should be bilingual. Since each Latino community is unique, it is impossible for us to provide a questionnaire that can be used in all circumstances.

Appendix A at the end of this chapter provides a comprehensive bilingual questionnaire that can be modified for your own local assessment. The questionnaire comes from the Santa Barbara Public Library. Adapt it to fit your local needs. For example, you may add different categories to the first question to cover the Latino subgroups in your community. We highly recommend that your questionnaire be reviewed by a bilingual person from your area; he or she may recommend modifications that will take into account the subtle language variations that can occur from one place to another. Additionally, before embarking on your community analysis, pretest your questionnaire with a smaller group to find out if you need to make further modifications.

As you know, one of the major problems with questionnaires in general is the low return rate. Generally speaking, you will get a higher return if you have a shorter questionnaire. As much as possible, avoid the temptation of asking too many questions. Your questionnaire need not be long in order to be effective; you only need to ask the right questions.

Step 2: Identify a Latino sample to study.

The second step is to identify Latino respondents to whom your questionnaire can be distributed. Let us say for discussion purposes that your universe is all the Latino households in your service area. For your results to have scientific validity, your questionnaire ideally would be distributed to a random sample of households generated from the entire universe of Latino households.

At first this sounds like an easy enough matter. What makes your task particularly difficult, however, is that there is no such thing as a database of all Latino households in your service area. Lists that are traditionally used in social science research (voter registration lists, property ownership records, telephone directories, criss-cross directories, and the like) all have their obvious biases and shortcomings.

In short, it is not feasible to identify all of the Latino households in your service area. Thus it is impossible to generate a truly random sample from the universe of Latino households. To deal with sampling problems such as these, social scientists use specialized sampling techniques (for example, cluster sampling and stratified sampling), but these techniques are very expensive. Most public libraries do not have the personnel or financial resources to perform these sophisticated statistical sampling techniques. Fortunately, your goal is not to be 100% statistically correct. Instead, your goal is to obtain valuable information that your library will use to its advantage in developing services and collections for Latinos in your service area—and to do this without spending a fortune! You can accomplish this by interacting as much as possible with a cross-section of Latinos in your community.

Many communities have distinct and recognizable Latino neighborhoods. You may already be familiar with the locations of such neighborhoods in your service area. Interacting with formal and informal Latino leaders or with social service providers in the community will also give you some useful information about where Latinos live.

Another useful source is (you guessed it!) the 1990 census. You may want to consult a series called the *1990 Census of Population and Housing: Population and Housing Characteristics for Census Tracts and Block Numbering Areas*, also known as "CPH-3."[3] There are 346 volumes in this series, with a volume for each state and territory, plus a volume for each of the metropolitan areas in the United States. Your library most likely owns at least the volumes that cover your service area, and probably additional volumes as well. This series will not be that useful for libraries serving sparsely populated areas, but will be more useful for other libraries because it provides data on the number of Latinos in the various census tracts and block numbering areas. Unfortunately, however, as with other census materials, this series will not be of much help if your service area has experienced dramatic Latino population growth rates since 1990.

Let us assume in this discussion that you have already identified a Latino neighborhood in your community. Since it may not be practical to distribute a questionnaire to each household in the Latino neighborhood, you need to identify a sample of households in that neighborhood. One possibility for identifying a sample is to divide the neighborhood into neighborhood blocks, and then use one or more blocks to serve as your target area. Your sample would include each household in the selected block or blocks.

Another strategy is to select a reasonable number of households in the neighborhood to be included in the sample. Let us assume that this particular Latino neighborhood has 200 households. If you want to reach 20% of the households, you need to distribute your questionnaire to 40 households. You could choose every fifth household in the neighborhood to be in your sample.

A third strategy is to obtain addresses from a variety of lists, and then generate a sample from this merged list. Vivian Pisano and Margaret Skidmore used this approach when they conducted a community analysis of Richmond, Virginia, back in 1978.[4] Their suggestions are still applicable to anyone doing such research today. In addition to using reverse telephone directories, they suggest that you obtain information from such community groups as schools, police–community liaison groups, community centers, ESL classes, public health agencies, neighborhood groups, social agencies, and churches. Creating a merged list from all these various sources, and then generating a sample from this merged list is not 100% statistically valid, but it may be the best approach.

Whichever sampling technique you use, your sample should resemble, as much as possible, Latinos in your community. If, for example, Latinos in your community have generally low levels of educational attainment, your sample should reflect this; therefore, you would not want your sample to be made up primarily of Latino college students.

Step 3: Distribute the questionnaires to your sample population.

Once a sample is selected, questionnaires are then distributed using one or more of the following methods:

- through the mail
- by hand delivery
- by personal interview
- by interview over the telephone

Usually surveys are conducted through the mail. Respondents answer the questions at their convenience and deposit the response in the mail. If you take this approach, you will get a higher return rate if you include a self-addressed, stamped envelope. You might consider including some other small benefit that encourages a response. You have probably received mailings from professional marketing firms that include a one-dollar bill as a small incentive to answering a questionnaire. You can do something similar, but with a library twist. For example, you can purchase inexpensive "Celebrate Latino Heritage" bookmarks from ALA and include them in your distribution packet. You can also consider including a coupon for a free book at your annual book sale. Small things like this can make a big difference.

Your survey can also be conducted in a one-on-one interview in person or by telephone call. An obvious factor to consider when using this interview approach is the language skill of the interviewers. If you decide to use this interview approach, you will need bilingual interviewers.

Assuming your library does not have enough bilingual interviewers to conduct this assessment, you will have to get outside assistance. Refer to Chapter 8 to identify potential partners to help you in this task. Local higher education institutions can provide the assistance you might need. Individuals with expertise in research methodology and/or with Spanish-language fluency are typically found here, and they are often willing to serve as consultants because of the service mission of the institution.

Another distribution method that libraries sometimes use in conducting a needs assessment is to distribute the questionnaire to Latino users as they enter the library. Distributing the needs assessment tool in the library is an inexpensive method that may work for libraries or branches in neighborhoods with very high concentrations of Latinos. In general, this approach has limitations concerning nonusers. This approach works if your sole intent is to study the information needs of current Latino library users. But if you are interested in attracting new Latino users to the library, it is essential to go out into the Latino community to conduct your analysis.

Step 4: **Collect the information and synthesize the results.**

Because most libraries have access to someone familiar with collecting and synthesizing data, we will not discuss this topic at length. It is critical, however, that you devote time and effort to distilling the collected information into a brief report. The report should specify the purpose of the study, the methodology used, and the results. The results section should itemize the concerns that Latinos have expressed in the survey. It might also be helpful to have a list of these needs/wants statements translated into Spanish for the benefit of interested Spanish-monolingual individuals in the community.

The Latinos in your community may express concerns in very general terms; they may be quite specific about others. One effective way to summarize these concerns in your report is to develop a series of "Latino needs/wants statements." Figure 9–2 on page 180 provides a few examples of needs/wants statements.

These needs/wants statements give life to your report. They are easy to read and understand, and they can provide very useful information to staff who use the results to develop programs, services, and collections for Latinos.

Step 5: **Publicize the results of your assessment.**

Conducting your needs assessment is sure to generate widespread interest in your findings. By all means, publicize your findings both internally and externally, and especially to the Latino community. Try to reach the Latino community through your local Spanish-language media, if this is available, to show your genuine interest in serving Latinos in your community and indicate that you are reviewing the results and are serious about making changes to benefit Latinos.

If access to the media is limited or nonexistent, use the flyer distribution method to share the information. Usually, the key points/results from your survey can be covered in a double-sided, one-page flyer.

Those who conduct surveys face three major limitations:
    they are costly
    they are labor intensive
    they are time-consuming

Nonetheless, if this is the methodology you choose, you can enlist volunteers to help and/or secure external funding to accomplish this task.

INFORMAL INTERVIEWS

Since questionnaries present some significant methodological and practical problems, you may want to try another kind of assessment. In this second method, your focus is on obtaining qualitative information by conducting one-on-one interviews. This type of assessment includes the following steps:

Step 1: Develop the interview questions.

Develop interview questions that address issues such as the perceptions of the library among Latinos, information needs of the Latino community, perception of barriers to providing services and collections, and suggestions from the Latino community on improving library services and collections.

The model questionnaire in Appendix A at the end of this chapter and the model focus group questions that we discuss in the next section provide some good ideas on the kinds of questions that you need to ask.

One major advantage of this technique is that you have the advantage of being able to ask open-ended and follow-up questions. Feel free to use the comprehensive model questionnaire and model focus group questions as starting points and modify them as needed to meet your own local, unique needs.

Step 2: Identify leaders in the Latino community.

Identify the recognized formal leaders (business, political, civic, social) from the Latino community itself. Latino leaders will be able to provide valuable information on their perceptions of Latino information needs. They will also be able to provide the names of other important Latino contacts, including both formal and informal leaders, for your assessment.

An excellent source of respondents is the local Spanish-language media (print, radio, television), if available. Leaders in this industry are usually well connected with the Latino community and therefore can provide useful information for your assessment and can provide further contacts. A side benefit of contacting the media is that you may get some free advertising. If there are no Spanish-language media in your community, a Latino columnist or Latino journalist may be employed by the local media. These individuals can be very helpful contacts.

Step 3: Develop a list of community resources.

Develop a list of agencies, organizations, and businesses in your community where you are likely to find willing respondents who can provide useful information about Latinos and their information needs.

Since religion is very important in Latino culture, many Latinos are likely to be church members. Consequently, you can get valuable information by interviewing religious and lay leaders in churches that have significant numbers of Latinos. Most will be very supportive of your efforts to reach out to the Latino community.

Also at the top of your list of possible interviewees should be K–12 and higher education administrators. Not only can these administrators be good sources of information themselves, they can also put you in touch with interested Latino faculty and students in their institutions.

If your community has businesses that employ a large number of Latinos, the human resources professionals in these companies may be a valuable source of employment information about Latinos in your community. Specifically, they are in a good position to tell you about particular occupations or skills that their companies need now or will need in the near future. You can use this information to guide the development of a self-help or job skills collection for Latino adults.

Step 4: Compile a list of events or places where significant numbers of Latinos typically congregate.

In the three previous steps, you identified important contacts (both Latino and from the larger community) who are knowledgeable about and can comment on the information needs of the Latino community. Interviewing these individuals can give you valuable insight, but bear in mind that these individuals, by definition, are elite members of the community. Such interviews may yield incomplete, or worse yet, erroneous information. Therefore, it is critical that your assessment include the viewpoints of Latinos from *all walks of life*.

There are numerous celebrations and festivals in communities around the country, many of which attract Latinos. Especially important are the festivals organized by the Latino community itself. Cinco de Mayo is a good example of a Mexican holiday celebrated by Latinos of Mexican descent. See Appendix A in Chapter 5 for a list of other holidays that may be celebrated in your community. Consider contacting your local festival organizers to set up a library booth where you can display examples of Spanish-language materials and promotional literature about your library. You can distribute brief questionnaires, interview passersby who take an active interest, and sign people up for library cards. A needs assessment does not have to be drudgery. Whenever possible, make it fun and enjoyable for everyone by conducting it in an informal, relaxed atmosphere.

Consider setting up a library booth at other places where Latinos congregate. For example, visit with local church leaders to ask permission to distribute questionnaires or conduct interviews at church after Sunday services. Also, many churches have annual festivals or bazaars which offer great opportunities to interact with the Latino community in a more relaxed, fun atmosphere.

Another place to set up a booth and interviewing area is the local supermarket. Check with the managers of supermarkets in Latino neighborhoods to ask if you can set up a booth on payday. Similarly, you can set up a booth at the local mall or shopping center, or even the local flea market.

Step 5: Remember to interview Latinos from all socioeconomic groups.

Your most difficult challenge will be to obtain information from the poor and the working poor. One of the more effective ways of accomplishing this is to compile a list of the directors of the various community agencies that assist those in need of financial assistance and/or other support services. Try to convince the directors of these agencies to provide you temporarily with a small area in the agency's waiting area for interviewing purposes. Remember that your library and these agencies are possible partners, and you may have something to offer them in exchange for making this temporary arrangement.

Step 6: Start conducting the assessment.

You can start by developing a schedule to interview the various contacts you have identified in the previous steps. If at all possible, we recommend interviewing the formal and informal Latino leaders first, thus signaling to Latinos and others that you consider the information needs of Latinos to be of vital importance. This approach will go a long way toward ensuring the success of your needs assessment and will facilitate your library's future interactions with the Latino community in general.

After interviewing the Latino leadership, you can proceed

to interview respondents that were identified in steps 3–5 above.

One of the major challenges in using this informal interview technique is that you must have enough bilingual interviewers to accomplish the task. When you go out into the community to conduct your assessment, you will encounter Spanish-monolingual, English-monolingual, and bilingual individuals, so you will need to recruit and train bilingual individuals for this assessment project.

The ideal is to have bilingual library personnel conducting the various interviews. However, this resource is not often available to you. The next best option is to conduct interviews using a two-person team that includes a library employee and a bilingual individual from the community.

Another challenge for your interviewers is dealing with open-ended questions. Some of the questions asked during the interview will be multiple-choice items which do not present much of a problem. The interviewer simply checks off the appropriate answer from the menu of choices. Other questions are much more open-ended. The best advice for interviewers is to take good notes during the interview and to write a summary paragraph after it is concluded.

Step 7: Compile the information and synthesize the results.

This step is a bit more difficult than the corresponding step in the questionnaire method, primarily because of the nature of interview data. In a questionnaire, the respondent typically selects an answer from a menu of choices which makes tabulating results a relatively easy process. However, in an informal interview, there may be lengthy responses to open-ended questions. You will need to keep track of these responses because these will give you valuable insights into Latino needs/wants. Finally, plan to develop Latino needs/wants statements, as suggested in Step 4 of the questionnaire method.

Step 8: Publicize the major findings of your interviews.

See Step 5 in the questionnaire section to review advice on this step.

Summary

In summary, informal interviews are informal assessments allowing you to concentrate your efforts on interacting with Latino and non-Latino leaders and with Latinos in the community from different socioeconomic backgrounds. These interviews can be conducted in a variety of settings outside the library. One major benefit of this approach is that your sincere interactions with a large number of Latinos is a strong and clear message that your library is serious about providing services and collections to this segment of the community. A side benefit is the interaction with the Latino community, allowing the library to take its first all-important step in marketing library services and collections to Latinos.

FOCUS GROUPS

A third type of assessment that is becoming more popular with libraries is the use of focus groups. This technique has been successfully used in libraries as varied as Denver Public Library, Salt Lake City Public Library, and Newark Public Library.

Focus group sessions are essentially group interviews during which a group moderator asks a series of open-ended questions designed to encourage participants to interact with the moderator and, most important, with each other. Perhaps one of the major reasons these sessions work so well is that most of us spend an enjoyable and significant portion of our daily lives in some kind of meaningful group interaction. Focus groups may tap into this social need.

Perhaps another reason they work so well is that sometimes people need to hear and acknowledge a variety of viewpoints on some issues before they form their own personal opinions. Our attitudes and perceptions of the world are shaped, in part, by the influence of people around us. In a focus group session, participants can

- listen and react to responses of the other members of the group
- change their minds as many times as they want, based on information they obtain from their co-participants
- attempt to influence the opinions of others
- learn directly from their co-participants about the wide range of opinions on certain issues

Fortunately, you need not spend a fortune to conduct focus group interviews. Successful focus group projects include three key components:

- focus grous members
- a focus group moderator
- focus group questions

Each of these three is discussed below.

Step 1: Hold one or more focus groups, each composed of six to ten individuals who share a demographic characteristic.

Many kinds of Latino focus groups are possible and useful in your needs assessment. For example, you can conduct Latino focus groups with young adults, business owners, ESL (English as a Second Language) class members, college students, Latino leaders, or (with skill, patience, and creativity) even children, to name just a few of the possibilities.

Since no one focus group has all the answers, you will not be able to rely solely on the input of just one focus group to gather all the information you need. Therefore, you will want to set up a variety of focus groups, each with participants sharing some demographic characteristic, in order to get a cross-section of opinion.

It is impossible to recommend a specific number of groups to convene. Eventually you reach the point at which the high cost of conducting more focus groups is not worth the added effort and expense. The proper number is reached when you feel you have a good cross-section of Latinos represented in your focus groups. This is a judgment call on your part. You can use your demographic data to help determine the optimum type and number of focus groups.

For the purposes of the following discussion, let us assume that you want to conduct a focus group session with the formal leaders in the Latino community. Your first step is to identify Latino leaders from a variety of organizations (such as K–12 and higher education, churches, professional groups, social agencies, and civic groups) who might be interested in participating.

The next step is to inform them of the library's intent to improve services and collections for Latinos. Describe the focus group process and invite them to participate. Since they are highly committed to Latino causes, you will probably have no trouble getting a number of Latino leaders to accept your invitation. Indicate that, if needed, a bilingual translator will be available during the session, and ask each participant if this service is needed. When you get at least six willing participants from a variety of organizations, you have successfully completed the first step.

Step 2: Use a focus group moderator to guide the group discussion.

If your moderator has formal and specialized training in conducting focus groups, this will help ensure the success of this project. Certainly, if you have such a resource, make use of it. If you have the financial resources to hire a focus group consultant, at least one company specializes in conducting Latino focus groups for public libraries.[5] Since most small and medium-sized libraries do not have the resources to hire someone to do this, you will probably rely primarily on in-house resources. Your library may be lacking in specialized focus group expertise, but you can easily make up for this with commitment and resourcefulness!

The most important qualifications for a moderator include:

- interest in conducting focus groups
- skill and experience in leading group discussions
- familiarity with library operations

In your library you can probably readily identify a number of individuals, including yourself, with these skills and attitudes whom you could recruit to take part in such a project.

Getting back to our example, since it is possible that one or more of the Latino leaders will be monolingual in Spanish, ideally your focus group moderator should be a bilingual/bicultural library employee. Realizing that this may not be a possibility right now, the next best option is for the focus group to be moderated by a library employee with assistance from a bilingual community volunteer.

Step 3: Provide the focus group moderator with a list of open-ended and broad-based focus group questions that can be used to lead the discussion.

Salt Lake City Public Library recently conducted focus group sessions to analyze the information needs of Latinos in that community. As with other materials in this manual, these questions can be used as a starting point and modified to meet your local, unique needs. The questions that were used in that assessment are included in Appendix B.

Once you have your three key components—focus group members, a focus group moderator, and focus group questions—you are ready to begin the assessment. Here are step-by-step suggestions for conducting a focus group:

Step 1: Select and equip a suitable site.

Select a suitably comfortable conference room in the library where the focus group can be conducted. Another possible area to conduct your focus group is in the Latino community itself. Many Latino organizations will gladly offer their meeting facilities for this purpose.

Before the participants arrive, make sure that the conference room is set up to facilitate interaction among all the participants. If possible, use a round table large enough to accommodate comfortably the moderator, all the participants, and, if necessary, the interpreter. Providing light refreshments will add to the comfort level. Provide tape and a flip-chart with large paper so that the moderator can take notes and tape them on the wall for everyone to see.

Step 2: Prepare the participants.

If you have both English-monolingual and Spanish-monolingual individuals, you will need the services of an interpreter. Translating from one language to the other will slow down the process; however, the benefits of providing this service is a signal that you respect each participant's language abilities and it is well worth the time and effort.

When all the participants have arrived, the moderator should introduce everyone involved in the focus group (or encourage self-introductions), provide a brief introduction to the focus group method, and present a brief overview of why the library is conducting this research. If needed, the bilingual interpreter translates during the session.

Next, the moderator should provide the ground rules on how the focus group session will be conducted. Here are some possible rules:

- Each individual has an opportunity to speak without interruption.
- Each individual has the right to an opinion and the right to express that opinion.
- Everyone has the right to agree or disagree with an expressed opinion.
- No one has the right to ridicule an individual's ideas or opinions.
- The moderator's role is simply to facilitate group discussion, not to take sides or settle any disputes that occur.
- Each individual has the right to change his or her own opinions at any time during the entire course of the session.
- To encourage full participation, each individual agrees that all personal opinions expressed during the session are to be considered confidential.
- Each participant agrees that there should be documentation of the significant points made during the session;

the moderator is responsible for this activity by making notations on the flip-chart for all participants to see, but maintains strict confidentiality by not linking specific comments to a specific individual.

- Each participant agrees to a maximum time limit of 90 minutes; if time constraints require the moderator to call for an end of discussion to a particular item, each agrees to move on to the next question.

These are only suggested ground rules. The moderator can make modifications to suit personal style.

Step 3: Conduct the session.

After setting the ground rules, the moderator asks the first question, encourages interaction among the participants, and then asks any appropriate sub-questions or follow-up questions. It is important for the moderator to make notations on the flip-chart to keep the group focused on the specific question and to provide a written record of the group's significant points.

When it appears to the moderator that the question has been fully discussed, the moderator should verbally summarize the main points brought up during the discussion and make certain that these key points appear on the flip-chart. This process is continued until all questions have been asked and fully explored within the 90–minute framework.

The moderator concludes the focus group session by thanking the participants for their time and effort and assuring them that their important ideas will be taken into consideration in planning programs, services, and collections for Latinos. After the session is concluded, the moderator gathers up the flip-charts with the written notations and provides the material to the person responsible for the overall assessment.

Step 4: Synthesize and summarize the results.

As in the case of the previous two assessment methods, it is important to synthesize the results of your focus group research. Since there is a written record of each focus group that summarizes the key points for each question, this task is relatively easy.

As we suggested in the two previous assessment methods, it will be helpful to summarize key points by developing a series of Latino needs/wants statements.

Step 5: Publicize the results of your focus groups.

See Step 5 in the questionnaire section to review advice on this step.

CONCLUSION

We have detailed three very general techniques for conducting a needs analysis of the Latino community in your service area—questionnaires, informal surveys, and focus groups. For each, we provided a brief overview of the methodology, discussed the advantages and disadvantages, and addressed the major challenges that await the library planner who is responsible for conducting such analyses with the Latino community. Although you will be required to devote human and financial resources to this process, we promise that the rewards greatly outweigh the costs.

There is no hard and fast rule for which of these three assessment techniques you should select. In fact, you may find it useful in your Latino needs assessment to use more than one of these techniques. Since many variables are involved (such as history and background of your library, history of the relationship between your library and the Latino community, financial and human resources available to conduct such analyses), you are in a better position to decide which technique, or combination of techniques, is best for your local situation. Finally, remember that you can write a grant proposal to obtain external funds to do a Latino community needs assessment.

Since this is not a library science research methods text, it is impossible to address each and every issue involved in needs assessment. We hope that this introduction encourages you to learn more about needs assessment techniques—which you will need to have in your toolkit because of the dramatically changing demographics of our nation.

NOTES

1. Richard Perez-Peña, "Big Cities Win Appeals Ruling on '90 Census," *New York Times*, 9 August 1994, sec. A1.
2. Salvador Güereña, "Community Analysis and Needs Assessment," in *Latino Librarianship: A Handbook for Professionals* (Jefferson, N.C.: McFarland & Company, 1990), 17–23.
3. U.S. Bureau of the Census, *Census of Population and Housing:*

Population and Housing Characteristics for Census Tracts and Block Numbering Areas, 1990, prepared by the Economics and Statistics Administration, Department of Commerce (Washington, D. C., U.S. Government Printing Office, 1993).

4. Vivian H. Pisano and Margaret Skidmore, "Community Survey—Why Not Take an Eclectic Approach?" *Wilson Library Bulletin* 53 (November 1978): 253.

5. Visions, Inc., conducts focus groups for libraries assessing needs of Latino users. E-mail communication, March 11, 1996, Carol Brey, President. Contact: 12065 José Cisneros Drive, El Paso, Tex., 79936; (800) 356–9622.

APPENDIX A
SANTA BARBARA PUBLIC LIBRARY QUESTIONNAIRE

1. **How would you identify your ethnic heritage?**
   1 ___ Mexican-American/Chicano
   2 ___ Mexican
   3 ___ Other Latino
   4 ___ Native American
   5 ___ Black
   6 ___ Asian-Chinese
   7 ___ Asian-Japanese
   8 ___ Asian-Filipino
   9 ___ Other Asian: _____
   10 ___ Decline to identify

2. **The public library is known as a place where one may check out books, magazines, or borrow records. The library is also a place where one goes or calls for information, and is also a place for special activities for children, cultural programs, and other services.**
   Do you know where the nearest library is located?
   1 ___ Yes
   2 ___ No

3. **Are you aware that all basic library services are free?**
   1 ___ Yes
   2 ___ No
   3 ___ Don't know

4. **Do you or a member of your family have a library card?**
   1 ___ Yes
   2 ___ No
   3 ___ Don't know

5. **In the past year have you visited or used any services of the Santa Barbara Public Library?**
   1 ___ Yes
   2 ___ No (go to #10)
   3 ___ Don't know (go to #10)

1. **¿De qué origen proviene usted?**
   1 ___ México-Americano/Chicano
   2 ___ Mexicano
   3 ___ Otro Latino
   4 ___ Indio
   5 ___ Negro
   6 ___ Asiático-Chino
   7 ___ Asiático-Japonés
   8 ___ Asiático-Filipino
   9 ___ Otro Asiático: _____
   10 ___ Prefiero no contestar

2. **La Biblioteca Pública es conocida como un lugar donde se presta libros, revistas, o discos. La biblioteca también es un lugar donde alguien puede llamar para información, y es un lugar para actividades especiales para niños, programas culturales, y otros servicios.**
   ¿Sabe Ud. donde se encuentra la biblioteca más cercana?
   1 ___ Sí
   2 ___ No

3. **¿Sabe Ud. que los servicios básicos de la biblioteca son gratuitos?**
   1 ___ Sí
   2 ___ No
   3 ___ No sé

4. **¿Tiene Ud. o alguien en su familia una tarjeta de la biblioteca?**
   1 ___ Sí
   2 ___ No
   3 ___ No sé

5. **Durante este año pasado—¿Ha Ud. visitado o usado cualquier servicio de alguna biblioteca en Santa Barbara?**
   1 ___ Sí
   2 ___ No (prosiga al #10)
   3 ___ No sé (prosiga al #10)

6. **Which of the following have you used or are you using? (check as many as apply)**
   1 __ Central Branch (40 E Anapamu)
   2 __ Eastside Branch (1102 E Montecito)
   3 __ Goleta Branch (500 N Fairview Av.)
   4 __ Carpinteria Branch (5141 Carpinteria Av.)
   5 __ Book Mobile
   6 __ Other _____
   7 __ Don't know

7. **Who in your household uses the library(s) you mentioned? (check as many as apply)**
   1 __ Self
   2 __ Spouse
   3 __ Children
   4 __ Other household members _____

8. **If you have used a Santa Barbara Public Library, what type of materials do you check out the most? (check as many as apply)**
   1 ___ Books, magazines, newspapers
   2 ___ Films
   3 ___ Records, cassettes
   4 ___ Art prints
   5 ___ Other
   6 ___ Don't know

9. **In the past year how often have you used a public library?**
   1 ___ At least once a week (go to #12)
   2 ___ At least once a month (go to #12)
   3 ___ At least once every six months
   4 ___ Don't know

10. **The following are a number of reasons why some people never or seldom (once every six months) use the library. Do you feel that any of them are true for you? (check as many as desirable)**
    1 ___ Library does not have the material I want
    2 ___ I am too busy to go to the library
    3 ___ I am not interested in the library
    4 ___ I buy my own books or magazines
    5 ___ Personal health problems make it difficult for me to use the library
    6 ___ I don't know about the library
    7 ___ The library is not open during the right hours
    8 ___ The library is hard to get to/no transportation
    9 ___ The staff at the library is not friendly
    10 ___ No one on the staff speaks my language
    11 ___ Other

11. **If you are not using the library, how could the library serve your needs and interests?**
    _____
    _____
    _____

6. **¿Cuál de las siguientes ha Ud. usado o usa actualmente?**
   1 ___ Biblioteca Central (40 E Anapamu)
   2 ___ Biblioteca Pública del Este (1102 E Montecito)
   3 ___ Biblioteca Pública de Goleta (500 N Fairview Av.)
   4 ___ Biblioteca Pública de Carpinteria (5141 Carpinteria Av.)
   5 ___ Biblioteca ambulante
   6 ___ Otra _____
   7 ___ No sé

7. **¿Quién en su hogar usa la biblioteca(s) que Ud. nombró? (marque todos los que apliquen)**
   1 ___ Yo solamente
   2 ___ Su esposa/esposo
   3 ___ Los niños
   4 ___ Otros miembros de su hogar _____

8. **Si Ud. ha usado su tarjeta bibliotecaria—¿Qué clase de materiales ha Ud. preferido?**
   1 ___ Libros, revistas y periódicos
   2 ___ Películas
   3 ___ Discos y cintas grabadas
   4 ___ Reproducciones gráficas de arte
   5 ___ Otro
   6 ___ No sé

9. **Durante el año pasado—¿Con qué frecuencia ha usted usado alguna biblioteca pública?**
   1 ___ Por lo menos una vez por semana (prosiga al #12)
   2 ___ Por lo menos una vez por mes (prosiga al #12)
   3 ___ Por lo menos una vez cada seis meses
   4 ___ No sé

10. **Por las siguientes razones, hay personas que nunca o raramente visitan la biblioteca—¿Cuáles le corresponden a usted? "Raramente" se considera cada 6 meses.**
    1 ___ La biblioteca no tiene los materiales que deseo
    2 ___ Estoy muy ocupado para usar la biblioteca
    3 ___ No estoy interesado en usar la biblioteca
    4 ___ Yo compro mis libros o revistas
    5 ___ No uso la biblioteca porque no me siento suficiente bien de salud para ir
    6 ___ No sé de la biblioteca
    7 ___ La biblioteca no está abierta durante el tiempo más conveniente para mi
    8 ___ Es dificil para ir a la biblioteca/hay falta de transportación
    9 ___ Los que trabajan en la biblioteca no son muy amables conmigo
    10 ___ Nadie en la biblioteca habla en mi idioma
    11 ___ Otro

11. **Si no usa Ud. la biblioteca—¿Cómo podrá la biblioteca servir sus intereses?**
    _____
    _____
    _____

12. **The following are some of the reasons people use the library. Do you (user)/Would you (nonuser) use the library for any of these reasons? (check all that apply)**
    1 ___ Read or borrow newspapers or magazines
    2 ___ Read or borrow books
    3 ___ Use or borrow materials other than books (films, language tapes, records, etc.)
    4 ___ Meet friends/drop off children/pick up children
    5 ___ Use the photocopy machine
    6 ___ Obtain information about community services
    7 ___ School assignments or other study purposes
    8 ___ Attend a children's library program
    9 ___ Job information
    10 ___ For a meeting
    11 ___ Reference or to have a question answered
    12 ___ Other _____
    13 ___ Don't know

13. **Which language or languages are spoken in your home? (check one)**
    1 ___ English
    2 ___ Spanish only
    3 ___ Both English and Spanish
    4 ___ Mostly English
    5 ___ Mostly Spanish
    6 ___ Asian language
    7 ___ Other _____

14a. **Do you or anyone in your household read in English, Spanish or in another language?**
    1 ___ Yes
    2 ___ No (go to #18)
    3 ___ Don't know (go to #18)

14b. **Who reads?**
    1 ___ Self
    2 ___ Other household members

15. **In which language do you prefer to read? (check one)**
    1 ___ English
    2 ___ Spanish
    3 ___ Both English and Spanish
    4 ___ Asian language
    5 ___ Other _____
    6 ___ Don't know

16. **What kinds of material do you prefer to read in your free time? (check as many as apply)**
    1 ___ Magazines
    2 ___ Newspapers
    3 ___ Foto novelas
    4 ___ Comic books
    5 ___ Books

12. **Los siguientes son unos ejemplos por los cuales las personas usan la biblioteca. ¿Usa usted o usaría la biblioteca para cualquiera de estos? (marque los necesarios)**
    1 ___ Para leer o pedir prestado libros
    2 ___ Para leer o pedir prestado periódicos o revistas
    3 ___ Para usar o pedir prestados otros materiales, además de libros, películas, cintas, discos
    4 ___ Para reunirse con amigos/o dejar a los niños
    5 ___ Para usar la maquina que hace foto-copias
    6 ___ Para obtener información de servicios en la comunidad
    7 ___ Para propósitos de escuela o estudio
    8 ___ Para asistir a un programa para niños
    9 ___ Para información de trabajo
    10 ___ Para una junta
    11 ___ Para referencia o contestación de preguntas
    12 ___ Otra razón _____
    13 ___ No sé

13. **¿Cuáles idiomas se hablan en su hogar? (marque una)**
    1 ___ Inglés
    2 ___ Solamente español
    3 ___ Inglés y español
    4 ___ Mayormente inglés
    5 ___ Mayormente español
    6 ___ Un idioma asiático
    7 ___ Otro _____

14a. **¿Lee usted, o alguien en su hogar inglés, español, o en otro idioma?**
    1 ___ Sí
    2 ___ No (proceda al #18)
    3 ___ No sé (proceda al #18)

14b. **¿Quiénes leen dichos idiomas?**
    1 ___ Yo
    2 ___ Otros en mi hogar

15. **¿En qué idioma prefiere usted leer?**
    1 ___ Inglés
    2 ___ Español
    3 ___ Inglés y español
    4 ___ Idioma asiático
    5 ___ Otro _____
    6 ___ No sé

16. **¿Qué clase de materiales prefiere leer en su tiempo libre?**
    1 ___ Revistas
    2 ___ Periódicos
    3 ___ Fotonovelas
    4 ___ Libros cómicos
    5 ___ Libros

17. **If you read books, what kind of books do you most often read?**
    1 ___ History
    2 ___ Religion
    3 ___ Animals
    4 ___ Crafts
    5 ___ Home making
    6 ___ Biographies
    7 ___ Studying language
       a) English _____ b) Spanish ____ c) Other ____
    8 ___ Travel
    9 ___ Mysteries
    10 ___ Plays
    11 ___ Short stories
    12 ___ Romance
    13 ___ Translation of U.S. best sellers
    14 ___ Stories or essays by Latin American authors
    15 ___ Books about Mexico/Chicanos
    16 ___ Literature
    17 ___ Adventure
    18 ___ Comic books
    19 ___ Politics
    20 ___ Other _____

18. **Which of the following newspapers do you read? (check as many as apply)**
    1 ___ Santa Barbara News Press
    2 ___ Santa Barbara News and Review
    3 ___ Los Angeles Times
    4 ___ Los Angeles Sentinel
    5 ___ La Opinion
    6 ___ La Voz del Pueblo
    7 ___ Excelsior
    8 ___ Other _____
    9 ___ Don't know
    10 ___ Don't read newspapers

19. **How many magazines do the members of your household currently subscribe to? (check one)**
    1 ___ None (go to #21)
    2 ___ One to two
    3 ___ Three to four
    4 ___ Five or more
    5 ___ Don't know

20. **Are any of these in Spanish or in another language?**
    1 ___ Spanish
    2 ___ Other language
    3 ___ English only
    4 ___ Asian
    5 ___ Don't know

17. **Si lee libros—¿Qué clase de libros lee más a menudo?**
    1 ___ Historia
    2 ___ Religión
    3 ___ Animales
    4 ___ Artesanía
    5 ___ Hogar
    6 ___ Biografías
    7 ___ Estudio de lenguaje
       a) inglés _____ b) español _____ c) otro _____
    8 ___ Viajes
    9 ___ Misterio
    10 ___ Dramas
    11 ___ Cuentos cortos
    12 ___ Romance
    13 ___ Traducciones de libros populares en inglés
    14 ___ Cuentos o ensayos por autores Latino Americanos
    15 ___ Libros sobre México/Chicanos
    16 ___ Literatura
    17 ___ Aventura
    18 ___ Libros cómicos
    19 ___ Política
    20 ___ Otro _____

18. **¿Cuál de los siguientes periódicos lee usted? (marque todos los que lea)**
    1 ___ Santa Barbara News Press
    2 ___ Santa Barbara News and Review
    3 ___ Los Angeles Times
    4 ___ Los Angeles Sentinel
    5 ___ La Opinion
    6 ___ La Voz del Pueblo
    7 ___ Excelsior
    8 ___ Otro _____
    9 ___ No sé
    10 ___ No leo periódicos

19. **¿A cuántas revistas se suscriben los miembros de su familia, actualmente? (marque uno)**
    1 ___ Ninguna (proceda al #21)
    2 ___ Uno a dos
    3 ___ Tres a cuatro
    4 ___ Cinco o más
    5 ___ No sé

20. **¿Son algunas en español, inglés, o en otro idioma?**
    1 ___ Español
    2 ___ Otro idioma
    3 ___ Solamente en inglés
    4 ___ Idioma asiático
    5 ___ No sé

21. What are your major sources of information?
1 ___ Radio
    a) Santa Barbara stations: _____
    b) Oxnard stations: _____
    c) Los Angeles stations: _____
    d) Other: _____
2 ___ Television
    a) Local station KEYT (channel 3 or 6) ___
    b) Los Angeles KMEX (channel 34 or 8) ___
    c) Other _____
3 ___ Newspapers and magazines
4 ___ Books
5 ___ Family and friends
5a __ Identify _____ Relationship _____
            _____   _____
            _____   _____
6 ___ Public library
7 ___ Social service agencies
8 ___ Other _____

22. Which one of the above do you rely on most?
1 ___ Radio
    a) Santa Barbara station: _____
    b) Oxnard stations: _____
    c) Los Angeles stations: _____
    d) Other: _____
2 ___ Television
    a) Local station KEYT (channel 3 or 6) ___
    b) Los Angeles KMEX (channel 34 or 8) ___
    c) Other
3 ___ Newspapers and magazines
4 ___ Books
5 ___ Family and friends
5a __ Identify _____ Relationship _____
            _____   _____
            _____   _____
6 ___ Public library
7 ___ Social service agencies
8 ___ Other _____

23. Are there times when you or someone in your household needs information on government services, health, or social services?
1 ___ Yes
2 ___ No
3 ___ Don't know

24. In your opinion, what kinds of social service information are needed by you or those in your household? (check as many as apply)
1 __ Information about schools and education
2 __ Information about job openings
3 __ Information on drugs and alcohol
4 __ Personal or family counseling
5 __ Where to get emergency food, clothes, money
6 __ Information on housing and landlord-tenant problems
7 __ Information on immigration and citizenship

21. ¿Cuáles son sus mayores recursos de información?
1 ___ Radio
    a) Estaciones de Santa Barbara: _____
    b) Estaciones de Oxnard: _____
    c) Estaciones de Los Angeles: _____
    d) Otras: _____
2 ___ Televisión
    a) Estación local KEYT (canal 3 o 6) _____
    b) Los Angeles KMEX (canal 34 o 8) _____
    c) Otras _____
3 ___ Periódicos y amigos
4 ___ Libros
5 ___ Familia y amigos
5a __ Idenifique _____ Relación _____
            _____   _____
            _____   _____
6 ___ Biblioteca pública
7 ___ Agencia de servicios sociales
8 ___ Otros _____

22. De los nombres ya mencionados—¿De cuál depende usted más?
1 ___ Radio
    a) Estaciones de Santa Barbara: _____
    b) Estaciones de Oxnard: _____
    c) Estaciones de Los Angeles: _____
    d) Otras: _____
2 ___ Televisión
    a) Estación local KEYT (canal 3 o 6) _____
    b) Los Angeles KMEX (canal 34 o 8) _____
    c) Otras _____
3 ___ Periódicos y amigos
4 ___ Libros
5 ___ Familia y amigos
5a __ Idenifique _____ Relación _____
            _____   _____
            _____   _____
6 ___ Biblioteca pública
7 ___ Agencia de servicios sociales
8 ___ Otros _____

23. ¿Existen ocasiones cuando Ud. o alguien en su casa necesita información acerca de los servicios del gobierno, salud o servicios sociales?
1 ___ Sí
2 ___ No
3 ___ No sé

24. En su opinión—¿Qué clase de información de servicios sociales son los que se necesitan en su hogar? (marque los necesarios)
1 ___ Información escolar y educacional
2 ___ Información acerca de oportunidades de trabajo
3 ___ Información acerca de drogas y alcohol
4 ___ Consultas personales y familiares
5 ___ Donde conseguir en caso de emergencia, alimentos, ropa o dinero
6 ___ Información sobre vivienda y problemas propietario e inquilino
7 ___ Información referente con ciudadanía e inmigración

8 ___ Legal counseling or assistance
9 ___ Information on low cost medical or health services
10 ___ Translations
11 ___ Information on recreational facilities or programs
12 ___ Transportation
13 ___ Where to get help in emergency or crisis situation
14 ___ Assistance in dealing with agencies
15 ___ Information on welfare
16 ___ Consumer information
17 ___ Other

25. **Are you aware that the library can provide you information, or refer you to agencies that offer information on these services?**
   1 __ Yes
   2 __ No
   3 __ Don't know

26. **Given your choice, what language would you prefer to use when asking for help at the library? (check one)**
   1 __ English
   2 __ Spanish
   3 __ Asian
   4 __ Other _____
   5 __ Don't know
   (Everyone must answer #27)

27. **Which of the following services offered by the Santa Barbara Public Library have you heard of? (check as many as apply)**

1 ____	Books	18 ____	Telephone ref/ services
2 ____	Story hours for children	19 ____	Reserves and interlibrary loans
3 ____	Magazines and newspapers	20 ____	Microfilm and microfiche
4 ____	Records and cassettes	21 ____	Large type books
5 ____	Films	22 ____	Civil service exam books
6 ____	Paperbacks	23 ____	College catalogs
7 ____	Children's books	24 ____	Community resource directory
8 ____	Reference books and services	25 ____	Genealogy material
9 ____	Young adult books	26 ____	Government documents
10 ____	Business reference section	27 ____	Local history files
11 ____	Service to shut-ins	28 ____	Maps
12 ____	Books in Spanish	29 ____	Telephone books
13 ____	Black studies books	30 ____	Community room
14 ____	Chicano studies books	31 ____	Member of Black Gold Cooperative Library system
15 ____	Art prints	32 ____	Spanish films
16 ____	Pamphlets	33 ____	Spanish records
17 ____	Periodical index	34 ____	Don't know

(Nonusers, go to #34)

8 ___ Información sobre el bajo costo de servicios médicos y de salud
9 ___ Consulta y asistencia legal
10 ___ Traducciones
11 ___ Información acerca de las facilidades de programas recreativos
12 ___ Transportación
13 ___ Donde conseguir ayuda en caso critico de emergencia
14 ___ Asistencia relacionada con agencias
15 ___ Información acerca del "Welfare"
16 ___ Información para el consumidor
17 ___ Otro

25. **¿Sabe Ud. que la biblioteca le provee información, o lo pone en contacto con las agencias que le ofrecen información en estos servicios?**
   1 ___ Sí
   2 ___ No
   3 ___ No sé

26. **De acuerdo a su gusto—¿Qué idioma preferiría usted cuando pregunta por asistencia en la biblioteca?**
   1 ___ Inglés
   2 ___ Español
   3 ___ Asiático
   4 ___ Otro idioma _____
   5 ___ No sé
   (Todos deben contestar #27)

27. **¿Cuáles servicios ofrecidos por la biblioteca conoce Ud.? (marque los que sean necesarios)**

1 ____	Libros	18 ____	Servicio de información por teléfono
2 ____	Hora de cuentos infantiles	19 ____	Préstamo de libros entre bibliotecas y reservas
3 ____	Periódicos y revistas	20 ____	Microfilm y microficha
4 ____	Discos y casetes	21 ____	Libros impresos con tipo grande
5 ____	Películas	22 ____	Libros para exámenes de servicios civiles
6 ____	Libros en rústica	23 ____	Catálogos colegiales
7 ____	Libros infantiles	24 ____	Directorio de recursos de la comunidad
8 ____	Libros sobre referencias y servicios	25 ____	Material genealógico
9 ____	Libros para adultos	26 ____	Documentos del gobierno
10 ____	Sección referente a negocios	27 ____	Archivos de historia local
11 ____	Servicios para personas recluidas	28 ____	Mapas
12 ____	Libros en español	29 ____	Directorios telefónicos
13 ____	Libros de estudio de la raza negra	30 ____	Salón de la comunidad
14 ____	Libros de estudios chicanos	31 ____	Miembro de la cooperativa bibliotecaria "Black Gold"
15 ____	Reproducciones gráficas de arte	32 ____	Películas en español
16 ____	Folletos	33 ____	Discos en español
17 ____	Indice de periódicos	34 ____	No sé

(Si no han usado la biblioteca pasar al #34)

28. Have you used this service? (check as many as apply)

1 ____ Books
2 ____ Story hours for children
3 ____ Magazines and newspapers
4 ____ Records and cassettes
5 ____ Films
6 ____ Paperbacks
7 ____ Children's books
8 ____ Reference books and services
9 ____ Young adult books
10 ____ Business reference section
11 ____ Service to shut-ins
12 ____ Books in Spanish
13 ____ Black studies books
14 ____ Chicano studies books
15 ____ Art prints
16 ____ Pamphlets
17 ____ Periodical index

18 ____ Telephone ref/services
19 ____ Reserves and interlibrary loans
20 ____ Microfilm and microfiche
21 ____ Large type books
22 ____ Civil service exam books
23 ____ College catalogs
24 ____ Community resource directory
25 ____ Genealogy material
26 ____ Government documents
27 ____ Local history files
28 ____ Maps
29 ____ Telephone books
30 ____ Community room
31 ____ Member of Black Gold Cooperative Library system
32 ____ Spanish films
33 ____ Spanish records
34 ____ Don't know

29. What do you feel are the four best things about the library? (check 4)

1 ____ Book collection
2 ____ Films, tapes, records, art prints
3 ____ Spanish-language collection
4 ____ Newspapers and magazines
5 ____ Reference services/collection
6 ____ Children's material
7 ____ Young adult materials
8 ____ Hours of service

9 ____ Staff
10 ____ Quiet atmosphere
11 ____ Library building
12 ____ Shelving arrangement
13 ____ Service in Spanish
14 ____ Adult material
15 ____ Other _____
16 ____ Don't know

30. Of these services, do any of these need improvement?

1 ____ Book collection
2 ____ Films, tapes, records, art prints
3 ____ Spanish-language collection
4 ____ Newspapers and magazines
5 ____ Reference services/collection
6 ____ Children's material
7 ____ Young adult materials
8 ____ Hours of service

9 ____ Staff
10 ____ Quiet atmosphere
11 ____ Library building
12 ____ Shelving arrangement
13 ____ Service in Spanish
14 ____ Adult material
15 ____ Other
16 ____ Don't know

28. ¿Ha hecho Ud. uso de estos servicios? (marque los que sean necesarios)

1 ____ Libros
2 ____ Hora de cuentos infantiles
3 ____ Periódicos y revistas
4 ____ Discos y casetes
5 ____ Películas
6 ____ Libros en rústica
7 ____ Libros infantiles
8 ____ Libros sobre referencias y servicios
9 ____ Libros para adultos
10 ____ Sección referente a negocios
11 ____ Servicios para personas recluidas
12 ____ Libros en español
13 ____ Libros de estudio de la raza negra
14 ____ Libros de estudios chicanos
15 ____ Reproducciones gráficas de arte
16 ____ Folletos
17 ____ Indice de periódicos

18 ____ Servicio de información por teléfono
19 ____ Préstamo de libros entre bibliotecas y reservas
20 ____ Microfilm y microficha
21 ____ Libros impresos con tipo grande
22 ____ Libros para exámenes de servicios civiles
23 ____ Catálogos colegiales
24 ____ Directorio de recursos de la comunidad
25 ____ Material genealógico
26 ____ Documentos del gobierno
27 ____ Archivos de historia local
28 ____ Mapas
29 ____ Directorios telefónicos
30 ____ Salón de la comunidad
31 ____ Miembro de la cooperativa bibliotecaria "Black Gold"
32 ____ Películas en español
33 ____ Discos en español
34 ____ No sé

29. ¿Cuáles son los cuatro servicios mejores de la biblioteca?

1 ____ Colección de libros
2 ____ Películas, cintas grabadas, discos
3 ____ Colección en idioma español
4 ____ Periódicos y revistas
5 ____ Colección de servicios de referencia
6 ____ Material infantil
7 ____ Material para jóvenes
8 ____ Horas de servicio

9 ____ Personal administrativo
10 ____ Ambiente silencioso
11 ____ Edificio bibliotecario
12 ____ Arreglo de la colección
13 ____ Servicios en español
14 ____ Material para adultos
15 ____ Otro _____
16 ____ No sé

30. De estos servicios—¿Cuáles cree Ud. necesitan mejorar?

1 ____ Colección de libros
2 ____ Películas, cintas grabadas, discos
3 ____ Colección en idioma español
4 ____ Periódicos y revistas
5 ____ Colección de servicios de referencia
6 ____ Material infantil
7 ____ Material para jóvenes
8 ____ Horas de servicio

9 ____ Personal administrativo
10 ____ Ambiente silencioso
11 ____ Edificio bibliotecario
12 ____ Arreglo de la colección
13 ____ Servicios en español
14 ____ Material para adultos
15 ____ Otro _____
16 ____ No sé

31. **If you use or have used the library, which of the following do you feel is most needed to meet your needs? (check as many as apply)**
1 ___ Larger book collections
2 ___ Larger nonbook collections (records, cassettes, films, etc)
3 ___ More newspapers and magazines
4 ___ Better reference service/materials
5 ___ Adult programs
6 ___ Children's books
7 ___ Longer hours
8 ___ More materials in Spanish
9 ___ More materials on the Mexican-Americans and their history
10 ___ More materials on the Black experience
11 ___ More materials on the Asian experience
12 ___ More materials on the Native American experience
13 ___ Spanish-language programs and services
14 ___ Library displays
15 ___ Bilingual/bicultural staff
16 ___ Other _____
17 ___ Don't know

32. **In general, the library staff seems to be:**
1 ___ Helpful
2 ___ Somewhat helpful
3 ___ Occasionally helpful
4 ___ Never willing to be of any help
5 ___ Other _____
6 ___ Don't know

33a. **If you use, or have used the library, on a scale of one to ten, do you consider the service of the Santa Barbara Public Library to be: (circle one)**

poor	inadequate	adequate	good	excellent
1 2	3 4	5 6	7 8	9 10

33b. **If 4 or below marked, why?**
_____
_____

34a. **Have you moved into Santa Barbara within the past year?**
1 ___ Yes
2 ___ No
3 ___ Don't know

34b. **How long have you lived in this neighborhood?**
1 ___ More than one year
2 ___ Less than one year
3 ___ Other

35. **Which of the following best describes your current employment? (check one)**
1 ___ Manufacturing or other industry
2 ___ Other blue collar positions
3 ___ Military
4 ___ Retired
5 ___ Not working at all

31. **Si Ud. usa o ha usado la biblioteca—¿Cuáles de estos servicios cree Ud. satisfacen sus necesidades? (marque las necesarias)**
1 ___ Engrandecer la colección de libros
2 ___ Engrandecer la colección de discos, cintas, películas, etc.
3 ___ Más periódicos y revistas
4 ___ Mejorar el servicio de referencia de materiales
5 ___ Programas para adultos
6 ___ Libros infantiles
7 ___ Extensión de horario
8 ___ Más materiales en español
9 ___ Más materiales sobre el México-Americano y su historia
10 ___ Más materiales acerca de la experiencia de la raza negra
11 ___ Más materiales acerca de la experiencia asiática
12 ___ Más materiales acerca de la experiencia de los indígenas de norte américa
13 ___ Servicios y programas en idioma español
14 ___ Exposiciones bibliotecarias
15 ___ Miembros del personal bilingües y biculturales
16 ___ Otro _____
17 ___ No sé

32. **¿En general, cómo considera nuestro personal?**
1 ___ De mucha ayuda
2 ___ Algo de ayuda
3 ___ Ocasionalmente de ayuda
4 ___ Nunca dispuestos a ayudar
5 ___ Otro _____
6 ___ No sé

33a. **Si Ud. usa, o ha usado la biblioteca, en la escala del uno al diez, ¿en qué posición considera Ud. los servicios bibliotecarios públicos?**

pobres	inadecuados	adecuados	buenos	excelentes
1 2	3 4	5 6	7 8	9 10

33b. **Si marcó menos que cuatro en la escala—¿Nos podría usted explicar brevemente por qué?**
_____
_____

34a. **¿Se ha usted mudado a Santa Barbara durante el año pasado?**
1 ___ Sí
2 ___ No
3 ___ No sé

34b. **¿Por cuánto tiempo ha Ud. vivido en esta vecindad?**
1 ___ Más de 1 año
2 ___ Menos de 1 año
3 ___ Otro

35. **¿Cuál de los siguientes describe mejor su ocupación? (actualmente)**
1 ___ Manufacturero u otra industria
2 ___ Otra técnica o vocacional
3 ___ Ejército militar

6 ___ Unemployed
7 ___ Professional—Educational
8 ___ Professional—Management
9 ___ Professional—Government
10 ___ Professional—Trades
11 ___ Professional—Sales
12 ___ Other _____
13 ___ Don't know

36. How many people are living in your home?
1 __ 1 to 2
2 __ 3 to 5
3 __ 6 to 8
4 __ 9 or more

37. What was your approximate total household income last year?
A 1 __ *[These letters were keyed to a governmental form.]*
B 2 __
C 3 __
D 4 __
E 5 __
F 6 __
G 7 __
H 8 __
I 9 __ Decline to state

38. How much education have you completed?
1 ___ 1 to 6 years
2 ___ 7 to 9 years
3 ___ 10 to 12 years
4 ___ 2 years of college (AA degree)
5 ___ 4 years of college (BA degree)
6 ___ Graduate school
7 ___ Vocational school
8 ___ Adult education
9 ___ GED completion
10 ___ ESL

39. What is your approximate age?
1 __ Under 15
2 __ 16 to 19
3 __ 20 to 24
4 __ 25 to 34
5 __ 35 to 49
6 __ 50 to 59
7 __ 60 and over
8 __ Don't know

4 ___ Retirado
5 ___ Desempleado
6 ___ Actualmente sin trabajo
7 ___ Profeción educativa
8 ___ Profeción administrativa
9 ___ Profeción gubernamental
10 ___ Profeción comercial
11 ___ Profeción de ventas
12 ___ Otro _____
13 ___ No sé

36. ¿Cuántas personas viven actualmente en su hogar?
1 ___ 1 a 2
2 ___ 3 a 5
3 ___ 6 a 8
4 ___ 9 o más

37. ¿Cuál fue aproximadamente su ingreso total el año próximo pasado?
A 1 __
B 2 __
C 3 __
D 4 __
E 5 __
F 6 __
G 7 __
H 8 __
I 9 __ Prefiero no contestar

38. ¿Cuál fue su educación total?
1 ___ 1–6 años
2 ___ 7–9 años
3 ___ 10–12 años
4 ___ Dos años de universidad
5 ___ Cuatro años de universidad
6 ___ Escuela universitaria de graduados
7 ___ Escuela vocacional
8 ___ Educación adulta
9 ___ Certificado de estudios generales
10 ___ ESL

39. ¿Cuál es su edad aproximadamente?
1 ___ Menos de 15
2 ___ 16 a 19
3 ___ 20 a 24
4 ___ 25 a 34
5 ___ 35 a 49
6 ___ 50 a 59
7 ___ 60 o más
8 ___ No sé

40. **In order to verify that I have conducted this interview, may I please have your name, address, and telephone number? We could also put your name on a mailing list to send you information about library programs.**

     Thank you very much for your time and cooperation. You have been very helpful.

Name _____ (optional)
Address _____
City _____
Telephone _____ ( ) No phone

Interviewer's signature

_____

Date _____

41. **Respondent is:**
    1 __ Male
    2 __ Female

42. **Census tract in which interview took place:**
                                    Block number: _____
    Time started _____ **Time finished** _____

40. **Para poder verificar que yo personalmente he conducido esta entrevista,—¿Por favor me podría Ud. dar su nombre, dirección, y teléfono? También podríamos poner su nombre en una lista de correo para enviarle información sobre los programas de la biblioteca.**

     Muchísimas gracias por habernos brindado su tiempo y cooperación, ha sido Ud. de muy gran ayuda para esta encuesta.

Nombre _____ (opcional)
Dirección _____
Ciudad _____
Teléfono _____ ( ) No tengo

Firma de entrevistador

_____

Fecha _____

41. **Respondiente:**
    1 ___ Masculino
    2 ___ Femenino

42. **Area censada:**
                                    Número de cuadra: _____
    Tiempo de comienzo _____ **Tiempo final** _____

APPENDIX B
MODEL FOCUS GROUP QUESTIONS

1. When members of your community think of the public library, what comes to mind?

    In general, how would you rate your community's awareness of library services, collection, and programming? Poor, good, or very good?

2. Are there any cultural barriers that impede the use of the library by your community?

    Possible barriers: Yes   No
    *   Language [communicating with staff]
    *   Language [collection]
    *   Library as a free lending library?
    *   Library as a place to obtain information?
    *   Library as a place for learners/students?
    *   Benefits of recreational use of the library?
    *   Fear of government agencies?
    *   Fear of fees, fines, charges for services?
    *   Illiteracy?
    *   Fear/unfamiliarity of technology?

3. How can the City Library erase any of these barriers?

4. How can the City Library improve our services to your community?

    Areas that need follow-up:
    *   Improvement in the collection?
    *   Improvement in programming?
    *   Improvement in general services?
    *   Technology?
    *   What is missing from our list of recommendations?

5. What would be the best way to get the word out about the City Library's services to your community?

    Possible follow-up questions:
    *   Where should the Library be displaying/posting library publicity?
    *   Would publicity in your community's native language prove useful?
    *   Are there any local newsletters that we should utilize?
    *   What neighborhoods should we target for our outreach efforts?
    *   What community events/meetings/organizations should the Library seek participation?
    *   Any suggestions on how to best register [for library cards] those members of your community who may not register on their own?

Permission to adapt and reprint granted by Salt Lake City Public Library.

5 PROGRAMS AND SERVICES FOR LATINOS IN YOUR COMMUNITY

CHALLENGE

Ingrid: *The good news is that the board has approved our policy statement regarding outreach services to Latinos. They also want us to begin thinking about integrating those services and programs and to look aggressively for external funds. The bad news is that I am feeling overwhelmed; I don't know where to start. We have no programs; we offer no special services to attract Latinos.*

Mario: *But, Ingrid, didn't you give the board a list of ideas for proposed programs and services that would be most beneficial for Latinos?*

Ingrid: *Yes, but they were just that—ideas.*

Mario: *I can understand your concern, Ingrid. But, we have to take this step-by-step. We can plan what we can do to attract our Latino community with current programs and services—and start there. Meanwhile, we can get ideas from our planned needs assessment and from some other libraries that already serve their Latino communities. We can also plan some programs to implement without special funds. Once we achieve some of those steps, we can start working on the external funding process. We can do it!*

It was difficult to decide where to place this chapter because you can become overwhelmed by what needs to be done. It could easily have been placed after the funding, staffing, or partnership chapters because all three chapters cover topics critical to the success of programs and services to Latinos. This is the ideas chapter, and what is useful to you will depend on your individual library circumstances. No matter where you are in the planning process, there are plenty of ideas from which to choose.

The purpose of this chapter is to give you many program and service ideas to attract and serve Latino residents in your community. Many of these suggestions are based on successful projects from all across the country, and some are just ideas.[1] Realizing that each idea has many implications—funding, staffing, partnership, material resources—we did not get into those specifically. There are other chapters that deal specifically with those implications. In this chapter, we just wanted to present ideas to give you a basis from which to start.

NITTY-GRITTY PROGRAMS AND SERVICES (BASIC SERVICES)

Planning, planning, planning. You will continue to read about planning throughout this book. Basic services are the place to start when planning services for your Latino community. Working hand in hand with basic services planning is knowing your Latino community (see Chapter 4). We suggest the following steps to help get you started:

Step 1: Identify existing basic services.

Sit down with your staff and identify the basic programs and services that are already available for Latino residents to use.

For example, many services such as circulation, general reference, readers' advisory, meeting rooms, children's programming, young adult, and adult programming are available to those Latinos who are either monolingual in English or bilingual. By basic services, we mean those services and programs already covered in your current budget; those basic services can be provided at no extra cost.

Step 2: Modify those basic services.

After you have identified those existing basic services and programs, you need to modify them to ensure that Latino residents in your community can benefit from them.

Let's take children's programming for example. If you are planning children's programming for the month of May, you may want to include activities for all children (non-Latino and Latino) around Cinco de Mayo activities. Activities could include a story hour around a children's book with Latino children characters and/or a piñata party that includes making piñatas.

Remember that you will need to know your community. If most of your Latino residents are Mexicano and Mexican American, the Cinco de Mayo theme is fine. However, if your residents are mostly Puerto Rican or some other Latino subgroup, you will need to find out what special events are popular and center similar activities around those times and events.

Step 3: Assess the marketability of basic services.

You need to determine which basic services can realistically be marketed to Latinos. As we mentioned earlier, almost all general services can be marketed to bilingual and English-speaking Latinos. However, you need first to highlight and market those basic services that you learned were important through the Latino community analysis efforts.

Step 4: Conduct targeted programming.

Programming around holidays is also a good way to attract Latinos of any age. Christmas, Easter, and Thanksgiving are some of the major holidays. Many of the libraries we visited also did Latino programming around "El Día de los Muertos" (The Day of the Dead).

Step 5: Set up library displays.

Another easy place to get started is library displays. Most public libraries develop periodic displays, exhibits, and art shows. Think about developing a display or exhibit that would highlight the Latino culture. Ask your formal and informal Latino community leaders to help you with ideas and materials. If there are Latino artists in the community, including young adults, invite them to display their artwork in the library. This is one of the best ways to introduce the library to the Latino community and to attract the Latino community to the library. It is a great ice-breaker.

Because your Latino community might have a variety of subgroups, you can do displays of national holidays. These displays are more effective in attracting Latino adults to the library. Also, if you have books about the various countries, display those. Almost all countries have an embassy in Washington, D.C. (As a point of clarification, Puerto Rico is a territory.) You can write to them and tell them what you would like to do. They might send you some posters, maps, small flags, and other materials to use in your displays. Appendix A at the end of this chapter lists and briefly describes some national Latino holidays for the various Latin American and Caribbean countries.

Step 6: Implement signage in Spanish.

Signage is a very basic service that can be done at minimal cost. If your library really wants the Latino community to feel welcome, there is no better way to do that than with Spanish signage in the library. With bilingual signage, you tell Latinos that you recognize and accept their cultural differences and want to serve them and that they are welcome in your library. Figure 5–1 on page 99 provides a Spanish translation for the Dewey Decimal Classification System signage.

Step 7: Export library card signup.

The library card application process is another basic service for Latinos that takes little, if any, additional funds. The process for signing up Latinos does not have to be in the library. This could be done with volunteers and a table set up at the grocery store, schools, post office, outside social services offices, after church, or at Latino festivals. Figure 5–2 provides text you can use to develop a bilingual library card application form. You can choose to design one bilingual form or two separate forms—one in English and one in Spanish. Whichever you choose, this sample text can be adapted to your local needs.

Step 8: Conduct open houses and tours.

Another no-cost or low-cost service is library open houses and tours designed specifically for the Latino community. You can work with another partner in the Latino community to organize them. If possible, these programs should be offered at times when the whole Latino family is available. Your focus groups, surveys, or interviews can help you determine the best time. We suggest you get a local food business to donate some food for an informal reception or coffee hour after the tours. Again, be creative to keep the costs low.

Step 9: Consider hiring a translator.

If you can find the funds, pay a bilingual resident to serve as an intermediary translator (between Spanish-speaking user and English-speaking library staff). An intermediary translator could work in the library for three hours once a week (for example, Thursday evenings from 5 to 8 p.m.). Even at an $8 hourly rate, that is only $1,200 per year. If that is still impossible, try to get some bilingual community residents to volunteer several hours a week. We suggest that you set a time and day to offer bilingual services. For example, every Tuesday and Thursday from 5 to 7 p.m. you could offer bilingual services. Basically, the volunteers would be able to translate wherever needed in the library during those hours.

If you do not have bilingual staff or volunteers available yet, then your staff needs to be prepared to provide basic services to Spanish-speaking Latinos until you can get appropriate staff and/or volunteers. Appendix B at the end of this chapter provides some basic Spanish phrases and the phonetic pronunciation.

Figure 5-1. Selected Dewey Decimal Classification in Spanish

000–009	OBRAS GENERALES		600–699	CIENCIAS APLICADAS
010	Bibliografías		610	Ciencias Médicas
030	Enciclopedias		612	Educación Sexual
060	Organizaciones		616	Enfermedades
070	Periodismo		618	Embarazo y Parto
100–199	FILOSOFÍA		620	Ingeniería, Electrónica
			629	Automóviles
130	Parapsicología, Ocultismo, Sueños		635	Horticultura
			636	Animales Domésticos
150	Psicología		641	Cocina
170	Ética		643	Mantenimiento de la Casa
180	Filosofía Medieval		646	Costura
190	Filosofía Occidental		649	Cuidado del Niño
			650	Negocios
200–299	RELIGIÓN		657	Contabilidad
220	Biblias		658	Administración
230	Teología Cristiana		670	Manufacturas
280	Sectas Cristianas		684	Carpintería
290	Otras Religiones, Mitología		700–799	ARTE, MÚSICA Y DEPORTES
300–399	CIENCIAS SOCIALES		730	Escultura
301	Sociología		740	Dibujo, Decoración
320	Ciencias Políticas, Ciudadanía		750	Pintura
330	Economía		770	Fotografía
340	Derecho, Inmigración		780	Música
360	Problemas Sociales, Criminología		796	Deportes
370	Educación		800–899	LITERATURA
400–499	LENGUAJE		810	Literatura Norte Americana
			822	Literatura Inglesa
420	Inglés		860	Literatura Española
460	Español		900–999	HISTORIA Y GEOGRAFÍA
500–599	CIENCIAS PURAS		910	Geografía
510	Matemáticas		920	Biografías
520	Astronomía		940	Historia de Europa
530	Física		972	Historia de México, Centroamérica, Cuba
540	Química		973	Historia de Estados Unidos
550	Geología		980	Historia de Sudamérica
560	Paleontología			
570	Biología			
580	Botánica, Plantas Medicinales			
590	Zoología			

Figure 5-2. Sample Bilingual Library Card Application Form Text

> Patron registration form/Formulario para la inscripción de usuarios

> Upon presenting this form and your driver's license or some other identification that will verify your name and permanent address, we are pleased to give you a library card. The card is free and most materials can be borrowed without charge. / Al presentar esta solicitud y su licencia de manejar o otra identificación que verifique su nombre y dirección actual, con gusto le daremos una tarjeta para la biblioteca. La tarjeta es gratis y no cobramos por prestar la mayoría de los materiales.

> Please print your name. / Por favor escriba su nombre.

> First name / Nombre

> Last name / Apellido

> Middle Initial / Inicial

> Mailing address / Direccíon

> Street / Calle

> P. O. Box / P. O. Box

> City / Ciudad

> State / Estado

> Zip code / Código postal

> Daytime telephone / teléfono del día

> Other telephone / otro teléfono

> Driver's license number / Número de licencia de manejar

> Do you desire materials in another language other than English? / ¿Desea Ud. materiales en otro idioma además de inglés?

> Which language do you prefer? / ¿Cuál idioma prefiere?

> I agree to be responsible for materials borrowed with this card, for fines incurred including charges for lost and damaged materials. / Me hago responsable por materiales prestados con esta tarjeta, por cualquiera multa incluyendo materiales dañados o extraviados.

> We need the signature of a parent or guardian for children in primary grades. / Necesitamos la firma de padre/madre o guardián para niños en la escuela primaria.

> Applicant's signature / Firma del solicitante

> Parent or guardian's signature / Firma de padre/madre o guardián

We have provided some steps to get started utilizing the resources and services you currently have. When you are ready to develop programs and services specifically for Latinos in your community, we offer below many ideas that have worked in public libraries with similar goals.

PROGRAMMING IDEAS

The purpose for this section is to provide all kinds of program ideas that you can adapt to fit your community's needs and your library's resources. Many of the ideas were developed by the librarians and staff in the public libraries we visited. As with the chapter on fundraising (Chapter 6), many of the program ideas we suggest are great external proposal ideas. The purpose for external funding is to achieve your ultimate goal of implementing those new programs in your library. For example, those programs that require bilingual speaking ability can be incorporated into a proposal to hire a bilingual librarian to implement your specific program ideas and other bilingual services—outreach, collection development, and reference, for example. Some of the ideas listed are also mentioned in the partnership and outreach chapters (Chapters 8 and 10).

CHILDREN'S PROGRAMS

Library personnel involved in providing library programs to Latinos in their community maintain that the best way to get Latino parents into the library is through children's programming because the Latino community is very family-centered. Here are some ideas for Latino children's programming.

Infants

Los Angeles County Public Library offered infant programming with infants and grandparents, called "Songs and Stories for Infants and Grandparents." Grandparents were given tips on how to read to infant children. Because the Latino culture emphasizes the extended family, this type of program recognizes the reality of working parents and focuses on grandparent and grandchild. The program could easily be bilingual to include non-minority grandparents and infants.

Preschool Children

In addition to the obvious idea of using bilingual story hours, we highly recommend bilingual fingerplays. If you do not have a bilingual staff person, invite someone who is bilingual to volunteer to do the fingerplays or to train staff to do them. You can also ask some Latino parents and grandparents if they remember any fingerplays from their childhood. Appendix C at the end of this chapter includes a few examples.

If you have favorite fingerplays that you use with your monolingual (English-speaking) children, ask a local Spanish teacher or a Latino to volunteer translating these fingerplays into Spanish. Also, you can get great ideas for bilingual story hour ideas and recommended books from articles like the one by Louise Zwick and Oralia Garza de Cortes.[2] Another very helpful publication is a book edited by Adela Artola Allen, *Library Services for Hispanic Children*, which discusses the entire range of library services for Latino children in public and school libraries.[3]

School Children

Summer reading programs are always a great mainstay of children's programming. If you can design your regular summer program to include bilingual activities or books, please do so. Bilingual programs and materials will definitely make some Latino children feel more comfortable with the program and will improve their self-esteem.

All kinds of music programs work well. Some libraries we visited made use of bilingual puppeteers and clowns. We realize that these resources may not be available for you right now, but it doesn't hurt to look for them in the Latino community. Another fun program idea is to show Disney films for a month. Many of your Latino children will probably be bilingual, and they will enjoy Disney films. This was a successful program at South Chula Vista (California) Library. You can introduce reading materials and activities on the theme or characters in each Disney film.

Programs on live animals are popular. Work with your local Division of Wildlife for programming ideas. At the East Los Angeles Branch of the Los Angeles County Public Library, which serves a community that is over 80% Latino (Mexican Americans and Mexican immigrants), the library hosted a children's program on live sharks one afternoon. Over 700 residents (children and adults) attended the program! You may not have sharks in your part of the country, but there are probably other animals available for use in library programming. If there is a local or regional pet store, form a partnership with the owners; they have all kinds of animals—ferrets, parrots, snakes, fish, and many more!

A program that would be great for instilling cultural pride involves the library and the local school organizing an exhibit of artwork by Latino children. Invite the children to submit their drawings around specific themes and display them in the library. Make sure to arrange the show by theme of drawings and age groups. Some suggested themes include family, friends, pets, and school. This program will definitely get the Latino adults into the library, so be prepared to have books on display that might be interesting to the adults, and encourage them to sign up for a library card!

El Paso Public Library provides a bilingual program on manners and etiquette for young children. It is very popular with children, and the parents love the idea that children are learning more about manners.

Oxnard (California) Public Library offers an innovative library research skills program that can easily be adapted by your library. It is bilingual at one branch and in English at another branch, and it was designed for Latino children in the community. The program is called the Junior Information Professional (JIP) program for children in grades 3–5. Then they graduate to the Junior Information Specialist (JIS) program for grades 6–8.

In these programs, children learn about 20 to 25 special reference books that can assist them with their homework assignments. The 45–minute classes are held every Saturday for ten consecutive weeks. The children are also taught basic research skills for their grade level. At the end of the program, there is a graduation ceremony with diplomas granted to the children. This program is so popular that the library has a waiting list of participants. The children love it because they are learning information that can help them with their homework; parents love it because their children are learning valuable library research skills.

The Oxnard Public Library works with the public schools in a partnership, particularly with marketing the program. However, word of mouth has made this program much valued. In addition, a questionnaire is sent to the children's teachers and parents asking them about their views on the program.

We loved this program idea! Additionally, the library benefits from the possibility that these bilingual children will become its future volunteers, pages, staff, and librarians.[4]

YOUNG ADULT (YA) PROGRAMMING

Most of the librarians we interviewed did not think they were doing enough for their Latino young adults and recognized the general difficulty in marketing the library to them through programming. Although the individual librarians were a bit apologetic, they had developed successful YA programs which we would like to share.

Newark Public Library did a program series called "Gente y Cuentos" (People and Stories) where they invited Latino young adults and senior citizens to come together to read certain works of Latino authors and discuss the books in Spanish from their own perspectives. It was a very successful program, particularly in promoting Latino intergenerational understanding. In addition, Newark Public Library sponsors a bilingual homework hotline for young adults.

New York Public Library branches have offered YA programs to Latino youth in theater, rap music, and button making, as well as book talks and discussion groups on peer pressure. Queens Public Library hosted a writer-in-residence program where Latino young adults were given creative writing workshops by the writer and encouraged to do creative writing.

Santa Monica (California) Public Library did a series of YA programs on self-esteem, assertiveness training, preparation for college, and health issues in the 90s. The library has offered Internet training programs to young adults. Also, it offered a career exposition with Latino professionals sharing their professional insights with the Latino youth.

El Paso Public Library has offered such YA programs as art workshops and martial arts demonstrations. The library also sponsors a Mardi Gras celebration where the youth decorated their bicycles and made costumes to wear.

Tucson-Pima Public Library offers its Latino young adults a Homeworkhelp Center and a program for rural youth called "Burgers and Books." In this B&B program, the young adults read books and the library staff hold bilingual YA discussion groups on such themes as careers, peer pressure, and drugs. Afterwards, Burger King, in partnership with the library, treats them to free hamburgers.

The Oxnard (California) Public Library formed a partnership with the local health clinic for its "Teens and Tots" program for teen mothers. The library provides programming on such topics as reading to children and how to use the public library, and displays self-help materials for the teen mothers.

The Lozano Branch of the Chicago Public Library, which serves a predominantly Latino community, developed chess clubs for its Latino youth. The program includes chess lessons and space for the clubs to meet and compete.

In general, music, animals, sports, and *food* will always attract young adults. We realize that young adults are a challenging group to attract to the library, but there is a definite need to reach out to them. With information technology developing as it is and with more public libraries offering Internet access, technology might also draw Latino young adults to the library.

Remember that, even if you do not have the expertise to offer YA bilingual programming, your marketing and publicity materials should still be bilingual. Parents who are monolingual in Spanish need to know about YA programs also. If they see a Spanish-language flyer on a bulletin board in the community describing a YA program, they can encourage their youths to attend.

ADULT PROGRAMMING

We have divided Latino adult programming into five areas—health, self-help and coping skills, legal, parenting, and general. Surprisingly, some programs have been very successful in some libraries and not so successful in others. Your Latino community needs analysis and/or focus groups can provide useful information on the types of programs that might be popular.

We recommend that at all adult programs you display a variety of adult materials including self-help materials. You can also provide reading lists for the adults to review. To promote library card registration, set up a table at the program.

Health

The East Los Angeles Branch (Los Angeles County Public Library) offered a program with the nearby health clinic. It provided bilingual programs and lists of suggested reading materials for pregnant Latino women. As we mentioned earlier, the Oxnard Public Library offers its "Teens and Tots" program.

Other health-related programs that have been successful include a nutrition workshop, CPR training, the importance of vaccinations for preschool children, Alzheimer's disease, AIDS, and household lead poisoning. A great idea is to organize a health information fair at the library. You can invite various health-related organizations to set up information tables. Both the library and these organizations can also provide various programs during the fair.

You have probably noticed that many of the programs listed are not vastly different from adult programming you are already offering. Almost all adult programming you currently offer would be of interest to your Latino adults. The difference is two-fold: your flyers and publicity materials should be bilingual, and your programs should be bilingual.

Self-Help and Coping Skills

This is probably the area most in demand by Latino adults. Most adults, in general, want to improve their lives (socially and economically); Latino adults are no different. Programs on starting your own business, minority contracting with the government, getting certified in daycare, applying for a small business loan, and paying for college should be very popular. Employment skills strategies—how to write a resumé, how to interview, how to dress for success—are also very helpful. Programs on improving job skills should attract Latino adults. Coping programs such as neighborhood watch or dealing with divorce, drug abuse, or domestic violence are also popular.

The East Los Angeles Branch of the Los Angeles County Public Library offered a series called "Domingos Alegres" (Happy Sundays). Government agencies such as the Housing and Urban Development agency set up a table in the library to assist low-income adults. The library then provided programs for the children while their parents were visiting with the agency of the day. In its programming, the library provided the Latino children with reading incentives such as book bags and balloons.

Legal

San Ysidro Branch Library (San Diego Public Library System) houses a small Legal Resource Center in the library and also works in partnership with various law groups to do programming in Spanish on immigration law, landlord/neighbor/tenant law, employee rights, patient rights, and citizenship. Other types of legal programming include bilingual programs on wills, living wills, and estate planning.

Parenting

Parenting skills programs can be popular. El Paso Public Library offers a read-to-babies program. Also, by conducting programs on the prevention of teenage pregnancy, drug prevention, CPR for infants, prenatal care, and the art of being a parent, the library has been able to attract Latino adults to the library.

General Programming Involving Literacy, General Equivalency Diploma (GED), and English as a Second Language (ESL)

One definite way of getting Latino adults to the library is to offer literacy, GED, and/or ESL programs. In the past, most of these programs were federally funded. In many cases, because the programs were so popular and successful, they have been integrated into the overall library program. If you already have a successful self-help program—literacy, GED, or ESL—you can provide for your captive audience a bridge from these areas to other adult programming and materials in the library. If your library cannot offer any of these three programs by itself, it can become a partner with agencies that can provide space and materials for the programs.

The El Paso Public Library's Literacy Center is very much an integral part of the library, especially at the Clardy Fox Branch. Most of the programming for the library is offered through the Literacy Center. The center offers citizenship classes, an adult reading club, and many other adult programs.

At the Queens Public Library, one of the largest and most successful programs is their ESL program. They teach approximately 3,000 students per year and half of them are Latinos. They offer 73 classes between the central library and its 62 branches. They also offer an

ESL component in which the students learn to read and write in English. One of the lessons in the ESL program includes instruction in using the library, and the overall ESL program includes a tour of the library and applying for a library card. The ESL program, which is structured around self-help and coping skills topics, is advertised through flyers distributed to over 350 city agencies in Queens.

The New York Public Library (NYPL) operates the adult reading and writing and ESL programs for Spanish speakers. NYPL's program, "Familias con Libros" (Families with Books), is a *family* literacy program consisting of four workshop sessions. The entire family attends and daycare is provided for the young children. Some of the programs consist of an introduction to reading to their children. Also, the family compiles a family photo album using family photographs from home supplemented with family photographs taken during the workshops. There are sessions in which parents talk in discussion teams about issues that they face. The parents are also given children's books and an almanac to start a home library. The best part of this program is that most of the parents become regular users of the library after the "Familia" workshop is over. This is the bridging we are talking about.

The Tucson-Pima Public Library supports the literacy and GED programs offered by other agencies. They purchase GED materials and house them at the various program sites which are not necessarily at libraries. The students check out these materials using the honor system.

In addition, Tucson-Pima wrote a grant proposal and received external funding for its family literacy program. The library provides services to mothers who are attending GED classes and also to their children who are attending the Head Start program. The mothers are given a library services orientation, a tour of the library, and a library card. The children at Head Start are provided with story times, and there are joint story times for children and their mothers. The library also offers the "Parents as Publishers" program, where GED mothers write short stories for their children and present them in book format. Tucson-Pima developed a beautiful bilingual booklet, "Let's Read Together," that provides a reading guide and a bibliography of books for the Latino parents to read to children of different ages. Because of its popularity, the overall family literacy program was integrated into the library's general programming and receives ongoing general library funding.

PROGRAMMING RESOURCES

Individuals or organizations play a vital role in helping the library offer programs. Most organizations or agencies will provide programming for free. Individuals, on the other hand, may not, especially if their program specialty is their livelihood. If that is the case, we suggest you operate by the four Ifs:

1. If you do not have funds to pay for programs, ask the individual to consider doing it for free.
2. If you can offer a small honorarium, do so.
3. If the individual does not waiver from a fee, try to negotiate a lower fee.
4. If you cannot negotiate a lower fee and you really want the individual, then ask an external funding source—for example, the Friends group, a local business, or a civic organization—for funds.

If you do not already have one, you need to develop a "Programming Resource File" that can either be a print file or a database file. This file should contain the names of individuals, organizations, or agencies that have done or are willing to do programs for the library. Figure 5–3 is a sample Programming Resource Form; adapt it as you see fit. Make sure, however, to update it as changes occur.

CONCLUSION

The program and service ideas presented in this chapter are by no means exhaustive. We encourage you to be creative also. Almost every library we visited presented a brand new idea we had not heard or read about. The important point in this chapter is to begin designing programs and services to fit your particular Latino community's needs. If at all possible, arrange for the programs to be bilingual or in Spanish. When you are ready, make sure that all your program flyers and publicity materials are bilingual.

Figure 5-3. Library Programming Resource Form

Individual/
Organization Name _____

_____

Address _____

Telephone _____   Fax_____

E-mail _____

Program Services Provided   _____

_____

_____

_____

Equipment Necessary   _____

_____

Other Special Requirements   _____

_____

_____

_____

Fee $ _____   Negotiable: _____ Yes   _____ No

Honorarium $_____

Notes:

NOTES

1. The following individuals were interviewed and provided information for this chapter and other chapters in this book: Juan Ortiz, Logan Heights Branch Library, San Diego, Calif., 6 June 1995; Jim Frazier, San Ysidro Branch Library (San Diego Public Library), San Ysidro, Calif., 6 June 1995; John Bishop, Jorge Castillo, and Jody Sawina, South Chula Vista Library, Chula Vista, Calif., 7 June 1995; Al Milo, Fullerton Public Library, Fullerton, Calif., 7 June 1995; Linda Chavez Doyle, East Los Angeles Branch (Los Angeles County Public Library), Los Angeles, Calif., 8 June 1995; Martha Garcia Almarzouk and Ninfa Duran, Santa Ana Public Library, Santa Ana, Calif., 8 June 1995; Wini Allard and Louix Escobar-Matute, Santa Monica, Calif., 9 June 1995; Sofia Marquez and Antonio Ramirez, Oxnard Public Library, Oxnard, Calif., 12 June 1995; Marge Fauver and Carol Keator, Eastside Branch Library, Santa Barbara, Calif., 12 June 1995; Hector Hernandez, Lozano Branch Library (Chicago Public Library), Chicago, Ill., 26 June 1995; Ismael Alicia, New York Public Libary, New York, N.Y., 8 August 1995; Adriana Tandler and Maria Fiol, Queens Public Library, Jamaica, N.Y., 9 August 1995; Ingrid Betancourt, Newark Public Library, Newark, N.J., 10 August 1995; Margie Sanchez, Armijo Branch Library (El Paso Pubic Library), El Paso, Tex., 21 November 1995; Mary Helen Michals and Martha Toscano, Clardy Fox Branch (El Paso Public Library), 21 November 1995; Fernando Racelis, Richard Burges Branch (El Paso Public Library), 22 November 1995; Ivonne Jimenez, El Paso Public Library, 22 November 1995; Liz Rodriquez-Miller and Amanda Castillo, Tucson-Pima Public Library, 13 February 1996.
2. Louise Y. Zwick and Oralia Garza de Cortes, "Library Programs for Hispanic Children," *Texas Libraries* 50 (Spring 1989): 12–15; Louise Y. Zwick, "Cuentos y Canciones Infantiles: Recordings in Spanish for Children," *School Library Journal* 35 (February 1989): 23–26.
3. Adela Artola Allen, *Library Services for Hispanic Children: A Guide for Public and School Librarians* (Phoenix, Ariz.: Oryx Press, 1987).
4. If you would like more information on this program, please contact Antonio Ramirez, Oxnard Public Library, 251 S. A St., Oxnard, CA, 93030-5712.

APPENDIX A
NATIONAL LATINO
HOLIDAYS

ARGENTINA

May 25   National Holiday (Revolución de Mayo)—commemorates the revolution of 1810 which initiated the move toward independence, finally achieved July 9, 1816

July 9   Independence Day—commemorates Argentina's declaration of independence from Spain in 1816

BOLIVIA

August 6   Independence Day—commemorates Bolivia's achievement of independence from Spain in 1825

COLOMBIA

July 20   Independence Day—Colombia defies Spanish authority and declares its independence

COSTA RICA

Sept 15   Independence Day—commemorates the achievement of independence from Spain in 1821

CUBA

Oct 10   Beginning of War of Independence—commemorates the commencement of Cuba's war for independence from Spain

CHILE

Sept 18   Independence Day—commemorates the end of Chile's allegiance to Spain in 1810 and independence in 1818

DOMINICAN REPUBLIC

Feb 27   Independence Day—commemorates the 1814 revolt against Haiti in which independence was regained and the Republic established under Pedro Santana

ECUADOR

Aug 10 — Independence Day—celebrates Ecuador's achievement of independence in 1822

GUATEMALA

Sept 15 — Independence Day—commemorates the achievement of independence from Spain in 1821

HONDURAS

Sept 15 — Independence Day—commemorates the achievement of independence from Spain in 1821

MEXICO

May 5 — Puebla Battle Day, or Cinco de Mayo—commemorates defeat of Napoleon III's forces in 1867

Sept 16 — Independence Day—Mexico claims independence from Spain in 1810 (the Republic was established Dec 6, 1822)

Nov 20 — Mexican Revolution Anniversary—anniversary of the overthrow of the dictatorship of Porfirio Díaz in 1910

NICARAGUA

Sept 15 — Independence Day—commemorates the achievement of independence from Spain in 1821

PANAMA

Nov 3 — Independence Day—celebrates Panama's independence from Colombia in 1903

Nov 28 — Independence from Spain—celebrates Panama's independence from Spain in 1821

Dec 8 — Mother's Day—consistent with the celebration of the Immaculate Conception, the people of Panama honor mothers on this day

PARAGUAY

May 14 — National Flag Day—beginning of a two-day celebration marking the achievement of independence from Spain in 1811

May 15 — Independence Day—celebrates the achievement of independence from Spain in 1811 (the second day of a two-day celebration)

PERU

July 28 — Independence Day—celebrates independence from Spain in 1821 (two-day celebration)

PUERTO RICO

Jan 11 — De Hostos's Birthday—celebrates the birth of the philosopher and patriot Eugenio María de Hostos (1839)

Mar 22 — Emancipation Day or Abolition Day—commemorates the abolition of slavery on the island in 1873

EL SALVADOR

Sept 15 — Independence Day—commemorates the achievement of independence from Spain in 1821

SPAIN

June 24 — King Juan Carlos's Saint's Day

URUGUAY

June 19 — Artigas Day—commemorates the birthday of General José Gervasio Artigas (1764)

Aug 25 — Independence Day—celebrates independence from Brazil in 1825

VENEZUELA

July 5 — Independence Day—celebrates Venezuelan declaration of independence from Spain in 1811

July 24 — Bolívar's Birthday—commemorates the birth of Simón Bolívar (1783), the "George Washington" of South America

APPENDIX B
SPANISH WORDS AND PHRASES FOR LIBRARY USE

PRONUNCIATION TIPS

There are many Spanish dialects, each with subtle differences in pronunciation. One example is the differences in pronunciation of the Spanish letter "v." Some Spanish speakers pronounce the "v" like an English "b," others pronounce it more like the English "v," and still others use a pronunciation that falls somewhere in between. Using these pronunciation tips, however, will enable you to be understood by most Spanish speakers.

Spanish Letter = Pronunciation:
a = ah (as in walk)
e = eh (as in leg)
i = ee (as in bee)
o = oh (as in bold)
u = oo (as in hoot)

ge = heh
gi = hee
ga, *go*, *gu* = gah, goh, gooh (hard g as in goat)
j = h
ll = y (as in yes)
r = (trill tongue slightly)
rr = (trill tongue heavily)
v = b
y = ee
z = s

BASIC WORDS

English	Spanish	Phonetic (Accent in CAPS)
one	*uno*	OO noh (OO as in hoot)
two	*dos*	dohs
three	*tres*	trehs
four	*cuatro*	KWAH troh
five	*cinco*	SEENK oh
six	*seis*	sais (rhymes with race)
seven	*siete*	see EH teh
eight	*ocho*	OH choh

eight	*ocho*	OH choh
nine	*nueve*	noo EH beh (oo as in hoot)
ten	*diez*	dee EHS
Sunday	*domingo*	doh MEEN goh
Monday	*lunes*	LOO nehs (oo as in hoot)
Tuesday	*martes*	MAHR tehs
Wednesday	*miércoles*	mee EHR coh lehs
Thursday	*jueves*	WEH behs
Friday	*viernes*	bee EHR nehs
Saturday	*sábado*	SAH bah doh
January	*enero*	eh NEH roh
February	*febrero*	feh BREH roh
March	*marzo*	MAHR soh
April	*abril*	ah BREEL
May	*mayo*	MAH yoh
June	*junio*	HOO nee oh
July	*julio*	HOO lee oh
August	*agosto*	ah GOHS toh
September	*septiembre*	sehp tee EHM breh
October	*octubre*	ok TOO breh
November	*noviembre*	noh vee EHM breh
December	*diciembre*	dee see EHM breh
no	*no*	noh
yes	*sí*	see
hello	*hola*	OH lah
goodbye	*adiós*	ah dee OHS
thank you	*gracias*	GRAH see ahs
you're welcome	*de nada*	deh/ NAH dah

LIBRARY-RELATED WORDS

your address	*su dirección*	soo/ dee rek see OHN
author (male)	*el escritor*	ehl/ eh scree TOHR
author (female)	*la escritora*	lah/ eh scree TOH rah
bathroom	*el baño*	ehl/ BAHN yoh
books	*libros*	LEE bros
boss (male)	*el jefe*	ehl/ HEH feh
boss (female)	*la jefa*	lah/ HEH fah
catalog	*el catálogo*	ehl/ cah TAH loh goh

check out	*tomar prestado*	toh MAHR/ preh STAH doh
children's room	*la sala de niños*	lah/ SAHL lah/ deh/ NEEN yohs
citizenship	*la nacionalidad*	lah/ nah see oh nahl ee DAHD
director (male)	*el director*	ehl/ dee rehk TOHR
director (female)	*la directora*	lah/ dee rehk TOHR ah
driver's license	*licencia de manejar*	lee SEHN see ah/ deh/ mah neh HAHR
entrance	*la entrada*	lah/ ehn TRAH dah
exit	*la salida*	lah/ sah LEE dah
fiction	*la ficción*	lah/ feek see OHN
fine	*la multa*	lah/ MOOL tah
left	*izquierda*	ee skee EHR dah
library card	*la tarjeta*	lah/ tahr HEH tah/ deh/ bee
	de biblioteca	blee oh TEH cah
magazine	*la revista*	lah/ reh BEES tah
non-fiction	*no-ficción*	noh/ feek see OHN
novel	*novela*	noh BEH lah
overdue	*vencido*	ben SEE doh
paperback	*el libro de bolsillo*	ehl/ LEE broh/ deh/ bohl SEE yoh
program	*el programa*	ehl/ proh GRAH mah
reference desk	*el mostrador*	ehl/ mohs trah DOHR/ deh/
	de referencia	reh feh REHN see ah
right	*derecha*	deh REH chah
signature	*la firma*	lah/ FEER mah
story hour	*la hora de cuentos*	lah/ OH rah/ deh/ KWEN tohs
table	*la mesa*	lah/ MEH sah
telephone	*el teléfono*	ehl/ teh LEH foh noh
time	*el tiempo*	ehl/ tee EM poh

PHRASES

Good morning	*buenos días*	BWEH nohs/ DEE ahs
Good afternoon	*buenas tardes*	BWEH nahs/ TAHR dehs
Good evening	*buenas noches*	BWEH nahs/ NOH ches
Welcome to the library	*Bienvenidos a la biblioteca*	bee ehn veh NEE dohs/ ah/ lah/ bee blee oh TEH cah
The librarian can help you.	*El bibliotecario* (male) *le puede ayudar*	ehl/ bee blee oh teh CAH ree oh/ leh/ PWEH deh/ ah yoo DAHR
	La bibliotecaria (female) *le puede ayudar*	lah/ bee blee oh teh CAH ree ah/ leh/ PWEH deh/ ah yoo DAHR
How are you today?	*¿Cómo está usted hoy?*	COH moh/ ehs TAH/ oo STED/ oy?
Do you speak English?	*¿Habla usted inglés?*	AH blah/oo STEHD/ een GLEHS?
I do not understand.	*No entiendo*	noh/ ehn tee EHN doh
Please speak more slowly.	*Por favor hable más despacio.*	pohr/ fah VOHR/ AH bleh/ mahs/ deh SPAH see oh
Please follow me.	*Por favor sígame*	pohr/ fah VOHR/ SEE gah meh

APPENDIX C
BILINGUAL FINGERPLAYS

UN HUEVITO – AN EGG

Este niñito compró un huevito (Hold up thumb)	This little child bought an egg
Este lo mandó asar (Hold up pointer finger)	This one put it in a pan
Este lo echó sal (Hold up middle finger)	This one sprinkled on the salt
Este lo revolvió (Hold up ring finger)	This one flipped it in the pan
Y el más chiquito se lo comió (Hold up little finger and wiggle)	The little one said, with a grin, "I will eat this egg if I can."

OJOS FEOS – SCARY EYES

Mira mis ojos grandes y feos (Circle thumb and index finger around eyes)	See my big and scary eyes
Ahora ten cuidado *¡Viene una sorpresa grande—* *Boo!*	Look out now A big surprise—BOO!

CONEJITO – LITTLE BUNNY

Aquí está un conejito con orejitas tan curiositas (Bend two fingers of one hand over the thumb)	Here is a bunny with ears so funny
Y aquí es donde vive en la tierra (Make a fist hole with the other hand)	And here is his hole in the ground
Cuando un ruido oye, levanta las orejas	When a noise he hears, he pricks up his ears

(Extend the index and middle
finger of first hand, and then
close them)

Y salta a su casa en la tierra.
(Jump fingers into fist
hole in other hand.)

And hops into his hole in the
ground.

CON LAS MANOS – WITH THE HANDS

Con mis manos	With my hands
Aplaudo, aplaudo, aplaudo	I clap, clap, clap
Y ahora las pongo	And now I lay them
En mi regazo. (Fold hands in lap)	In my lap.

CONEJITO – LITTLE BUNNY

(Make fingers of hand run up
the arm and take hold of ear as
you are saying all 4 verses)

Conejito que corre	Run little rabbit
Que sube, que te alcanza	Climb right up here
Que te pilla y	He is so hungry
Te tira la orejita.	He nibbles at your ear.

CINCO CALABACITAS – FIVE LITTLE PUMPKINS

Cinco calabacitas sentadas en un portón (Clasp hands and use one hand—5 fingers for 5 pumpkins)	Five little pumpkins sitting on a gate
La primera dijo: (hold up 1 finger) *"Se está haciendo tarde."*	The first one said: "My it's getting late."
La segunda dijo: (hold up second finger) *"Hay brujas en el aire."*	The second one said: "There are witches in the air."
Le tercera dijo: (hold up third finger) *"No le hace."*	The third one said: "We don't care."

La cuarta dijo: (hold up fourth finger) *"Es una noche de espanto."*	The fourth one said: "It's Halloween fun."
La quinta dijo: (hold up fifth finger) *"¡Corramos, corramos!"*	The fifth one said: "Let's run, let's run!"
Ooooo hizo el viento (Wave arms)	Ooooo went the wind
y se apagaron las luces (Clap hands)	and the lights went out
Las cinco calabacitas	The five little pumpkins
¡Corrieron a esconderse! (Run fingers behind back)	Ran to hide!

Permission to reprint fingerplays granted by Los Angeles County Public Library from *Vivan Los Niños! A List of Materials for Use with the Mexican-American Child*, Los Angeles County Public Library, March 1980.

6 MONEY, MONEY, WHO'S GOT THE MONEY?

CHALLENGE

Board Member:	*Ron, congratulations on the board's approval of the library's plan to begin offering services to Latinos. I am worried, though, that there won't be enough funds to do this and still serve our regular users.*
Ron:	*I understand your concern. I think we can offer many of our existing services to Latinos. But you're right—Latino users will also require some different services. We discovered this when we held those Latino focus groups. We took that into consideration and have developed a fiscal plan that will allow us to integrate some of those specialized services into our present budget. To expand into other services, we are probably going to pursue some external funding.*

The one thing that you will constantly have to address, externally and internally, is this funding issue. Serving Latinos in your community might indeed be new for your library; what is not new, though, is the fact that Latinos in your community have already been paying for those library services through their tax dollars. For whatever reasons, they have not become library users.

Latinos in your community, in one way or another, contribute to the tax base that funds city/county services provided by such departments as fire, police, and libraries. You will find yourself saying this over and over to other residents in your community. In fact, it will become second nature to you as will your rationale for serving Latino residents. That is what we want.

Internal funding and external funding are the major emphases in this chapter. Additionally, we include grant-writing tips to get you started in developing some creative projects, and we showcase a few externally-funded library projects designed to serve the Latino community.

INTERNAL FUNDING

While state aid is essential to the ongoing support of public library services, the major funding for public library services is local taxation. Since minorities are taxpayers and have a right to library services and programming, it makes good political and educational sense for libraries to factor them into their budgeting plans as resources, services, and programs are being developed.[1]

Internal funding is the money provided to the library through general funds. We define general funds as those moneys generated from a tax base that the library receives on a yearly basis from its funding agency.

PLANNING

Planning is absolutely crucial for any funding issue. You will find that you are not able to implement all at once everything you want to do for Latinos in your community. Your plan should be a plan of the future but must also address your present situation.

By planning to deal with today's realities and to project for future needs, you will be able to provide a broader range of services for Latinos. We strongly recommend a phase-in process using the following three questions as a guide:

- What can you do right now without taking additional funds from your library's current general fund budget?
- In priority order, what do you plan to do to integrate services to Latinos in your community within your library's general fund budget?
- For the future and in priority order, what do you plan to do to secure and use external funds for the library?

Overall, and at some point, funds should include targeted moneys for services and programs, materials, and personnel to provide library services to Latinos in your community.

When developing your plan, first identify the services you want to provide, at some point, for Latino residents. This is a wish list of sorts. At this stage, don't get bogged down and overwhelm yourself by worrying about *how* you are going to provide those services. Just list all the services you would like to offer to Latinos.

Second, delineate the services that are already available to Latinos under your current budget. You will need to sit down with your managers and/or staff to determine this. For example, services such as circulation, general reference, readers' advisory, meeting rooms, children's programming, and adult programming are already available to those Latinos who are either bilingual or monolingual in English. These services are already covered in your current budget at no extra cost.

Third, add to this list low-cost items that will make Latinos want to come into and use your library. Items could include funds for bilingual signs, outreach activities, some special children's programming, and so on. Again, prioritize those items using such criteria as

- Is it important to the Latino community (for example, a program on income tax advising)?
- Will it be popular and of high interest (for example, a bilingual puppeteer)?
- Is it doable and expedient?
- Can you share resources (for example, forming a partnership with a social service agency to provide some relevant programming)?

Next, plan to integrate into your general fund some of the services you have listed for Latinos in your community. This calls for rethinking the use of some of your general funds.

For example, let us say that your library has earmarked funds from your general fund for eight years to develop your children's collection. You have just completed your fifth year and still have three more years in that collection development project. You might want to take two-thirds of the next three years' funds and devote them to purchasing Spanish and bilingual children's materials to enhance your children's collection. Remember that bilingual materials are as useful to English-speaking children as they are to Latino children.

Another example includes sharing the funds available for adult general programming. Let's assume that you have budgeted a specific amount to offer adult programming each year. You can take a percentage of those allocated funds to offer bilingual programs to all adults. Again, depending on the general nature of those topics (for example, wills, hospice care, teenage pregnancy prevention), these bilingual programs can be beneficial to those Latino adults who are monolingual in Spanish as well as to those non-Latino adults who are monolingual in English.

These are examples of how you can begin to offer services using current general fund moneys to attract Latinos. However, don't forget that original list of Latino services. You may have listed services that have not fallen in the planning and funding schedule we just provided. Those are the services that, most likely, will take extra funds not available through your general fund budget, and that's okay. You at least now have a plan for providing services to Latino residents in different phases. You also know where you need to apply your current funds and when to seek external funds to augment your general budget. It just takes some planning, rethinking/redesigning, and initiative. You can do it!

EXTERNAL FUNDING

One of the best ways to get money for providing creative projects and services for Latinos in your community is through external sources. Most public libraries will not be able to develop and provide all services needed by Latinos by relying solely on general fund, tax-based dollars. If you want to do more than what can be done within your existing budget, you will have to think of other ways to fund some of your projects. One of the best ways to supplement your general funds is to pursue external funding aggressively.

We define external funding as any moneys coming from any source outside of your tax-supported general fund. These external funds could come from private sources—such as corporations, foundations, individuals—or they could come from government entities other than the one that funds your library. Your external funds could come from your Friends of the Library or your library foundation, if you have one, or they could come from library money-making projects. We even consider library discretionary funds—money from fines, lost books, or copier services—as external funds. However, you will have to check on your funding agency's fiscal rules to make sure there are no restrictions on use of such funds.

Many people are intimidated by proposal writing. Writing grant proposals, working with your Friends group or library foundation, contacting external private and public funding agencies will take much time and effort. However, the payback in getting a project funded can be substantial. For example, if it took a total of $960 (48 hours of total staff time at an average of $20 per hour from beginning to end) to submit a proposal for funding, and if you received funding based on that proposal for $38,000, you have increased your investment nearly 40 times! When you look at fundraising from that perspective, it becomes well worth your time.

We know that it is difficult to handle rejection. Unfortunately, that is a fact of life in fundraising. However, when you do get a proposal funded or a project supported by an external group, you tend to forget your last rejection.

PROPOSAL WRITING

We want to focus on grant writing as a major method for obtaining external funds. This is a quick lesson in Grant Writing 101. There are many books on proposal writing; we suggest you refer to some of them if you need a more in-depth discussion.

Again, many different organizations—private, public, and nonprofit—provide funds for other organizations, usually through a competitive process. Funding organizations will have general guidelines or criteria, such as:

- The applicant organization must be nonprofit.
- They may restrict the use of their funds to supplant your general fund budget.
- They may restrict the use of funds to support an existing project/ service.
- They may specify pilot projects that will be supported by the library or the library's internal funding body after the external funds run out.
- They may provide topical guidelines dealing with funding specific subjects areas (such as science, humanities, art).
- There may be funding and time limitations.
- They may have very specific proposal guidelines and format (such as page restrictions).

You will find that you can usually live with the general criteria or restrictions.

So, what kind of proposal is attractive to funding organizations? We would like to share our proposal philosophy. First of all, after you determine that you have met all the general guidelines and criteria, you need to start thinking about other criteria, such as

- demonstrated need
- creativity
- buzz words or words *du jour*

For the sake of this whole grant-writing discussion, let us offer a hypothetical situation: Your library has committed to reach out aggressively to Latinos in your community. You have completed your planning process and one of your priorities is service to Latino children and young adults. You have incorporated some services for them into your general fund budget but now are pursuing external funding sources.

The first thing to consider is identifying a special need—in this case something to do with serving Latino children and young adults. You can probably identify something right this moment off the top of your head.

Let us start with demonstrating *the need*. In many cases, need is related to problem solving. That is, you recognize a problem and there is a definite need to solve that problem.

Again in our hypothetical scenario, you are bothered by the reports and articles you have been reading concerning the high Latino youth dropout rate in your community and in the state. You are also concerned about the growing illiteracy rate among teenagers. You know that there is a strong correlation between literacy and educational success. You also know that public libraries should work closely with schools to assist in providing supplementary library services. So you have decided to create an afterschool, bilingual, homework help center sponsored by the library.

To illustrate your point concerning need, use whatever published data you can find on local and national educational attainment levels that will allow you to draw inferences about the literacy rates of Latino young adults in your community (see Chapter 3). You need such data to show a definite need.

You also conducted some focus groups in your Latino community and have the summaries of those group discussions which overwhelmingly show that the community is concerned about its children and teenagers and would like your library to assist them in some way. This is another strong demonstration of need. Having shown sufficient need for your idea, you can move on to creativity.

Most funding organizations do not want to fund something that does not seem creative or that is already part of a current project. You are convinced that something needs to be done to help solve a problem; however, you need a *creative idea* to help solve the problem. The concept of a homework center in a library, you have found, is new to the state. In fact, the school districts have been unable to fund such a service. So, in a sense, your idea is very creative from a library service point of view.

Even more creative is the fact that you have chosen to locate this homework center where it is most needed—in the Latino neighborhood—and to make it bilingual. Now you have really mastered creativity!

So far, you have shown a strong need in your proposal; and you have come up with a creative idea to meet that need. Now you need to build in the *buzz words* or *words du jour*. Using such words will effectively strengthen your proposal.

In our hypothetical scenario, buzz words you would use throughout your proposal could be *illiteracy, dropout rates, graduation success, children at risk, teenagers at risk,* and *crime prevention*. Because your idea shows commitment to serving the Latino children and young adults in the community, don't be afraid to use those buzz words.

Demonstrating a strong need coupled with a creative idea or solution to solve a problem are the basics for a proposal. Now you are ready to move on to the next steps.

Proposal Format

Other parts of a proposal tend to follow conventions specific to proposal writing. However, we want to make sure you understand the importance of each part of a proposal. Figure 6–1 provides you with a sample proposal format. Following is a brief discussion of each item in that proposal format.

1. Title Page

    The title page includes the title, the name of the organization submitting the proposal, and the contact person. We recommend that the title says what the project is—but try to make it catchy. For our hypothetical scenario, the title might be "From Dropout to DropIN: A Library HomeworkHELP Center."

2. Introduction/Background

    The introduction can be brief. Here you identify the *local problem* (for example, high dropout rate of Latino youngsters). If you did any preliminary research on the proposed topic, you

---

Figure 6-1. Sample Proposal Format

1. Title Page

2. Introduction/Background

3. Demonstration of Need

4. Purpose

5. Description of Project

6. Goals and Objectives

7. Project Activities

8. Activities Timeline

9. Budget

10. Evaluation

11. Support Letters

would include it here. For example, you could cite an article that describes the success rate of a minority tutoring project.

3. Demonstration of Need

    The demonstration of need tells the reader *why* you need to do the project. For example, here you could elaborate on the problem of Latino high school dropouts—how it affects illiteracy, the economy, and so forth. Use your local demographic data here.

4. Purpose

    For the purpose of your project, you need to tell the reader what you want to accomplish in order to help solve a problem. For example: *The purpose of the HomeworkHELP Center is to provide academic assistance to at-risk Latino students, thereby increasing the high school graduation rate of Latinos in the community.*

5. Description of Project

    Describe the proposed project in layperson's terms. Make the description succinct but effective; use your buzz words.

6. Goals and Objectives

    The goals basically include much of what was stated in the "Purpose" text; goals are usually in numerical format. The objectives tell *how* you will accomplish each goal. We strongly recommend that each objective be demonstrable. Demonstrable, in the broadest sense, means that if something is done you can prove it. See Figure 6-2 for an example.

Figure 6-2. Sample Project Goal and Objective

Goal 1. To provide a site where Latino children can come in to get help with their homework.

Objective A.   By November 1997, a site will be selected and prepared to house the HomeworkHELP Center.

7. Project Activities

   A list of activities is optional. However, the more information you can provide without overwhelming the reader, the more it shows careful thought and planning, and the fewer questions the reader will have. We recommend that you follow the same format as under "Goals and Objectives." Using that previous example, Figure 6–3 shows an activity example.

8. Activities Timeline

   Some people prefer to use a chart that shows the term of the project in months and then lists the activities. Figures 6–4a and 6–4b provide a timeline schematic; an outline also works well. This timeline again gives the proposal reader a clear indication of a carefully planned project that recognizes specific timelines to complete the project.

9. Budget

   Include whatever costs it takes to complete the project. Sometimes external funding organizations will have guidelines that you need to be aware of, such as:

   - Dollar for dollar match—This means that if they fund you for $38,000, the library must match it by $38,000. Usually the external funding organization doesn't care where you get the money, just that there is a match. Also, the match might be a cash match, an in-kind match, or a combination of both.
   - In-kind costs—Some external funding agencies will allow you to show your in-kind contributions. For example, you can show the percentage of the salary of anyone donating time to the project or you can show the amount of non-

---

Figure 6-3. Sample Project Goal, Objective, and Activities

Goal 1.   To provide a site where Latino children can come in to get help with their homework.

    Objective A.   By November 1997, a site will be selected and prepared to house the HomeworkHELP Center.

        Activity 1.   Prepare the specifications for the HomeworkHELP Center site.

        Activity 2.   Work with City Facilities Department to find an appropriate site.

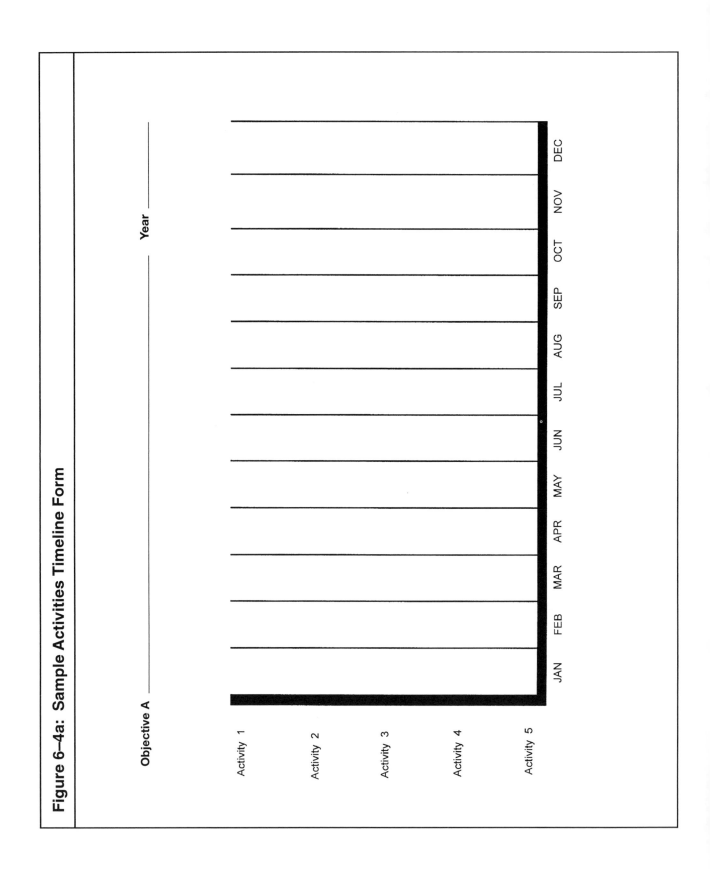

Figure 6–4a: Sample Activities Timeline Form

Figure 6–4b: Sample Activities Timeline Form—Completed

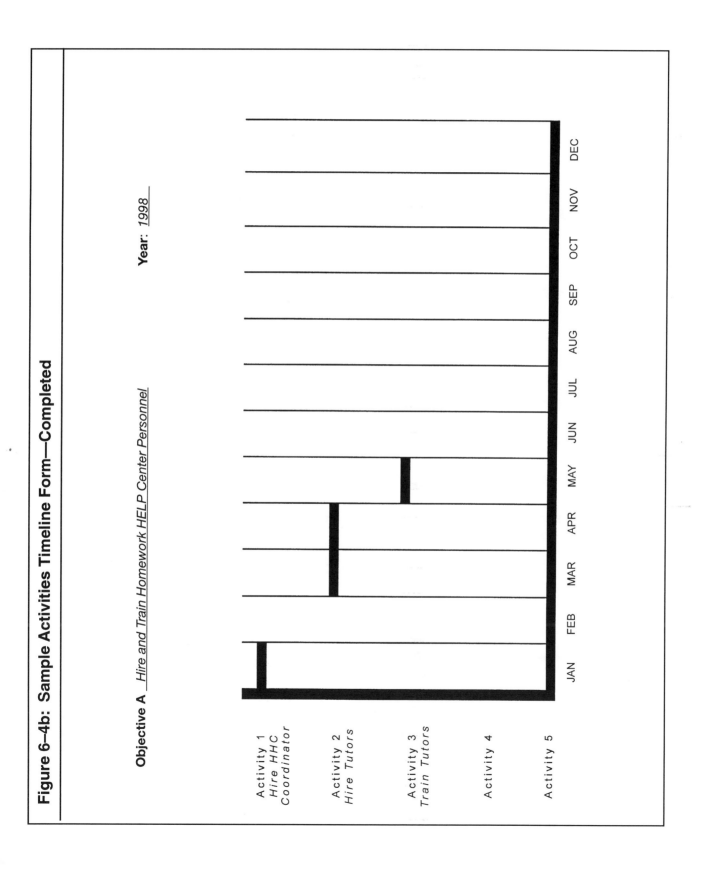

cash match the library will provide (such as books or equipment).

- No indirect or overhead costs—The external funding organization wants to make sure that every dollar it awards goes to funding the project and does not go to supplementing fixed costs of the library or salaries of individuals not working on the project.
- No support for any type of equipment or salaries—Usually the funding organization does not want to buy library equipment or pay for salaries.

Figure out what it will take to complete the project down to the last activity and dime. Remember that most proposal readers are very astute. Do not pad the project budget—they will figure it out.

One of us was once on a reading team for an external funding agency, and a library that submitted a proposal wanted funds for starting a literacy program. Its budget costs seemed in line until, at the very end, the library requested ten desktop computers. Nowhere in the proposal did the library say how or where those PCs would be used to do any literacy-related activities nor what kind of computer software would be needed. The project was funded, but funds were denied for nine of the ten PCs.

In this budget section, we recommend you err on the side of too much information rather than not enough. For example, enter a budget item accordingly:

1,000 Spanish/bilingual children's/YA books
  [$20/book x 1,000 books] $20,000
Rental of HomeworkHELP Center facility
  [700 sq.ft. @ $15/sq.ft. x 5 years] $52,500

10. Evaluation

After you have told the external funding agency what you want to do, how and when you are going to do it, and how much it is going to cost, you are now ready to tell them how you will determine if the project is successful. That segment is the evaluation mechanism.

One of the most common mistakes made by libraries submitting proposals at the local, state, and national levels is providing a weak evaluation component or none at all. Most external funding agencies usually require the applicant to address evaluation, but many submitting organizations do not pay enough attention to this component. If you follow the process we outlined in the goals, objectives, and activities sections, it is not difficult to design a very strong evaluation component. Again, this is a step-by-step process. Following are some suggested evaluation measures:

- Meeting goals and objectives—If your objectives are measurable, then half of the evaluation process is done. Part of your project evaluation will be showing whether or not each goal and objective was met and how.
- Evaluation from participants—This is another effective evaluation procedure. Devise a sample evaluation form that could be completed by the Latino students using the HomeworkHELP Center. Tell how and when you plan to use it.
- Evaluation from project staff—Although this step can be perceived as subjective and possibly self-serving, it is still a viable way to evaluate the project. Most people are honest in sharing the successes and setbacks of a project.
- External evaluation—Either your library or the external funding agency may want to bring in an external evaluator(s). If you decide to do it and there are costs related to this method of evaluation, build the cost for external evaluation into your proposed budget.

These are just some of the evaluation measures you can include in your proposal. The point is, do not underestimate the effect of a good evaluation component in your proposal.

11. Support Letters

We strongly recommend that you include support letters in the appendices of your proposal. Using our scenario of the HomeworkHELP Center, we recommend including letters from members of the Latino community—Latino students who would benefit, your local school administration and teachers, community agencies, and parents. Make sure to enclose a copy of the proposal when you write to an organization or individual asking for a support letter. If the proposal is not finished, then send them a brief proposal executive summary highlighting the proposal components.

Ideas for external funding need not be as elaborate as a HomeworkHELP Center. An idea could be as simple as asking for funds to develop a collection of Spanish and bilingual children's books. Our point is that it often takes pursuing outside funds to get some special projects started for Latinos in your community. For example, Tucson-Pima Public Library has been very successful in securing external funding for library projects and then getting those projects integrated and funded internally.

SOURCES FOR EXTERNAL FUNDS

One of the most common library funding sources for years has been LSCA (Library Services and Construction Act), now named LSTA (Library Services and Technology Act). Most states receive LSTA funds that are administered by the state library in each state. Some state libraries have restricted how LSTA funds can be used, but for the most part LSTA funds have been available to fund creative projects.

At one time, there were funds—Major Urban Resource Library (MURL)—for those public libraries that served a population over 100,000. Consider what Denver Public Library and Oxnard (California) Public Library did with their MURL funds. Denver allocated all of its MURL funds for a certain number of years to develop a very strong children's collection of Spanish and bilingual materials. Oxnard Public Library used a combination of MURL and LSCA funds to build its Spanish/bilingual collection, and it now has the largest collection of Spanish materials between Los Angeles and San Francisco!

There are other possible external sources. Research the private, philanthropic organizations based in your state. Contact them to find out their funding cycles and the guidelines for submitting proposals. Ask them to send the appropriate information to you.

Next check the services organizations in your service area and their regional headquarters. For example, the Rotary Clubs in Colorado, in conjunction with Pizza Hut, funded a statewide Read-Aloud program that encouraged any nonprofit organization, including libraries, to apply for funds to promote reading to children.

Check the corporate sector also. It doesn't matter, for instance, that the corporation is located in the city and your library is a small rural library, as long as the corporation does statewide marketing. If the corporation has a community relations or philanthropic department, it may be willing to fund a much-needed program for your local community. Such a program is great public relations for the corporation. Don't be timid about approaching nationwide businesses. Many national corporations have regional or state offices, and that is the place to start.

Look at other nonprofit organizations at all levels—local, state, and national—that fund outside projects. For example, a state humanities council can be approached by a library in a rural part of the state. Such a library could request funds to bring minority humanities scholars and/or authors residing in the state to offer some bilingual, Latino-related humanities programming to its community.

Other national government agencies, such as the Department of Education through LSTA funds, provide funds for innovative projects. Check their RFP (Request for Proposal) guidelines. Maybe your library and another agency closely related to the department issuing the RFP can design an innovative project partnership to serve Latino residents.

Don't forget your local Friends of the Library, if you have one. They can designate a particular fundraising effort to help your library meet the needs of Latinos in your community.

EXTERNAL FUNDING SUCCESS STORIES

This is another exciting part—sharing with you some of the success stories of libraries and their externally-funded projects to serve their Latino communities. Most specifically, we wanted to share some of the successful LSCA projects geared to the Latino community. First are two success stories; second, other projects that were funded throughout the country.

TWO LSCA SUCCESSES

The first story involves the Conejos County Library outside of La Jara, Colorado. Conejos County is the poorest rural county in the state of Colorado and small in population. This library serves a county of 7,452 residents where over 62% of the residents are Latinos. Of the total residents, 48.6% speak a language other than English; it is a safe assumption that the language is Spanish. Thirty-four percent of the Latino families fall below the poverty level.

The director, Maria DeHerrera, has one of the most successful LSCA records in the state; her success rate in the past decade surpasses some of the largest public libraries' LSCA success rates. By including some of Maria's proposal ideas funded for this very small county library, we hope to give you some encouragement!

One crisis the Conejos County Library's community faced was the problem of an extraordinarily high suicide rate among Latinos. Maria received funding for a proposal that included forming partnerships with county agencies and the nearby small college to bring in programming on suicide prevention and other related issues and to purchase related materials on suicide prevention.

Maria had another project in mind, but she needed additional funding from external sources to fill an unmet need. Her library didn't have many children's materials for the Spanish monolingual and bilingual Latino children. A proposal she wrote allowed her to enhance her small children's collection with materials in Spanish and Spanish/English.

Once Maria started building her Spanish children's collection, she was concerned that Latino preschool children were not coming into the library. She wrote a proposal for LSCA funding that provided her library the funds to offer off-site read-alouds to the at-risk Latino children in the local Head Start program. Her partnership with this organization helped make this read-aloud program a huge success. Once she got the preschool children hooked on books, they became avid library users.

Maria tried to solve another community problem by seeking external funding for a library-based, computer skills development project. The Latino adults in the community were unable to upgrade their job skills to compete in the job market because they didn't have access to the latest computer technology. Only a few Latinos in the community could afford to purchase a PC and relevant software for home use. Maria's LSCA proposal requested funds to purchase four complete PC systems along with supplemental job skills software packages that included word-processing software and tutorials, resumé-writing software, and the like. Again, this project was very popular with her Latino community. All of Maria's proposals identified a specific need for the Latino community.

The Conejos County examples illustrate that even the smallest of libraries can be successful in obtaining external funding to provide library services to Latinos. Our second LSCA funding story occurred in California. Probably one of the most successful LSCA multi-year projects dealing with library services to minority communities was the California State Library's Partnership for Change (PFC) program. The mission of the PFC program was to assist California libraries in analyzing and restructuring their community library service programs and policies to respond to the ethnic and cultural diversity of their communities.[2]

Since this project provided services to all people of color, many Latinos throughout California benefitted from the project. Many of the libraries we visited were PFC libraries. For some, the PFC project got them started in effective outreach that not only dramatically increased their Latino user base but also strengthened their Latino political base.

Although PFC funds were provided for only a limited time, most libraries were able to integrate some of these services to Latinos into their general library programs. That is to say, many boards of trustees and funding agencies agreed to fund, at some level, and to integrate some of the services produced through the PFC program. That is what external funding is all about—providing the library the financial ability to develop special services and programming that increases library usage and popularity, especially from a new user base such as the Latino community. Some of these services should eventually be incorporated into the library's general services and funded through local general funds.

Remember our discussion in Chapter 3 about presenting a strong rationale? Developing an additional political base for the library from the Latino community was one of them.

We found that, for the most part, PFC libraries were able to integrate some critical Latino services. However, the hardest cuts came in staffing. So the services that were integrated were those services that could continue to be offered without specialized PFC staff. One lasting effect of the PFC programs was the cultural awareness training that was provided to library staff. That training has had a long-term beneficial effect on staff and their treatment of minority users.

OTHER FUNDING IDEAS

In our two LSCA success stories—Conejos County Library and the PFC statewide program in California—we shared with you two extremes. Tiny Conejos County Library serves the poorest county in a remote, rural part of Colorado; the PFC program served mostly large, urban communities in California. We wanted you to get a sense that size may not mean much when competing for external funds.

In this section, we want to share other ideas that were successful in raising external funds for the library. We describe some externally funded LSCA projects in Colorado, New Jersey, and Illinois. However, these scenarios could easily be situated in any state with Latino and other minority populations and could be funded with other external funds besides LSTA.

Colorado Successes

Adams County Library system received funds to develop a collection of multimedia Spanish language materials for at-risk Latino youth—preschool through high school. Aurora Public Library, one of the largest library systems in Colorado, received funds to provide bilingual reading materials for preschool and elementary-level children.

The Lake County School District, which is located in a remote mountainous region of Colorado, developed a partnership with Lake County Public Library and Colorado Mountain College to deal with a large increase in Lake County's Latino population. These libraries received funds to address multicultural diversity by providing Lake County residents with Spanish-language and multicultural materials.

Pueblo Library District, which serves over 100,000 residents and has always had a large population of Latino residents, found an alarming number of functionally illiterate residents (over 10%), most of whom were Latinos. The district received external funding to provide materials and establish a literacy program that would help combat that illiteracy rate. The funds also enabled them to hire adult tutors to work in the literacy program.

Saguache County Public Library, located in the same rural mountain valley as Conejos County Library and ranked in Colorado's lowest one-third of counties in terms of income levels, received funds to develop a collection of Spanish materials and to develop an aggressive outreach program for the community.

Denver Public Library (DPL), the largest public library system in Colorado, received a large LSCA grant to provide off-site read-alouds to at-risk (mostly minority) preschool children at Head Start centers, crisis centers, and shelters in metropolitan Denver. The grant funded special library programs, including storytellers and musicians, to encourage minority families to use the library. Subsequently, DPL received funds to work with minority parents and their children in a read-to-me–type program.

Weld County Library District received external funds to improve the Spanish-language skills of its staff. In an effort to increase services to the Latino community, the library also used some of those funds to purchase Spanish-language materials.

Westminster Public Library, which serves a suburb northwest of Denver, received LSCA funds to use its bookmobile staff one day a week to provide a bilingual storytime for Latino children. The grant also funded the purchase of 300 Spanish children's books for its collection. In addition, Westminster received a separate grant to establish a core collection of Spanish-language materials for adult library users.

These are just some projects that were funded based on proposals submitted by Colorado libraries to provide services to their Latino communities. These examples should give you some ideas for your own future proposals.

Two Other Funding Successes: Newark Public Library and Chicago Public Library

Many library projects have been funded to help libraries serve their multicultural communities. If you need financial assistance taking that first step to develop library services to Latinos, then you might consider submitting a planning grant proposal similar to the one submitted by Newark Public Library. Newark's population consists of 90% minorities and 10% whites. The library received a planning grant to conduct a thorough community analysis of its Latino community. The project headed by Ingrid Betancourt used census data and the following methodology:

1. Identify Latino community leaders and interview them individually about library services.
2. Use focus groups with translators in meetings in the community and in the library.

3. Develop a list of recommendations based on all the input, and thus enable the library to address the needs of Latinos in Newark.

Newark also received funds to start a pilot project that was eventually integrated into the general library services and budget. That project provides a Spanish "hotline" that is open all the hours the library is open and that provides bilingual staff to answer reference questions and supply community information. This project is located in the public library's Sala Hispanoamericano which is a special facility in the library housing Latino materials and services.

The Chicago Public Library (CPL) has also been very successful in external fundraising. CPL was aggressive in the area of literacy funding. Using external funds, CPL produced a manual on how to teach Spanish literacy and supplied literacy materials in Spanish and English.

In the area of children's services, CPL received federal funds to train monolingual English-speaking children's librarians to incorporate Spanish elements into their children's programs. Another effort by CPL to train non-Latino staff to serve Latinos in the community received external funding. This project provided the funds to offer Spanish-language classes for library staff working in Latino neighborhoods.

CPL also received external funds to provide programs and materials on subjects important to new Latino immigrants. In addition, the Friends of CPL funded the purchase of educational toys and kits intended to encourage Latino family learning and development of prereading skills. These are just a few of the successful proposals for which CPL received funding.[3]

Many other types of projects have been funded by external grants. Grants have been received by libraries to purchase materials in several formats dealing with life-coping skills—job information, housing needs, citizenship exam preparation assistance, computer skills, and translation services. Grants have been received to provide cultural programs featuring music, films, guest speakers, and ethnic performers. One project was funded to train library personnel in the language and cultural values of the immigrant community to enhance services to the bilingual residents. Funds to assist libraries in providing tutors for ESL (English as a Second Language) programs have been granted. In addition, external funds were provided to develop outreach programs that brought library materials and information to rural Latinos.

These are ideas for you to consider. Remember that the basic rule for writing a proposal for external funding is to help solve a problem or to meet a strong need. We encourage you to submit your proposal. You really have nothing to lose and a lot to gain for your library and Latino community if you are funded.

CONCLUSION

For public libraries, funding is a constant challenge. Many compete with other local government agencies for limited available funds. Consequently, there are never enough dollars to provide every needed program. However, there is no excuse for not aggressively looking for external funds and for not integrating some library services for Latinos.

We hope this chapter has given you some ideas of where and how to pursue funding from external sources. Additionally, you now are aware of the types of projects that have been successfully funded. For those of you who are novices to the proposal-writing process, the outline we provided delineating the proposal mechanics should get you started.

Think positive, be more assertive, and don't let any rejection deter you. Usually reading teams will let the library know of a proposal's weaknesses. Deal with their suggestions and resubmit the proposal and/or submit the same proposal to another external funding source. You will never experience the joy and satisfaction of being notified that your project was funded unless you submit a proposal. Go for it!

NOTES

1. National Commission on Library and Information Services, *Report of the Task Force on Library and Information Services to Cultural Minorities* (Washington, D.C.: U.S. Government Printing Office, 1983), 68.
2. California State Library, *Helping California Libraries Respond to Change,* a brochure prepared by the California State Library (Sacramento, Calif.: California State Library, n.d.), 5.
3. Hispanic Services Committee, *Hispanic Services: A Practical Manual for the Public Librarian* (Chicago: Chicago Public Library, 1990), 99–102.

7 MAY I HELP YOU? THE IMPORTANT ROLE OF LIBRARY PERSONNEL

CHALLENGE

Mrs. Foster: *Roberto, I think it's great that you've checked out lots of books this year. Your teacher says that your reading level has gone up three grades; you should be very proud of that. I hope you continue your reading this summer at the public library.*

Roberto: *I really love to read, Mrs. Foster, and you've always encouraged me to come into the school library. But I don't use the public library. A couple of years ago, my mom took us to sign up for the summer reading program, and the people working in the library laughed at her because she doesn't speak English very well. My mom was really embarrassed, and we've never gone back. I trade comic books with my friends in the summertime.*

Mrs. Foster: *I'm really sorry to hear that, Roberto. But I know the new library director who was just hired there about six months ago. She's talked to me about how to get more Latinos involved in using the library. I think things are really starting to change there. Why don't you meet me at the library on Saturday, and I'll introduce you to her and show you around the library? Bring your mom, too.*

It is important to have staff and volunteers who are Latino, first and foremost. If that is impossible, libraries that want to serve their Latino community must, at least, have white staff who have undergone training to respect and be aware of the Latino culture; and be sensitive to those cultural differences.[1]

Staff, more than library materials, have the most profound effect on library users. How staff treat people who walk in the door can determine whether or not those people will return to use the library. It is what we call setting the tone of the library. Unlike school libraries, public libraries do not have a captive audience.

Probably the most serious mistake any library can make is not to sensitize its staff to cultural awareness and ethnic diversity issues. In the Latino culture, Latinos prefer to establish some type of personal relationship before they ask for help. That personal relationship could easily be eye contact and a friendly smile.

This chapter discusses the issue of library personnel. We cover ideas from the best-case scenario (and how to get there) to the realities of an all-white staff and how to help them. We also offer tips on the recruitment of minority personnel. Latino library trustees and internal Latino advisory committees are also addressed in this chapter.

LATINO TO LATINO: THE BEST-CASE SCENARIO

In our visits to the various libraries around the country that were noted for providing exemplary services to their Latino community, the most pressing point was the need for bilingual staff. Without hesitation, people interviewed in these libraries were adamant about the need for bilingual Latino staff.

Because much of the work that needs to be done to attract Latinos in your community to the library requires the ability to speak their language and to understand their Latino culture, having bilingual and bicultural Latino personnel on the staff is obviously the best-case scenario. One could argue that a non-Latino who is bilingual could be as effective. We are not denying that such staff members can be effective, but the best-case scenario for staffing is to have some bilingual Latino personnel. Why is that? For the most part, Latino library personnel have the following characteristics that would be hard to match:

- They grew up with and know the local Latino culture (albeit there are many subcultures among the Latino population in this country).
- They are very aware of the cultural differences between the predominant white culture and the Latino culture and can adjust to those differences.
- They are often easily and *visibly* identifiable among the Latino community you are striving to serve.
- They offer a sense of commonality (for example, physical characteristics, heritage) that automatically establishes a sense of trust among the Latino community.
- They know and speak the local vernacular Spanish language.
- They are familiar with and often live in the Latino community.
- They bring a sense of purpose and commitment to serving the local Latino community.
- They can be good role models for Latino children and young adults.

How else can bilingual Latino library personnel serve the library and the community? They can do effective outreach in the Latino community. They know of Spanish-speaking individuals in the community who can assist the library with bilingual programs. They, themselves, can offer bilingual programming, such as children's story hours in Spanish, as well as design and write the bilingual flyers that advertise the various bilingual programs being offered. They can do effective collection development and processing of Spanish-language materials. Additionally, they can serve as public-relations liaisons to the Spanish-language media.[2]

RECRUITING LATINO LIBRARIANS

One of the most difficult challenges is recruiting Latino librarians. This is a challenge no matter the type of library. First of all, there are very few Latino library professionals relative to the 22.4 million Latinos living in this country. This is where the challenge begins.

Let's assume that you were successful in getting some extra librarian positions funded to help you concentrate on developing services to your Latino community. Your recruitment efforts demand planning a strategy that will be successful. We have some tips for planning that strategy.

Write your job announcement to allow for the expansion of the pool of candidates. That is, write the job announcement so that the minimum qualifications are indeed the minimum. If someone with two years experience can do the job as well as someone with five years of experience, then require only two years of experience.[3]

On the other hand, if the position requires a special skill, then be specific. If you want a librarian who can communicate with the Latino community, do Spanish-language programming, and buy Spanish-language materials, then you need to make fluency in Spanish a requirement. You should also provide added compensation to employees who have these special bilingual abilities.

Once the job announcement is ready to go, you need to plan strategically where to advertise. Depending on the size of your community, you might be successful in finding some Latinos with MLS degrees. Usually your chances are much greater in finding Latino paraprofessionals from your local community. Nonetheless, it does not hurt to advertise the professional position locally.

Word of mouth is another effective local strategy. Ask your local Latino residents—business people, educators, community leaders, government employees—for referrals. You never know who might have a second cousin with an MLS who just might be interested.

We recommend that you contact the placement officers at the library and information studies programs in areas that have some concentration of Latinos. These officers can usually provide names and addresses of Latino alumni and current Latino students. A list of those library programs are included in Appendix A at the end of this chapter.

REFORMA (National Association to Promote Library Services to the Spanish-Speaking), an American Library Association (ALA) affiliate, distributes a quarterly newsletter to its 700–plus members. You can advertise your position there. REFORMA also manages an Internet discussion group (called REFORMANET) which posts job announcements. You can find more information on REFORMANET in Chapter 11.

Cultivating your own staff is a very effective way to increase the number of Latino professional librarians. Although this is a long-term solution, it is still doable. The strategy is to support Latino paraprofessionals already on your staff in getting their MLS degrees. Once they achieve that goal, they should be next in line for assuming professional positions as librarians.[4]

There are a variety of ways to do this. Providing tuition reimbursement/incentives is one way. The Denver Public Library has been aggressively promoting the "grow-your-own" concept. It basically pays for its employees to attend library school. Another incentive is to provide release time for your employees to attend classes that are only offered during the workday.

Scholarship opportunities are also a possibility for recruiting Latino MLS graduates. For example, the Colorado State Library's advisory board has provided scholarship funds to attend library school. The recipients must have demonstrated a commitment to working with minorities. On the national level, the American Library Assocation's Spectrum Initiative is providing 50 scholarships for minorities for three years.

RECRUITING LATINO PARAPROFESSIONALS

We have provided some tips on how to find Latino librarians. However, we recognize that, for various reasons, you may not be able to hire Latino librarians. If you have personnel funds but cannot afford to hire a professional Latino librarian, then consider hiring and training Latino paraprofessionals.

When developing the job description for a paraprofessional staff position, we recommend that you make bilingual ability in Spanish a requirement. That is the only way to attract someone who meets your library's primary need—bilingual competency. Your commitment to serve Latinos will be demonstrated and solidified when you follow through with this bilingual requirement and are able to hire a bilingual Latino paraprofessional.

In developing the job announcement and in order to get Latino residents to apply, do not make experience in a library a requirement.

This requirement will automatically eliminate almost all Latinos. Also, understand that the more requirements you list, the more Latinos you eliminate. For example, there may be a Latino individual who can help in bilingual translation of programs, services, and promotional materials; who can canvass the Latino community in the library's outreach efforts; and who can be trained to offer story hours and work various service desks. However, if you make "typing 50 words per minute" or "experience with personal computers and/or word-processing software" a requirement, you might eliminate many qualified Latino applicants.

Remember that you are making an investment when you hire a Latino paraprofessional. That person will bring special characteristics to the library—bilingual ability and inside knowledge of the Latino community and culture. In return, you must commit to the time it will take to train this individual in the library-related duties and responsibilities that will make him or her successful in the library.

We recommend that you advertise in the local and area newspapers. If there is a Spanish-language newspaper, advertise in that. See if you can get someone to translate the job announcement into Spanish for that newspaper. If there are Spanish-language radio and/or television stations in the area, advertise there too.

We have one other advertising tip. Put the job announcement in flyer format and distribute and post flyers throughout the Latino community. You need to get the information directly to the community from which you want to draw.

Last but not least, rely on word-of-mouth referrals. Ask staff, Latino library users, educators, Latino business people, and others for referrals. People will usually only refer others to you who are capable, dependable, and responsible.

RECRUITING LATINO VOLUNTEERS

Another pool of Latino personnel who can help you in providing services to their community is the volunteer pool. Most public libraries, especially in smaller communities, do not have a high staff turnover rate. Consequently, very few permanent staff positions—professional or paraprofessional—become vacant. This aspect, along with budget limitations, is a real barrier in hiring additional permanent staff—Latino or not—and it is beyond the library's control.

Volunteers are vital to most libraries. There is no reason for the scope of your volunteer base not to include bilingual Latino individuals. This is definitely the next best thing to hiring permanent Latino staff.

Latino volunteers should come from the Latino community, and speaking Spanish should not be their only responsibility. The library needs to train them to work adequately in the library and to do outreach for the library in the Latino community.

How and where do you find Latino volunteers? Here is where a lot of time and dedication takes place. First of all, how do you regularly enlist non-Latino volunteers from your community? Try using similar methods in the Latino community.

Following are some tips for recruiting Latino volunteers to help you in your efforts to serve the Latino community:

- Check among your current staff. They may know of Latinos who might be willing to volunteer or who might be able to help you find Latino volunteers.
- Find out who the formal and informal Latino community leaders are. Enlist their help. Some may have friends or relatives who might be willing to volunteer in the library.
- Check with the church leaders and religious organizations most frequented by the Latino community for volunteer referrals.
- If you already have Latino users in your library, ask them for referrals. In fact, if some of them are adults or young adults, see if they would be willing to volunteer some time.
- Check with other organizations and government agencies that provide services to Latinos. They can help with referrals.
- Don't forget to check with the local junior high and high schools. If the high school has Spanish classes or a Spanish club, members may be willing to volunteer to do bilingual story hours or translate after school during scheduled hours.
- If your community has a recreational center that is frequented by Latinos, go there to recruit volunteers.
- If your community has a senior citizen's center, recruit Latino senior citizens as volunteers. Libraries, in general, have real success with senior volunteers.
- Cooperate with your local judicial system and use community service workers. East Los Angeles Public Library averages about 100–150 hours per month using these workers, and those hours are very important to the library's overall operation.
- Advertise in the local media for bilingual volunteers. If there are any Spanish-language media, make sure to advertise there also.
- Invest in your young adults. They are a great source for building a volunteer base. They can effectively assist in your bilingual story hours and your summer reading programs.

We want to share some success stories of volunteer programs using young adults. For example, the Logan Heights Branch library in San Diego has only young adults as volunteers. They are absolutely crucial to the operation of the library because there are only two full-time staff members to serve a community of over 20,000 residents. Juan Ortiz, the branch manager, recruits local youths already using the library for his volunteer staff. They are as young as ten years old with the average age being 13 years old. They volunteer one hour per day, two days per week, and must have their homework and chores completed before they can come to work. They choose their days (Monday and Wednesday or Tuesday and Thursday).

Ortiz maintains that he could not offer the services or the hours of operation if it were not for his young adult volunteers. Most of them also stay with him until they are old enough to work elsewhere in a paid, part-time job.

Another successful example is the New York Public Library's (NYPL) volunteer program using young adults. First of all, the New York Public Library's volunteer groups reflect the neighborhoods of the branch libraries. Consequently, many of the volunteers are Latinos. NYPL has a young adult bilingual volunteer group called the "Junior Lions" who work with advanced adult ESL (English as a Second Language) clients. In addition, the Junior Lions hold discussion groups called conversational programs.

One other advantage NYPL has found concerning its volunteers has been their political activism. This volunteer activism has been instrumental in successful letter-writing campaigns to keep or restore service hours in the various NYPL branches.

We have one word of caution, however. If your professional and paraprofessional staffs are represented by unions, be careful about how you use your volunteers. Otherwise, bilingual volunteers are a source that can be very important to the services you offer or want to offer to your Latino community.

We acknowledge that all this takes time and that you need to be aggressive about your volunteer development efforts. However, it will pay off one way or another. For example, if you already have an established group of Latino volunteers, you also have a pool of potential employees when a position does become vacant; you have basically grown your own! You already have a good sense of the Latino volunteer's work ethic, sense of responsibility, attitude, capabilities, and community reputation.

Even with a pool of Latino volunteers, you are still faced with the fact that your current permanent staff is 100% non-Latino. How do you handle the challenge of preparing them to serve your underserved Latino community?

WHITE TO LATINO: REALITIES OF NON-MINORITY STAFFING

When we do our workshops on library services to Latino populations, one of the advantages is the immediate interaction we get from our participants. It is during those interactions that we are confronted with the real-life challenges that face them. For example, at a workshop in Kansas, a white librarian from a very small farming community in Kansas explained why she was attending our workshop. Her community had experienced an influx of Latino immigrants who were working in the local meat-processing plants. The Latino immigrants brought their families, and the community's population increased by 25% as a result of that influx.

Her challenge began when the Latino immigrant children started coming into the library with their mothers, and no one on her staff felt they were offering adequate services—not to mention that they didn't speak Spanish. Providing that scenario, the librarian said that her all-white staff was very small and that they had been with her for years and would probably retire from the library.

This is the reality that many of you may be facing. So what can you do? You can't lay off or fire a long-time employee because that employee doesn't have the characteristics (such as Spanish-speaking ability) you so desperately need. Well, you do the next best thing, which is to work with your staff to help them understand the importance of serving Latinos in your community. This alone is not an easy task, and it is especially difficult if you are dealing with institutional racism.

Some of you will understand the realities of institutional racism. Institutional racism is racism that is embedded in the institution—school, library, organization, or community. Institutional racism occurs when the values, customs, behaviors, and attitudes of one group are so fixed that the institution becomes intolerant of any group different from itself.

Do not be surprised if this occurs in your library; you need to be prepared to deal with it. Because library staff are so instrumental in the success of libraries, you have to work with your staff so that they understand the purpose and rationale for needing to serve the Latino community.

STAFF DEVELOPMENT AND TRAINING

Staff development becomes an important part of what you do. Here are some tips for getting your staff prepared:

1. Use the same rationale for your staff that you prepare for your external groups (see Chapter 3). In fact, you have to convince your staff before you can convince others in the community.
2. Involve your staff in all aspects of developing these services. This process will make your life easier because you have the necessary staff buy-in to be successful.
3. If the opportunities are available, have your staff sign up for conversational Spanish at your local community college or college/university. Provide release time for them to attend classes; reimburse tuition fees. If funds are an issue, write a proposal for funding (see Chapter 6) that includes such items as tuition reimbursement and staff training to talk and work with Latino users.
4. If there are no colleges nearby that offer Spanish courses, bring someone in to teach your staff relevant Spanish words and phrases necessary in a library environment. Again, include this staff training component in your proposal to acquire funds to begin serving Latinos in your community.
5. If some staff members have developed some fluency in Spanish, offer a pay differential for that expertise.
6. If tips 3–5 are impossible, adapt a phonetic Spanish manual of library phrases. Appendix B at the end of Chapter 5 provides some library-related, Spanish-language words and phrases.
7. Strongly urge your state library or regional library systems office (if you have regional systems in your state) to provide appropriate staff training to help your library serve your Latino community. Chicago Public Library developed the following workshops that enabled library staff to serve their Latino communities better:[5]

   - developing library services for Latino children
   - developing a reference collection in Spanish
   - using bilingual concepts in storytelling
   - training staff on cultural awareness and sensitivity
   - developing a core collection of Spanish adult fiction
   - training staff on various Latino cultures

8. Most of the time, the American Library Association's (ALA) Annual Conference and other specialized conferences (for example, REFORMA) will have various programs dealing with library services to Latinos and/or minorities, ranging from the aforementioned types of topics to recruitment and retention of minority personnel. If you or your staff do not normally attend these conferences, it would be a good investment to send someone who can attend all the relevant programs and then return and share the information. Better yet, the person can

provide some internal staff training based on the conference programs. *American Libraries*, the ALA professional journal, also provides a synopsis of the various conference programs by subject category in the issue published just before the ALA Annual Conference.

9. Use Latino personnel from other organizations and city/county agencies to assist you in staff development, especially with cultural sensitivity and ethnic awareness matters.

10. Enlist volunteers from the Latino community to help you with staff development. Organize a panel of local Latino citizens to discuss their Latino culture (music, food, celebrations, and dance, for example) with your staff. Latinos, like all minority groups, are willing to share their culture in efforts to help the predominant group understand and accept them more.

Preparing staff to serve your Latino community is a must, whether you have bilingual staff or not. The tips we have provided should help you get started in relevant staff development.

RECRUITING LATINO TRUSTEES

The matter of Latino trustees is best covered in this chapter on library personnel. Having Latino representation on your board of trustees can be one of the best ways for your library to have the leverage to encourage, develop, and implement the necessary services for Latinos in your community. Additionally, one of the best ways for any public library to know and serve its minority community is to ensure minority representation on its decision-making body. Latinos should be encouraged to apply or should be recommended to the authority that appoints library trustees.

INFORMAL RECRUITING

Canvass your churches, social organizations, and government/social services agencies for recommendations. In every Latino community there are formal and informal leaders. Some of your formal leaders may be minority business owners, directors of agencies and organizations, educators, or government employees.

Informal leaders can also be effective trustees. These may be parents, church activists, or members of the Parent Teacher Organization, all of whom have demonstrated leadership capabilities in their everyday lives and have genuine interest in the well-being of their Latino community and the whole community in general. Look, too, for adult Latino library users who have attended and actively participated in library programs you have offered.

In addition, your library staff may have recommendations for Latino representation. Those recommendations could include any of the categories of people just mentioned.

FORMAL RECRUITING

Use your local newspaper, radio station, and/or promotional flyers to announce board openings. However, you need to be specific in encouraging members of the Latino community to apply for board positions. Distribute the flyers to popular spots in the Latino community—minority businesses, church bulletin boards, local grocery stores, gas stations, and daycare centers, for example. Human nature is such that people who read the advertisements will think of formal and informal leaders who would be excellent candidates. They, in turn, will contact those leaders and encourage them to submit their names as nominees.

If a library sincerely wants Latino board representation and follows some of the tips mentioned, there will be a response from the Latino community. There is a word of caution, however. You want to make sure that the names that go forward are indeed the names of Latino individuals who would take the position of trustee seriously and would do a good job for the library and the Latino community.

This process of identifying Latino nominees is no different from the process you use in finding non-Latino nominees to fill board positions, except that you may have the limitation of not knowing very many Latino community members. Nonetheless, it is probably in your library's best interest to identify and submit several Latino candidates to the appointing authority whose responsibility it is to select the best candidate for the board.

LATINO TRUSTEE SUCCESS

Getting a Latino on your library's board of trustees is only half the challenge. It is in everyone's best interest for the library administration to nurture, respect, inform, and educate that Latino trustee. What you already have is a leader by virtue of reputation and/or position in the Latino community. You need to continue to develop the leadership skills of that Latino trustee.

Your Latino trustee is the lifeline to your Latino community. That trustee will be the liaison who will assist the library in such matters as:

- identifying potential Latino staffing prospects
- recommending effective programming to attract your underserved Latino community
- working on good pubic relations between the library and the Latino community

- developing library and Latino partnerships/networking with individuals and organizations

INTERNAL LATINO ADVISORY COMMITTEES

If you are eventually able to hire a number of Latino staff members, then we strongly recommend that you encourage them to establish an internal Latino advisory committee. This type of committee can enhance your total library organization and can help recruit new Latinos and retain the Latinos already employed. We are aware of at least two effective internal Latino advisory committees—Chicago Public Library's Hispanic Services Committee and Denver Public Library's (DPL) Hispanic Steering Committee.

The DPL Hispanic Steering Committee, which has the support of the DPL administration and DPL's Library Commission, has been involved in all aspects of library services to Denver's Latino community. The committee has developed an annual local Latino authors series and hosted a community reception for noted Latino authors, such as Rudolfo Anaya and Manuel Ramos.

The DPL Hispanic Steering Committee has presented programs at the Colorado Library Association annual conference and at the REFORMA National Conference. Members of the Hispanic Steering Committee also have developed and offered community workshops on Mexican genealogy and citizenship.

The DPL Hispanic Steering Committee has developed strong partnerships with external organizations. With the Colorado Chapter of REFORMA (National Association to Promote Library Services to the Spanish-speaking), the committee has participated in an adopt-a-school program, where members of both groups participate in bilingual read-alouds in a predominantly Latino elementary school. The committee has also developed partnerships with the Mexican consulate and the Denver Public School Bilingual Parent Advisory Committee.

In the area of recruitment, members of the Hispanic Steering Committee have been involved in identifying and recruiting other Latinos to the DPL organization. They are also involved in recruiting Latino nonusers to the library. They attend various Latino cultural events in Denver and promote DPL services and library card applications.

In Appendix B at the end of this chapter, we have included the mission, goals, and bylaws of the DPL Hispanic Steering Committee to give you an example of the structure of an internal Latino advisory committee. If your library has adequate Latino staffing, we recommend that you encourage the development of such a committee. With encouragement and proper guidance, this type of advisory group can assist your library in achieving and enhancing its goal of providing library services to Latinos in your community.

CONCLUSION

All library personnel—your non-Latino staff and whatever Latino staff, volunteers, and trustees you might have—are crucial to your library's success in attracting and serving your underserved Latino community. Again, they set the tone for your library. Consequently, something as simple as eye contact and a friendly smile can make your Latino users feel welcome. The challenge at the beginning of this chapter gives you a good indication of the effect staff attitudes and demeanor have on a potential library user, regardless of that user's color or ethnic background.

You need to recognize the importance of staff training and to develop partnerships with others to help provide that training. Remember to apply for external funding to help pay for the personnel costs associated with the design and implementation of programs and services for Latinos in your community and/or to do outreach into that community. Even if those funds are temporary, you can at least get started on this important feature of your overall library services.

NOTES

1. Juan Ortiz, interview by Camila Alire, Logan Heights Branch Library, San Diego, Calif., 6 June 1995.
2. Hispanic Services Committee, *Hispanic Services: A Practical Manual for the Public Librarian* (Chicago: Chicago Public Library, 1990), 51.
3. Ray E. Peterson, *Recruitment and Retention of Minority Personnel and Trustees in Public Libraries* (Denver, Colo.: Colorado Department of Education, Office of State Library and Adult Education, 1996), 17.
4. Peterson, *Recruitment and Retention*, 17.
5. Hispanic Services Committee, *Hispanic Services*, 73.

APPENDIX A ACCREDITED LIBRARY AND INFORMATION STUDIES PROGRAMS LOCATED IN GEOGRAPHICAL AREAS WITH LATINO POPULATIONS

California State University, San Jose

Emporia in the Rockies, Denver, Colorado (Emporia State University, Emporia, Kansas)

Florida State University, Tallahassee, Florida

Pratt Institute, Brooklyn, New York

Queens College, Queens, New York

Texas Woman's University, Denton, Texas

University of Arizona, Tucson, Arizona

University of California at Berkeley

University of California, Los Angeles

University of North Texas, Denton, Texas

University of Puerto Rico, Rio Piedras, Puerto Rico

University of South Florida, Tampa, Florida

University of Texas at Austin

APPENDIX B DENVER PUBLIC LIBRARY HISPANIC STEERING COMMITTEE

Mission Statement

To assist the Denver Public Library in its Mission "to inform, educate, inspire, and entertain," by exploring and implementing ways to bring about increased use of the Library and its branches by the Hispanic community,

> Explore outreach opportunities and techniques.

> Explore ways to better serve the Hispanic community.

> Explore ways to make the Library more "user friendly" to the Hispanic community.

Goal 1: To assist the staff in bringing about increased involvement of the Hispanic community in all programs and activities.

    A. Create Hispanic focus groups, posing up-dated questions.

    B. Increase the number of volunteers through recruitment of Hispanics of all ages.

    C. Meet with Hispanic community groups and leaders.

    D. Work with the schools in Hispanic communities.

    E. Establish ties with the Branch Library staff to learn from their successful cultural programs, implementing their strategies in customer service to the Hispanic community.

Goal 2: To assist the staff in understanding, realizing, and capitalizing on the potential of the rich diversity of the Hispanic community.

    A. Explore staff development in the areas of cultural awareness, diversity of the Hispanic community, Hispanic community activities, organizations, and the Spanish language.

    B. Explore ways to make knowledge of a second language an asset.

By-Laws of the Denver Public Library Hispanic Steering Committee

Article I

The official name of this organization shall be "Hispanic Steering Committee" and shall be abbreviated as HSC throughout these by-laws.

Article II—Business and Purpose

1. To enhance library service to the Hispanic community.
2. To serve as a link of communication between the Hispanic community, the Hispanic staff, and local Hispanic organizations with DPL.
3. To represent Hispanic staff members of DPL and promote advocacy on Hispanic issues.
4. To promote Hispanic staff development through training, recruiting, and promotion.

Article III—Membership

1. HSC will have five officers.
2. Terms for all officers shall be two years. To ensure leadership continuity, the Chairperson and Secretary will be elected for terms beginning in even-numbered years; the other three officers will serve two years, beginning in odd-numbered years. Elections shall be held in October and terms will begin and end the first of January. No officer shall serve two consecutive terms.
3. Membership is open to ALL staff members—attendance of at least 3/4 of the meetings held per year must be met in order to maintain voting privileges.

Article IV—Officers

1. Officers of the HSC shall be: Chairperson, Vice-chairperson, Events Coordinator, Historian, and Secretary.
2. Nominees must be present in order to be eligible for office.
3. All officers shall be elected in October by the members of the HSC. All officers' terms shall be two years.
4. Voting procedures shall be as follows:
   A. Option to closed ballot.
   B. Option to vote by show of hands.
5. Duties of officers:
   A. Chairperson—Calls and presides over meetings and appoints committees.

B. Vice-Chairperson—Presides when Chairperson is absent or when Chairperson gives up the Chair to the Vice-Chairperson.

C. Events Coordinator—Calls and presides over meetings of the Events Committee, plans and coordinates special events.

D. Secretary—Takes roll call and reads minutes. Prepares, signs, and distributes minutes to members prior to meetings.

E. Historian—Handles all correspondence and maintains archive of documents re: HSC activities.

Article V—Meetings

1. Meetings shall be held once a month, first Wednesday of each month.

2. The Chairperson shall call special meetings as needed.

3. Quorum—In order to have a meeting, there must be half of the total officers (three or more) attending.

4. Meetings are open to ALL staff members. Any person wishing to make a statement on any issue of concern must be recognized by the Chairperson in advance of meeting.

Article VI—Order of Business

1. Call to order
2. Roll call
3. Minutes of previous meeting
4. Chairperson's report
5. Old Business
6. New Business
7. Committee reports
8. Notification of next meeting
9. Adjournment

Article VII—Change in By-Laws

These by-laws may be changed at any regular meeting, or special meeting of the membership called for that purpose, by a majority vote of HSC, provided that notice of such proposed change is given at the preceding regular or special meeting, and a copy is made available to every HSC officer.

3 PARTNERSHIPS

CHALLENGE

Nancy: *Now that we have a plan that outlines the services we want to offer to attract Latinos, I'm concerned that we'll be short of resources, particularly staffing and program expertise, to provide those services.*

Jackie: *I know where you're coming from. But we need to think positively and make use of the resources available in the community. Remember when we worked with the police department to offer neighborhood watch programs in the library? We advertised the programs, supplied the room, and provided a display of books dealing with home and personal safety. The police department provided staff with the program expertise.*

     That's exactly how we should work to serve Latinos. To be successful, we need to reach out and develop partnerships with relevant groups, organizations, and individuals.

Partnerships, partnerships, partnerships. We use this term interchangeably with collaboration and networking. We cannot emphasize the partnership concept enough. Partnerships are all about a different kind of networking that libraries may or may not be used to. They are absolutely crucial to your success in offering programs and services to your Latino community. Most public libraries already have some external partnerships established to help in some library programs for the general public.

One of the strongest themes we found when we visited various libraries throughout the country was the strong partnerships the libraries had established with other groups in the community. They all had one goal in mind—meeting the needs of Latinos in their community.

In this chapter we discuss the importance of partnerships and offer tips on how to establish external partnerships with organizations in and outside the Latino community. We provide a list of the types of groups with which you can establish partnerships and we offer a multitude of real-life examples of successful library partnerships from across the nation.

PARTNERSHIPS=MUTUAL BENEFIT

A partnership implies a relationship between two or more partners in which cooperation in a venture or challenge is mutually beneficial. In the case depicted at the beginning of this chapter, the public library's challenge is to meet the information needs of its underserved Latino community. The library's partner is probably saddled with a similar challenge. Therefore, it behooves you and your partner(s) to collaborate to meet those needs.

Partnerships are formed because neither partner necessarily has all the resources to meet its challenges on its own. Those resources include any or all of the standard resources—human, time, facilities, and financial—with which we deal.

ESTABLISHING A PARTNERSHIP

First of all, we recognize that going out into the Latino community may be new to some of you. That is why we are very specific about what to do and how to do it. As you accept this challenge of forming new partnerships, keep reminding yourself that it will be mutually beneficial for the library and your partner. Following are some general suggestions for facing this challenge:

1. Plan this activity. Remember in Chapter 6 when we talked about planning for services and funding? You can add another aspect to that planning process—identify the library programs and services that require an external partner and list the partner possibilities.
2. Once you have the list of potential partners for appropriate Latino programs and services, get the name of the head of the organization and his/her proper title, mailing address, and telephone number.
3. Do your homework on each group/organization you plan to approach. Some of the organizations you approach may have clients besides Latinos; others may have only Latino clients.
4. Develop a letter to send to each group requesting their assistance. Figure 8–1 is a sample of such a letter. If you come from a small community, a phone call may suffice. However, you may need to approach organizations at the county level for assistance. If that is the case, the letter would be best. Follow up with a telephone call.
5. Develop a short survey form to accompany the letter. Figure 8–2 is an example of such a form. Feel free to modify it to fit your library/community needs. The results of the survey can be used to develop a community organization/agency database for pos-

---

Figure 8-1. Sample Letter to Local Organizations

February 1, 1998

Mr. Joe Baca
Director
Housing and Urban Development
123 Park Street
Somewhere, Colorado 80000

Dear Mr. Baca:

The Somewhere Public Library recognizes the need to assist all our residents with their information and recreational reading needs. We are in the process of extending our library services to our underserved Latino community. We realize that services are long past due, and we are aggressively trying to meet those needs.

I understand that HUD has a series of programs that you offer to the community on housing issues such as tenants rights, home safety, and effective weatherization. I also understand that you have been challenged with finding sites that are open in the evening to offer these programs. The public library could help you with this and offer some additional benefits to your programs. Would your agency be interested in cooperating with the public library in a partnership that would enhance assistance to our Latino community?

I am including a short form that should take no more than ten minutes for you to complete and return. Someone from my administration or I will personally contact you as a follow-up to the survey.

The Somewhere Public Library looks forward to talking with you about a possible partnership to benefit our Latino community.

Sincerely,

Mary Little
Director

Figure 8–2. Sample Community Organization/Agency Partnerships Form

1. Organization/agency name _____

   _____

2. Name of head/contact person _____

   _____

3. Address _____

4. Telephone _____

5. Fax _____

6. Description of organization:

   _____

   _____

   _____

   _____

   _____

7. Services and/or programs offered by your organization:

   _____

   _____

   _____

   _____

8. Would your organization be willing to work in a
   partnership with the public library to help meet the information needs of our
   Latino community? ___ Yes ___ No

   Comments:

   _____

   _____

   _____

sible partnerships with the library; to establish a bilingual directory of organizations and agencies for the Latino community's use; to send mailings announcing library events and programs; and to ask an organization to distribute items such as library program flyers. The form can also easily be adapted and sent to individuals with whom the library might want to establish a partnership.

Update the database information at least annually. This would be a good project for a staff member or volunteer who has certain database software knowledge and skills.

6. You can also develop partnerships with organizations that would not necessarily be involved in providing programs but would be supporting programs. We are talking particularly about local businesses such as grocery stores, restaurants, and bakeries, as well as the media (newspapers, and radio and television stations). We suggest that you keep a print form or database of these resources. Figures 8–3a and 8-3b are samples of a form for supporting partners.

DEVELOPING MUTUAL PROGRAMS/SERVICES

Once you have a database of partners and are ready to proceed further in collaborating on some programs and/or services, some general guidelines may be useful. To further illustrate our point, we will elaborate on the hypothetical scenario provided in Chapter 6 where your library wrote a proposal to fund the HomeworkHELP Center. In this chapter, assume that you received the necessary funding to establish this center and its services. The local school district has agreed to be one of the partners in this venture. Here are some general guidelines for you to consider and/or adapt:

1. Sit down with your partner and set your mutual goals/objectives/activities for the program (these are probably already listed in the proposal you submitted). In general, the library wants the program to be helpful and successful in the Latino community; the school district wants more at-risk Latino students to graduate.

More specifically, the library may set numerical goals that are easily evaluated. For example: *In the first year of operation, the library will sign up and tutor 25 Latino junior and senior high students.*

The school district's goal could be: *The school district will recruit and supply two tutors in all the major subject disciplines that are offered in the junior and senior high school curricula.* (Remember, hypothetically, your grant included the funds to hire these tutors.)

Figure 8-3a. Sample Local Business Resource for Library Events Form

Business _____

Address _____

Phone Number _____ Fax Number _____

Contact Person _____

DATES	LIBRARY EVENT	RESOURCES PROVIDED	RESTRICTIONS	THANK YOU SENT

Figure 8-3b. Sample Local Business Resource for Library Events Form—Completed

Business   _Martinez Grocery_

Address   _123 Main Street, Somewhere, CO_

Phone Number   _462-3511_   Fax Number   _462-3512_

Contact Person   _Rudy Martinez_

DATES	LIBRARY EVENT	RESOURCES PROVIDED	RESTRICTIONS	THANK YOU SENT
2-15-98	Latino Community Library Open House	Donuts and punch	No delivery/ must pick up	2-25-98
5-5-98	Cinco de Mayo Celebration & Program	Paper plates, tableware, etc.	No delivery	5-10-98

2. Once the goals/objectives/activities are agreed on, you and your partner need to agree on who is responsible for what activities and the timeline for those activities.

3. Don't forget the costs. Both the library and its partner need to agree on the related costs. Again, these are probably delineated in the proposal. Nonetheless, it is important that the responsibility of expenses and costs be mutually agreed on.

4. To protect both partners, agree to everything in writing. A contract is not necessary; a letter specifying all the above would suffice to avoid any misunderstandings.

5. Some of the partnerships you will establish will be with organizations/agencies that are operated by Latinos solely for Latinos. How you approach and work with them can make or break your efforts. Following are some tips for the novice to consider:

   - If you are not that familiar with Latino culture and customs, get the advice of someone who is. Identify a Latino you respect in the community; you can probably think of one right this minute. Contact that person to help you for advice on the best ways to approach certain Latino organizations or individuals.
   - Be sincere about the library's commitment to reach out to the Latino community; if you are not sincere, that community will see right through you.
   - Be assertive, but not pushy. If you don't get a response via the survey form, call the organization and talk to the director or head. The letter is more a letter of introduction; don't be deterred if you don't get an immediate response.
   - As a follow-up, visit the local organization, agency, or group. Taking the time to do this demonstrates a real interest and commitment on the library's part. It also enables you to put a face with the name and to communicate with these contacts at other events; it personalizes your efforts.

These general guidelines will get you started in your efforts to form community partnerships in efforts to serve Latinos.

IDENTIFYING POSSIBLE PARTNERS

No matter the size of your community, you will be surprised by the number of organizations and individuals with whom you can collaborate. We list below some organizations/individuals for you to consider.

PUBLIC EDUCATION

Public education includes the gamut of K–12 and higher education institutions. It also includes the various organizations within those institutions, such as clubs—honor societies, Spanish clubs, business clubs, specific Latino student clubs, and other service clubs that work on community projects. In addition, there are Parent Teacher Organizations, university faculty spouses clubs, and college fraternities and sororities. The public library serving its Latino community should be considered as a potential partner in the projects of any of these organizations.

If your school district supports a bilingual education program, then establishing partnerships with the bilingual education director and teachers is crucial. These individuals can be instrumental in providing Spanish-language assistance. You can hire them, if library funds are available, as translators for programming and for promotional materials. If there are no funds, you can ask them to volunteer. In exchange, the library could provide special story hours for children in the bilingual education classes.

Do not forget about the school administrators or their boards at each level of the public education sector. These are also important groups that could lend support to education/public library partnerships.

SOCIAL SERVICES AGENCIES

Various government agencies (such as the Social Security office, job services office, health/medical clinics, legal aid, welfare office, migrant services, or immigration services) already provide services to the Latino community. These are agencies where you can find your formal and informal Latino leaders or information about those leaders.

These agencies can provide expertise that would be very relevant for programs in the library. They can also be vehicles for promoting library programs and services to the Latino community via newsletters and bulletin boards.

OTHER SERVICE ORGANIZATIONS

Other service organizations could include ESL (English as a Second Language) and literacy programs. Both of these services are very popular with Latino immigrants, and if they are not offered by the library, then collaboration with these groups is essential. The library has many support services (materials and programs) that can be of benefit to Latino clients.

CHURCHES AND RELIGIOUS ORGANIZATIONS

Find out which churches have a considerable number of Latinos as parishioners. Introduce yourself to the clergy of the church; establish a professional relationship between the church and the library. The same goes for religious organizations or clubs. With these clubs, you will be working directly with their membership.

Once a relationship is established, churches are great for advertising library programs to the Latino community. Library programs can be listed in the church's newsletter and on church bulletin boards. If the church has a bazaar, the library can request to set up a bazaar booth staffed by Latino library staff or volunteers to talk about library programs and encourage library card applications.

FINE ARTS ORGANIZATIONS, MUSEUMS, GALLERIES

The partnerships with these organizations are limitless. Collaboration with any of these groups could include joint art and museum exhibits, multicultural programs and festivals, or fine arts programs for Latino children and adults.

POLICE AND FIRE DEPARTMENTS AND SOCIETIES

Again, with these organizations there are many possibilities of joint projects serving all age groups of Latinos. Because these organizations often share a funding pie with the public library, their respective boards/ commissions welcome collaborative efforts to serve the Latino community.

PROFESSIONAL ASSOCIATIONS

Associations like the local bar association and the medical association can be instrumental in providing library programs on topics that are relevant to the Latino community. Other professional groups might include certified public accountants, realtors, bankers, engineers, dentists, veterinarians, and nurses. Additionally, in larger communities or in surrounding areas (more than one community), there may be professional associations whose members are primarily from the Latino community. Don't be afraid to approach any of these groups. They usually have similar goals, such as trying to meet the needs of the minority communities, and are very willing to share their expertise with the library.

COMMUNITY SERVICE CLUBS

Clubs such as Kiwanis, Lions, Soroptimist, Jaycees, and Sertoma also are involved in service projects to the community. They provide excellent resources, especially human resources, for collaborative programs.

THE FRIENDS OF THE LIBRARY

If you have a Friends of the Library group in operation, it can be a great partner! We encourage you to approach your Friends group with creative ideas that the library would normally not be able to accomplish and/or fund alone.

LOCAL BUSINESSES

Fast-food chains (such as McDonald's, Kentucky Fried Chicken, Burger King), as well as grocery stores and other local businesses in small communities are usually willing to collaborate with the public library on their efforts to reach the Latino community. Because the Latino population in most communities continues to increase in size, these collaborative efforts provide great marketing and advertising for the local businesses. They may not be willing to give the library funds, but they are usually more than willing to provide free supplies and food for library programs and events.

DAYCARE CENTERS

Daycare centers are great partners with which to collaborate on developing programs for preschool children. They are a human resource for bilingual story hours and are also another link to Latino parents. They can assist in marketing all your programs to Latino parents, by distributing flyers, hanging posters, and including library program announcements in their newsletters to parents.

SPORTS TEAMS/INDIVIDUAL ATHLETES

With Latinos becoming major players in such sports as baseball, soccer, and boxing, these groups might be great partners in library programming efforts. Also, sports training programs/schools (such as martial arts, gymnastics, and tennis) should be approached as potential partners.

SUCCESSFUL PARTNERSHIPS IN ACTION

Now on to some success stories. We mentioned earlier that the libraries we visited had very strong partnerships with groups in their communities. We want to share some of those successes.

NEWARK PUBLIC LIBRARY

The Newark Public Library collaborated with the Newark school system and the board of education to focus on those schools with large concentrations of Latino students. One result of that collaboration was the homework hotline established by the library.

The library has also worked with the New Jersey Performing Arts Center, which is located in the same area as the central library. They have collaborated on Latino cultural programming. Most recently, the library and the Newark Museum hosted a Puerto Rican artist-in-residence. The artist developed an exhibit/program of his works and provided art workshops for the children. Finally, the library has also enlisted the Hispanic Bar Association to offer programs on various legal issues.

OXNARD (CALIFORNIA) PUBLIC LIBRARY

The Oxnard Public Library has established partnerships with the local health clinic, the Department of Housing and Urban Development (HUD), and the Legal Aid office. It always involves local restaurants and bakeries as partners in supplying the food or treats for library events, especially those events targeted to Latino children. The library collaborates with the local television and radio stations for free PSAs (public service announcements) on programs and events in Spanish.

SANTA ANA (CALIFORNIA) PUBLIC LIBRARY

The Santa Ana Public Library has developed very strong partnerships with educational institutions. For example, the library offers a series of Teacher Open Houses both at the public schools and at the library. Librarians do presentations for the teachers, which include a bibliography of children's books in the library. In addition, they have a strong partnership with the Parent Teacher Organization; the library provides a bibliography of parenting materials in the library. With the University of California, Irvine, the library participates in its "Kids and Science" programs. The library also has active partnerships with other city agencies. It supplies library materials for an agency's program themes, and it participates in the programs by talking about relevant library services.

The Santa Ana Library also formed a partnership with Kenny Rogers Roasting Chicken restaurants in its "Read to Succeed" program. The restaurant chain donated $250 to the program and distributed 15,000 program bookmarks at the restaurants. The children received a 50–cent coupon to the restaurants for each book they read.

Another interesting partnership was developed between the library and the Mexican consulate. The library has hosted Mexican traveling exhibits in the library which were sponsored by the consulate. Also, the library has invited civic organizations to assist with children's programs and these partnerships have steadily grown.

QUEENS PUBLIC LIBRARY

The New Americans Program staff at the Queens Public Library maintains that its partnerships and outreach go hand in hand; and, consequently, the staff members follow an aggressive program in developing partnerships. They make a point to visit the agency with which they want to collaborate and then follow up with telephone calls. They also distribute a questionnaire for the agency to complete that describes the agency and its services; this agency information is entered into a database. The library published a 200-plus-page directory, *Guide to Local Services Offered in Immigrant Languages of Queens,* which is arranged by ethnic group and indexed by agency name, type of service, and geographical (neighborhood) location. Queens Public Library also works closely with public schools and ESL (English as a Second Language) programs in other agencies.

EAST LOS ANGELES PUBLIC LIBRARY

Like many other public libraries in California, East Los Angeles Public Library works very closely with the public schools since most school library services have been virtually eliminated in California. Additionally, the library developed an innovative partnership with the nearby health clinic. The library does programming with the health clinic for local residents on various health issues. The library developed another strong partnership with the two colleges that serve the East Los Angeles area—East Los Angeles College (a two-year institution) and California State University-Los Angeles. These partnerships have developed because of the library's Chicano Resource Center which is heavily used by professors and students of both institutions.

NEW YORK PUBLIC LIBRARY (NYPL)

NYPL views partnerships as crucial to the success of its services. For example, it collaborates with an organization called Riverside Language Program which provides teachers for the library's ESL programs. For the library's "Familias Con Libros (Families with Books)" programs, the library collaborates with local daycare centers to provide the necessary daycare during the program. NYPL also has a partnership called CLASP (Community Library and Schools Project) in which public librarians initially visit the schools, the teachers, and administrators. Once a partnership is established, the library invites school classes to the library and also works with Latino parents to apply for library cards. NYPL is proud of its partnerships with various local Latino authors who are invited to do some library programs.

FULLERTON (CALIFORNIA) PUBLIC LIBRARY

One of the more innovative partnerships Fullerton Public Library developed involves St. Jude's Hospital. Besides assisting the library in collection development of health-related materials, the hospital shares its healthmobile schedule and route with the library's bookmobile. Consequently, when the healthmobile makes its rounds in the Latino community, the library's bookmobile is right behind providing library services to families who are waiting for healthmobile services. What a great idea to enhance services to the community! The Fullerton Public Library also collaborates with various agencies within Orange County to offer young adult programming. Again, like other California public libraries, the library works very closely with the schools; this library concentrates on regularly serving the first through sixth grades.

EL PASO (TEXAS) PUBLIC LIBRARY

The Literacy Center in the Clardy Fox Branch has formed strong partnerships with several agencies. The center works with a local community college which also holds ESL and literacy classes. In addition, the center collaborates with the El Paso Citizenship Task Force to offer citizenship classes one night a week at the library. The local Friends of the Library group, which is actually an empowered literacy group, works with the center and the library on joint projects.

SAN YSIDRO BRANCH LIBRARY, SAN DIEGO PUBLIC LIBRARY

San Ysidro, the last community stop before entering Tijuana, Mexico, has a library that works in a well-developed partnership with the County Law Library, the Latino Bar Association, the California Western Law School, and volunteer Latino lawyers from San Diego. This collaboration includes supporting the library's "People's Law School" program which offers pro bono programs in Spanish for Latino residents. Additionally, the library cooperates with one of the city's other agencies in the "MACworkers Summer Project" which provides jobs for Latino young adults. The library is one of the agencies that employs these youths, and consequently, they return to use the library after they complete the program.

TUCSON-PIMA PUBLIC LIBRARY

We want to highlight Tucson-Pima Public Library's success in establishing partnerships with other city/county government agencies. These government partnerships have fostered the development of teams whose members include a librarian and individuals from other city/county departments, such as parks and recreation, water, and social services. They work together to learn what each entity offers and how they can help each other. Library director Elizabeth Rodriquez-Miller was so instrumental in leading these government agency partnerships that she was promoted to assistant city manager!

LOGAN HEIGHTS BRANCH LIBRARY, SAN DIEGO

Because the Logan Heights library is small and minimally staffed, it relies heavily on its partnerships. Some of its partners include the Boys and Girls Clubs, legal services, the Parent Teacher Organization, and the police department. One strength of the partnerships involves the library and various community organizations using each other for mutual letters of support for various purposes (such as grant proposals, budgetary issues, or hearings). In addition, other mutual benefits include community organizations actively using the library to meet their information needs. For example, Youth Opportunity Unlimited, a community organization, brings its students to use the library; later on, the library uses these students to distribute promotional flyers. The library also meets with and solicits advice from community organization partners prior to conducting its community analysis.

BENSONVILLE (ILLINOIS) COMMUNITY PUBLIC LIBRARY

We were unable to visit the Bensonville Community Public Library but it is worth discussing because of its innovative development of partnerships. It is involved in a multiple partnership program, the "Bensonville Intergovernmental Group's Lifelong Learning Community," which includes city departments, such as parks and recreation, and the elementary, junior high, and high schools. Each partner has established its version of a lifelong learning center; the library's center focuses its efforts on combatting illiteracy in the Latino community.

The library also formed the Family Literacy Council which works together on literacy issues with such organizations as churches, schools, Head Start, social services agencies, and various community organizations. When the city established a Neighborhood Resource Center in the Latino community, the library collaborated with the center to establish a small Spanish and bilingual collection, to offer library programming at the center, and to do home visits using the center for referrals. The Bensonville Library also collaborated with the Illinois Department of Employment Security to establish a Job Search Club for Latino residents seeking employment.[1]

These are just a few examples of the many successful partnerships between public libraries and other organizations and agencies working together to serve their Latino residents. A library should be able to offer more services and/or programs if it collaborates with various partners in the community to share resources—human, financial, facilities, and programs—to reach out to its Latino community.

CONCLUSION

Remember that partnerships are mutually beneficial. It must be advantageous for both partners to become involved in a partnership. A public library is one organization, by virtue of its mission and service orientation, with which it is easy to collaborate. Because the Latino population in this country is rapidly increasing and because Latinos are becoming more aware of service agencies, it is essential that those agencies work together to meet the various needs of the Latino community. You do not have to do it alone. Plenty of other organizations in your community feel the same urgency to serve Latino residents. The tips, ideas, and examples we have provided will get you started on your way to developing productive and long-term partnerships.

NOTES

1. Jill Rodriquez and Maria Tejeda, "Serving Hispanics Through Family Literacy: One Family at a Time," *Illinois Libraries* 77 (Fall 1996): 331–335.

9 STARTING A COLLECTION FOR LATINOS

CHALLENGE

Manny: *I've reviewed the local Latino demographics and the results of the needs assessment that we recently conducted. I'm better informed about Latinos in our community and their information needs, but I'm not exactly sure where to go from here. I want to spend our collection development funds wisely, so I've looked in all the standard reviewing sources; but I don't see many reviews of Latino materials. How can I find out about good materials so that I can order them?*

Laurie: *Here's another problem. Our regular book vendor has a few more Spanish titles than in the past, so that's improving. But we have pressing needs* now. *It certainly looks like we need to take a different approach to collection development if we want to be successful in meeting the information needs of Latinos.*

What a luxury it would be if you had unlimited resources to purchase all the library materials that you want for all your patrons, and unlimited resources to catalog, process, and provide access to such a collection. The real world of limited resources requires you to spend your collection development funds wisely. Like all public libraries, yours has many needs to meet, and you try to obtain the very best library materials for your patrons within the constraints of your budget.

The challenge Manny and Laurie face illustrates a problem that has been plaguing libraries for many years. Unfortunately, there still are not many published reviews of Latino materials, and the situation is not likely to improve significantly in the near future. A few standard reviewing sources are beginning to devote more attention to Latino materials than in the past. The semiannual En Español Book Review column that appears in the January and July issues of *Library Journal* is a good example; another source to consult is *School Library Journal*, which publishes reviews of Spanish materials in the February, August, and November issues. Still, reviews are few and far between. Individuals in charge of identifying materials for Latino users will not be able to rely solely on these trusted reviewing sources.

Traditional book jobbers are making some progress, but they are not able to supply everything that your library needs. Like other players in the publishing industry, book jobbers see great profit potential in the large Latino market; and they are beginning to respond to the high demand for Latino materials. Because of this growing demand, jobbers will likely make steady progress toward providing access to materials in Spanish. The challenge you face is that Latinos in your community have pressing needs now. To meet these needs today, you need to adjust your collection development practices.

Clearly, a different approach to collection development, one that is more eclectic, is required. The main challenge is that this approach can be very time-consuming and often frustrating for those in your library responsible for collection development and acquisitions. We hope that the practical tips and advice offered in this chapter will make your collection development efforts a bit easier and more rewarding.

MANAGEMENT ISSUES

We need to cover several management issues pertaining to collection development:

- reviewing collection development policies and practices
- linking collection development to the results of the needs assessment
- establishing advisory groups
- dealing with the lack of Spanish skills among collection development staff
- encouraging the development of support systems

How you deal with these management issues will have a significant impact, either positive or negative, on your collection development efforts.

COLLECTION DEVELOPMENT POLICIES AND PRACTICES REVIEW

The first management issue is to review your official collection development policies. Some well-meaning policies unintentionally impede the development of collections for Latino users. If you have a formal collection development policy, you need to review it to identify practices and procedures that are potential barriers to your multicultural collection development efforts.

If it does not already do so, your policy should clearly indicate that your library collections are for the benefit of everyone in your service area and that some information needs in your community can only be met by purchasing library materials that are bilingual or in languages other than English. We provide two model statements in Figure 9–1. Including this idea in your collection development policy is a clear signal that you are serious about meeting the information needs of all your citizens. Additionally, a policy statement will give you much-needed backup in case a few angry members of your community complain about the noticeable increase in the number of Spanish-language materials in your library.

In addition to reviewing your formal collection development policy, you may want to review systematically your collection development practices and procedures. Luis Herrera and Albert J. Milo have identified a number of these practices and procedures that hinder the development of collections useful to Latinos.[1] For example, some libraries require that library materials be selected from reviews in standard reviewing media, such as *Library Journal* and *Booklist*, before they can be ordered. Since many of the items that meet the information needs of Latino populations are never reviewed, this requirement is a discriminatory barrier to Latino collection development efforts and should be removed from official policies.

There are other well-meaning practices in official collection development policies that unintentionally create barriers to developing effective and useful Latino collections. If your policy forbids purchasing items from small or specialty presses in the United States, publishers and distributors outside the country, neighborhood bookstores, or

---

Figure 9-1. Model Diversity Statements to Include in Collection Policies

1. General statement for all groups:

   Somewhere, USA, is a racially, ethnically, and linguistically diverse community. To meet the educational, informational, and recreational needs of all our residents, Somewhere Public Library purchases and provides access to library materials that are produced in the different languages spoken in this community.

2. Specific statement for Latinos:

   One of Somewhere Public Library's goals is to provide a library collection that serves all its residents. Most of the materials purchased by the library are in English. To meet the goals of those in our community who wish to learn or practice Spanish, and to meet the unique educational, informational, and recreational needs of the many Spanish-speaking Latino residents in our community, Somewhere Public Library purchases and provides access to Spanish-language and bilingual (Spanish-English) materials for children, young adults, and adults.

conferences and book fairs, you are effectively shutting your library out of significant sources of materials that meet the information needs of Latinos. If such prohibitions are mentioned in your library's collection development policies, they should be eliminated. As a manager, your role should be to remove barriers and to facilitate Latino collection development.

LINKING COLLECTION DEVELOPMENT TO LATINO INFORMATION NEEDS

A second management issue is making certain that your collection development efforts are linked very closely to the results of the Latino community demographic analysis and needs assessment. You will gain much-needed support and assistance from the Latino community by showing that your attempts to meet their identified needs are sincere. By all means, gain allies in the Latino community by publicly advertising that you are responsibly and enthusiastically attempting to develop a collection that will meet the needs as identified in the community analysis.

Since each Latino community's needs are unique and since each library is unique, it is not possible for us to tell you specifically what should be in your collection, nor can we provide any formula that can tell you what percentage of your collection development budget to devote to Latino material collection. You and your staff are ultimately responsible for developing a collection that meets the unique blend of needs identified in your Latino community assessment.

Latinos in one community may want you to concentrate mostly on improving the English reading skills of their young children. In another community, there may be an overwhelming concern about providing more recreational materials for young adults. Latinos in still another community may want you to purchase mostly newspapers and magazines from various Central and Latin American countries, rather than books. Perhaps Latinos in your community will want you to devote most of the available resources to purchase Spanish-language, self-help materials for adults. These are just a few of the many possibilities.

Your job would be a relatively easy one if there were only one overriding need expressed in the Latino community. However, your needs assessment will undoubtedly show that your service area has a heterogeneous Latino community with a variety of information needs. To meet these very diverse needs, you will probably be purchasing library materials for all age groups in many different formats. The material will probably be in both English and in Spanish, for all literacy skill levels, for a variety of educational and income levels, and possibly, for individuals from different Latino subcultures. This is quite a challenge for the small or medium-sized library!

Fortunately, your analysis of Latino demographics and your local needs assessment will help you determine where the greatest needs are—and will enable you to develop the library's collection for Latinos, based not on any preconceived ideas of what might be needed, but on the needs expressed by members of the Latino community during the needs assessment. For example, in 1985 the Queens Public Library conducted an extensive public opinion project, "Say Sí," where they found that their Latino residents were not using the libraries. Based on that analysis, they were able to focus on collection development. Now Queens Public Library has seven branches housing strong Spanish-language collections.

As an administrator, you will need to develop a plan that shows how your library will allocate collection development funds to meet these needs. This plan does not need to be lengthy to be good. It should be readily understood by managers, library employees, the board of trustees, the media, leaders in the Latino community, and the general public. It should include a list of needs identified by the community (see the Latino needs/wants statements described in Chapter 4). This list should be accompanied by library strategies to meet each of the identified needs with budget allocations assigned to each strategy. Figure 9–2 provides two examples of a needs/wants statement with a collection strategy and a budget allocation.

We realize that developing such a list is much easier said than done. What will be especially challenging is that your library does not have the resources to do everything that is needed. Consequently, the needs will have to be prioritized, and resources allocated accordingly. Since there will be many needs and not enough resources at any one time for the library to meet them, consider phasing in some of your resources over a period of time. Remember your collection development plan should keep you focused.

It is impossible to obtain everything that is needed all at once; nonetheless, it is essential that you make a good-faith effort to allocate resources where they are needed most. In the end, you will be thankful that your library devoted the necessary time and energy toward the Latino community needs assessment. Now you can channel your limited funds to the areas that are considered to be a high priority by the Latino community.

ESTABLISHING AND LISTENING TO A LATINO ADVISORY GROUP

If you are just starting to develop a collection for Latinos, then you may find it helpful to establish a voluntary Latino advisory community group that can, among other things, provide input and feedback on your collection development efforts. You can share your ideas on the allocation of resources with members of this advisory group to get feedback on and support for your library strategies and budgetary

---

Figure 9-2. Sample Needs/Wants, Collection Strategies, and Budget Allocations

1. Specific need/want example:

Need/Want Statement:	Latino young adults in our community want Spanish-language magazines.
Collection Strategy 1:	Library will purchase 10 Spanish-language magazines for Latino YA males.
Budget Allocation:	10 Spanish-language magazines at $40/each = $400.
Collection Strategy 2:	Library will purchase 10 Spanish-language magazines for Latino YA females.
Budget Allocation:	10 Spanish-language magazines at $40/each = $400.
Total Budget:	$800

2. General need/want example:

Need/Want Statement:	Latinos in our community want their elementary school children to read and have an appreciation for both English and Spanish.
Collection Strategy:	Library will purchase bilingual recreational books for elementary school children.
Budget Allocation:	100 books at $30/each = $3,000.
Collection Strategy:	Library will purchase bilingual language instructional audiotapes for children.
Budget Allocation:	50 audiotapes at $25/each = $1,250.
Total Budget:	$4,250

allocations. Consider establishing an advisory group of Latino young adults to give you ideas on library materials that will help attract this hard-to-reach clientele.

Members of advisory groups can provide direct assistance in any number of ways:

- They can peruse appropriate publisher or distributor catalogs and make recommendations to the selectors.
- When new books are processed, they can prepare bilingual hand-outs or bibliographies publicizing the new arrivals.
- They can review the newly acquired materials and write bilingual articles about them for your library newsletter.
- They can be involved in organizing Spanish book reading clubs based on the new arrivals.

Your local situation will inspire you to think of other possible uses for this advisory group. Remember that this advisory group can also serve as one of your *political action* groups when needed.

SELECTORS AND THEIR KNOWLEDGE OF SPANISH

Another important management issue to be concerned about is the probable lack of Spanish skills among your current selectors. In all likelihood they do not read or understand Spanish, which obviously makes selection difficult. As if this were not a serious challenge in itself, they also do not have the skills to distinguish between the many variations of Spanish. The Spanish that is spoken and written in one Spanish-speaking country may be somewhat different from the Spanish that is spoken and written in another Spanish-speaking country. Similarly, there are Spanish dialect differences within the very diverse Latino communities in this country.

Your selectors who are unfamiliar with Spanish will have difficulty choosing Spanish library materials that are the most appropriate for Latinos in your community. What does all this have to do with developing a collection for Latinos? Just as an English-speaking American might have a little difficulty with British English or with English from several hundred years ago, so too might an American Latino have some difficulty reading books in Spanish from different Central or South American countries. If the language is too difficult, the material will not be used or enjoyed. Generally speaking, the selector should try to select materials that are closest to the vernacular used by Latinos in the community, but this is not an absolute rule.

Bilingual materials also present a problem to English-monolingual selectors. Because of high demand for bilingual materials, publishers and distributors are scrambling to meet this need. While this response has resulted in improved availability of bilingual materials, there are also a number of inferior books currently on the market. Unfortunately, English-monolingual selectors will not be able to judge the quality of these books. This is not an easy problem to solve.

As we have mentioned before, the best solution is to have bilingual and bicultural library staff who can make these quality judgments. The next best solution is to provide opportunities and incentives for your selectors to learn Spanish. Also, you can encourage your selectors to interact with and get advice from bilingual individuals in the community. Remember to enlist bilingual volunteers to assist in this process.

Even if all the above steps are taken, every now and then a few unwanted books will still make their way into the library collection. When this happens, acknowledge it, accept it, use it as a learning experience, and then move on.

ENGLISH LANGUAGE MATERIALS

Even though we spend much time discussing Spanish-language materials and because these materials are more problematic for libraries, you cannot assume that all Latinos want or need Spanish or bilingual resources. A significant number of English-speaking Latinos have very limited Spanish speaking and reading skills. Consequently their preference will be for English-language materials on a wide variety of subjects.

Your collection probably already addresses many of the needs of Latinos whose first language is English. Make sure that your collection includes English-language materials about the history of Latinos in the United States with particular emphasis on the history of the particular subcultures represented in your service area. It should also include a collection of literary works by U.S. Latino authors writing in English, as well as a collection of English translations of major literary works from the Spanish-speaking world. The chapter on resources (Chapter 11) provides some assistance in this area.

SUPPORT SYSTEM FOR SELECTORS

One final management concern that we would like to address is the development of a support system for your collection development staff. Most likely, starting a Latino collection from scratch will necessitate change, some of which could be drastic. Some of your staff will respond quite well; others may have a more difficult time. You need to provide a supportive atmosphere to ensure that your staff can develop skills and confidence in these new endeavors. Useful strategies include the following:

- Establish in-house quality circles or teams to discuss Latino collection development issues and resolve any problems that arise.

- Support attendance at national, regional, and state conferences and workshops where Latino collection development issues are discussed.
- Provide opportunities for staff to meet and interact, formally and informally, with others in the immediate area who are dealing with similar issues or who have special skills.
- Cooperate with other libraries and library associations to bring outside speakers and experts to local workshops and conferences.
- Provide funds, opportunities, and incentives for employees to learn Spanish.
- Encourage collection development staff to interact with the Latino community and solicit ideas on improving the library's collections.

Your library's overall success in collection development may very well depend on how you deal with the management issues discussed above. Being aware of these issues and dealing constructively with them will establish and nurture a positive framework for your collection development efforts.

ADVICE FOR SELECTORS

In this section, we provide tips for selectors who are responsible for developing your library's collection for Latinos. If developing Latino collections is a new area for you, you will be absolutely amazed at the variety of available materials. In current catalogs you can easily find translations of Stephen King novels, romance books, self-help books for adults, reference books of all types and for all ages, bibles and other religious materials, translations of Isaac Asimov, detective novels, ESL (English as a Second Language) materials, Spanish-language versions of Indiana Jones comic books, fotonovelas (adult comic books), translations of best sellers, and Spanish classics from the Americas and from Spain, to name just a few of the many interesting selections.

When we presented our workshops, we prepared and distributed various lists of recommended titles for Latinos in each of the various age groups. Fortunately, we no longer need to compile such lists because a growing number of American publishers and distributors are making it easier for small and medium-sized libraries to obtain such materials. Compared to even just a few years ago, the availability of and access to materials, especially books, for Latinos of all ages has greatly improved. Consequently, these publishers and distributors are able to supply many of the materials needed by many small and medium-sized libraries beginning to develop collections for Latinos. If the recent past is an indicator, then we will see more distributors and publishers entering the market; and an even greater variety of materials to purchase is likely to be the result.

DISTRIBUTORS

Appendix A at the end of this chapter lists the major United States-based distributors that have significant interest and experience in Latino book distributing. Since these distributors realize they are dealing primarily with English-speaking selectors, the catalogs are written in English. Probably no single distributor will be able to meet your diverse needs. We suggest that you contact each one of the distributors. Each will gladly send you a catalog and put you on its mailing list. By reviewing the offerings of a number of competitors, you will be able to do comparison shopping. Another benefit of reviewing catalogs and other mailings from a variety of distributors is that you will get a broad view of the available materials.

When you start to receive and review these catalogs, you will find that each company is unique. Some are very general in scope, offering materials for all age groups, in all formats, including English, Spanish, and bilingual titles. Some distributors are much more specialized. Some have strengths in certain areas (such as children's literature) or formats (for example, reference books in Spanish). Some distributors offer special services to attract business from libraries. For example, some offer volume discounts to libraries, and some even have approval plans. Some distributors can even provide MARC records for you to enter into your catalog for a small additional fee.

This segment of the book industry has been and will continue to be dynamic. Innovative companies will flourish; others will go by the wayside. Some companies will respond better or more quickly than others to market demands. New, specialized distributors could emerge to capture untapped markets. What is true about a particular distributor today may not be true in the near future.

Because there is a variety of distributors, and because changes in this industry can happen so quickly, it is impossible for us to recommend any particular distributor for specific types of material. Instead we provide a chart (see Figure 9–3) that you can use to track distributor offerings. When you receive catalogs and mailings from the various companies, we suggest that you review them and make notations on the tracking chart.

Here is a list of questions to ask yourself when reviewing a catalog from a distributor:

Figure 9-3. Latino Distributor Tracking Chart

Company	Provides books for which ages?			Provides nonprint materials? (Check all that apply)				Provides magazines?	Provides fotonovelas?	Catalog contains informative English annotations?	Catalog contains complete publication date information?	Company provides MARC records?
	Children	YA	Adult	Audio	Video	Kits	Software	Yes/No	Yes/No	Yes/No	Yes/No	Yes/No
1.												
2.												
3.												
4.												
5.												
6.												
7.												
8.												
9.												
10.												
11.												
12.												
13.												
14.												
15.												

- Does the distributor sell materials for all different age groups, or does it specialize?
- Does the distributor sell materials in different formats (such as recordings, videotapes, CD-ROM and other electronic formats, kits)?
- Does the distributor offer core collections?

A number of distributors offer core collections that can contain up to several hundred books, primarily for children and young adults, at a less expensive price than if each title in the collection were purchased separately.

Some distributors develop their Latino core collections based on officially adopted lists of titles that are endorsed by a public education agency. For example, the California Department of Education has an official recommended reading list of Spanish materials.[2] Other distributors have developed their own core collections based not on officially adopted lists but on such market factors as expected library demand, availability, price, quality of material, and reputation of publisher.

Purchasing a core collection is a relatively inexpensive way to develop immediately a beginning collection for Latino children and young adults. Depending on the size of your library, you may even consider purchasing multiple sets of these core collections.

- Does the distributor sell specialized materials, such as fotonovelas?

    Fotonovelas are pulp-magazine books in comic-book style published in Mexico that are very popular among some Latino young adult and adult immigrants. Many Latinos come to the library only for fotonovelas but they eventually use other library materials and services.
- Does the distributor sell magazine subscriptions?
- Does the distributor offer special services to libraries, such as approval plans or library discounts?
- Does the distributor offer MARC records?
- Does the distributor's catalog contain informative English-language annotations?
- Does the distributor have a local sales representative for your area?

Although we highly recommend the use of distributors because they are able to supply many of the needs of small and medium-sized libraries, we would be doing a disservice if we did not list some of the possible problems selectors will encounter when relying on distributor catalogs:

- Some distributors do not provide informative English-language annotations in their catalogs.
- Since distributors are in business to sell products, the catalogs do not provide objective reviews.
- A few distributors do not provide the date of publication information in their annotations.
- With some distributors, it is difficult to identify the age group for which an item is intended.

For these reasons, it is helpful, though not often possible, to view the materials in person. Some distributors have approval plans that give you the opportunity to review items and to return them if you decide they do not meet your needs. If your library is within reasonable driving distance of one or more of these distributors, the sales representatives are often willing to show you samples of their products right in your library. If possible, attend these sessions with members of your Latino advisory group; they can review the materials and make recommendations.

Another way to get firsthand exposure to a wide range of materials is to meet with the distributor representatives at conferences. Many of these distributors are exhibitors at American Library Association conferences and at other library association conferences around the country. These are great opportunities to make professional contacts and to review personally the materials they have on hand.

If you are fortunate to have the funds to travel to Mexico, consider attending the Guadalajara International Book Fair that usually takes place in November or December of each year. This conference attracts over 9,000 attendees from a variety of professions interested in Spanish-language materials. If your library cannot afford to send someone to Guadalajara, then perhaps you could arrange for recent attendees from a larger public library in your area to report on their experiences.

AUDIO AND VIDEO DISTRIBUTORS

Many of the Latino book distributors listed in Appendix A at the end of this chapter, also provide a variety of audio and video materials. Additionally, other companies specialize in providing an assortment of audio and video materials for Latinos. There are instructional, educational, and recreational resources on a variety of topics. Each of these companies is unique. One may have a strength in providing materials to a particular age group. Another may have strong collections in recreational video recordings, but little in educational material. We recommend that you obtain a current catalog from each of these specialized distributors. Appendix B lists the distributors of specialized Latino materials. Also, you can use the matrix chart in Figure 9–4 to keep track of the strengths of a particular company.

Figure 9-4. Audio/Video Distributors Matrix

Directions:

Distributors offer audio and video materials for a wide variety of Latino language and age groups. When reviewing a distributor's catalog, note the type of material offered for the various Latino groups, and enter the company name in the appropriate cell on the chart.

When completed, you will have a handy reference chart of companies that provide materials for specific Latino language/age groups.

	Types of Materials			
	Audio		Video	
Latino Group	**Recreational**	**Educational**	**Recreational**	**Educational**
Spanish-speaking Children				
English-speaking Children				
Spanish-speaking Young Adults				
English-speaking Young Adults				
Spanish-speaking Adults				
English-speaking Adults				

PUBLISHERS

In this chapter, we have emphasized distributors because they can provide a wide range of materials from domestic and international sources. In addition to distributors, a number of United States–based publishers are interested in Latino materials, and they are also eager to sell you their products. You can find a directory of these publishers in Appendix C. We recommend that you obtain catalogs from each of these publishers. By examining recent catalogs and mailings, you can develop an appreciation for the wide variety of publishers in this market. Some primarily publish Spanish materials; others concentrate on publishing English works by or about Latinos. Most are in the private sector, but a few are affiliated with universities, and a few are nonprofit. Some offer more academic titles, while others are more interested in the mass market. Each has something valuable for your Latino materials collection.

SELECTION/EVALUATION CRITERIA

Every book on developing library collections mentions selection or evaluation criteria, and this book continues the tradition. Most likely, your collection development policy addresses this topic. Typical criteria for the selection and evaluation of materials are value, need, format, price, and availability. These are useful criteria, but they do not specifically address Latino materials. In this next section we provide some useful criteria for selecting or evaluating Latino materials for children and young adults.

EVALUATION OF LATINO CHILDREN'S MATERIALS

Though written in 1981, Robert Haro's discussion of criteria for evaluating books for Latino children is still valid and useful today.[3] When evaluating an item for this age group, Haro suggests that selectors consider the following questions:

- Is it relevant and enjoyable to young Latino readers?
- Is it well written and well illustrated?
- Are there positive characters with whom children can identify?
- After reading the book will the child feel a sense of pride?
- Is the item authentic and realistic from a Latino perspective?
- What are the credentials of the writer?
- Is there racial bias?
- Is there sexual bias?
- Is the language understandable?

- If a book is bilingual, is the text in both languages of equal quality?

EVALUATION OF LATINO YOUNG ADULT MATERIALS

Here are some questions suggested by Adela Artola Allen that can be used to evaluate materials for Latino young adults:[4]

- Is the book relevant to the Latino experience?
- Is the book authentic from the Latino perspective?
- Is the perspective from the point of view of the Latino character or from the Anglo observer?
- Are the people, relationships, and culture stereotyped in a racist manner?
- Do the language and dialogue imply a put-down of Spanish?
- Are historical data accurate and in political perspective?

APPLICATION OF EVALUATION CRITERIA

We include two sets of questions above because they are useful supplements to criteria typically found in collection development policies. However, in your day-to-day practice of collection development, it is impossible to inspect personally each and every title before selecting it. Few of us have the time or energy to ask all these questions of each and every book we are considering for purchase. Because of the time constraints, the evaluation criteria would actually be more helpful after you have developed your beginning, core collection. Some books will not circulate as often as others. The evaluation criteria can help you determine if these low-use books are appropriate for your library's collection. If not, they can be replaced by others that might be more popular.

THE CENTER FOR THE STUDY OF BOOKS IN SPANISH FOR CHILDREN AND ADOLESCENTS

One valuable resource that provides some general guidance to selectors is the Center for the Study of Books in Spanish for Children and Adolescents (Centro para el Estudio de Libros Infantiles y Juveniles en Español), based at the California State University, San Marcos. Dr. Isabel Schon, director of the center, is a leading authority on the subject of Spanish books for young readers. Since 1991 the center has sponsored annual conferences on Spanish books for children and young adults. Another reason to contact the center is that for a small fee it provides recent bibliographies of recommended children's and young adult materials. Further information on the center can be found in Chapter 11.

Sometimes it is the first step in a journey that is the most difficult. We hope that these collection development tips will help you get started.

LATINO COLLECTION ACCESS

Now that you have some ideas on how to get started, you need to plan to provide physical and intellectual access to all the wonderful materials you will purchase. A number of challenges will need your attention.

SITE SELECTION

First, you will need to select a site in your library for the new materials. To focus attention on the new collection, you may want to designate a site in your library very close to the entrance. Wherever the location, it must be at least as attractive as other areas of the library. Be sure to include proper bilingual signage to direct users to the collection. If you want to name this area, you could call it the "Spanish-Language Collection" or "Latino Collection" (not "Foreign Language"). You might consult your advisory group to ask if they have other suggestions.

MATERIALS PROCESSING

One problem you will encounter is that some of the materials you purchase may not be shelf-ready when they arrive in technical services. Some of the bindings will not be of the quality that is typically found in the United States. Similarly, the paper quality may not be as good. Be prepared to spend more on processing time and supplies than you would with traditional materials. When you start receiving materials, it will be easier to judge how much of a challenge this will be. You will then be better able to budget for this extra activity.

MATERIALS CATALOGING

Think what it must feel like for a monolingual, Spanish speaker to walk up to a typical online catalog. There are nothing but English-language commands or menu options with an impatient cursor flashing on the screen. What may seem to you like an ordinary, everyday matter—performing a subject search in an online catalog—can be a frustrating experience for others with limited English skills.

In an ideal world, every library would first have an automated library system with a multilingual interface that would be easy for all patrons to use. Second, the bibliographic database that your library uses to obtain cataloging records would have an accurate and complete MARC record for each item you purchase, no matter the original language of the item. Third, the bibliographic records for all Spanish-language items in your library would contain both Spanish and English subject headings.

Among the libraries that have developed catalogs that are user-friendly to Latinos are San Antonio Public Library and the Queens Borough Public Library. CARL Corporation, Inc. and San Antonio Public Library have jointly developed a Spanish-language interface to its children's catalog. "Catalita" has been operational since May 1997. Queens Borough Public Library allows users to search the library's catalog in Spanish (and other languages) and to access its community services database. These are exciting developments! Since there is much to learn about how such systems work, it will be fascinating to see how these two projects develop in the future.

Like most libraries, yours will probably not have a Spanish-language catalog interface for quite some time. Since you will be relying on your English-only catalog for the foreseeable future, you need to make some adaptations, so that you can provide access to Spanish materials.

One of your major challenges will be to catalog the Spanish-language materials that you have purchased. Be prepared to spend more on this activity than you do with traditional materials. Recently there has been much concern expressed on the REFORMANET electronic discussion group about the lack of cataloging records for Spanish-language materials in very large bibliographic utilities like OCLC. If this is a concern for OCLC-member libraries, your library, like most other small and medium-sized public libraries, will probably find it challenging to find suitable bibliographic records for the Spanish-language materials you purchase.

You will find that no matter which database you use to obtain bibliographic records, there will be a significant number of Spanish-language items for which there are either no cataloging records available or for which the records will need modification. For many Spanish-language items, this means you will have to modify existing records, do your own original cataloging, find some alternative methods for obtaining the needed bibliographic records, or a combination of all three.

As we have mentioned before, the best solution is to have bilingual individuals on your staff; they are best able to review and understand Spanish-language materials, search for matching records in whatever source your cataloging department uses to obtain bibliographic records, make modifications to bibliographic records if necessary, and do any original cataloging that is required.

Realizing that such staffing may not be possible, you have some alternatives:

- Purchase MARC records from the specialized Latino distributors. The distributors realize that cataloging Spanish-language materials is difficult for the smaller libraries; a few distributors are able to sell MARC records for the items they sell, at a reasonable price.

- Contract with a nearby source (for example, an academic library, library consultant, or library cooperative) who has experience in cataloging Spanish-language materials.
- Review the cataloging records for the same or similar Spanish-language items in the databases of larger, metropolitan libraries that have larger Spanish collections.
- Hire a bilingual person or recruit a bilingual volunteer from the community (such as a local Spanish teacher) who can assist the cataloger.

One major decision you will have to make is whether or not to add Spanish subject headings to the bibliographic records of Spanish materials.[5] This is obviously an added expense, but in the long run it may be the best option. If, sometime in the near future, your library system vendor provides a Spanish-language version of the OPAC, Spanish-speaking patrons will be able to search the catalog in their native language. If you remain with an English-language OPAC, which will probably be the norm for quite some time, including Spanish-language subject headings in your bibliographic records for Spanish materials will provide better access. As an example, you can have your automated system generate author, title, and subject cards for the Spanish-language materials which can then be filed in a card-catalog placed near the collection itself. Your system could also generate a printed catalog in book format.

Another way to improve access is to produce attractive bibliographies written in Spanish, describing the Spanish-language materials in a wide variety of topics that are of current or lasting interest. These guides to the collection can be placed near the collection itself and also near the reference desk. An added benefit of these guides is that you can use them as public relations pieces when you go out into the Latino community. This is a project that can be taken on by the Latino advisory group. Another inexpensive way to improve access is to provide a Spanish-language overview of the Dewey Decimal System near the collection (see Chapter 5, Figure 5–1).

An online catalog with English-language commands or menus can be an impenetrable barrier to access, but it doesn't have to be. There are creative ways to make it work for Latinos. Every library is struggling with these access issues. State libraries, regional library systems, and state library associations can do their part by providing practical workshops on these challenging technical services issues.

CONCLUSION

In this chapter we have provided some guidance on how to start a Latino collection and how to provide access to it. It is clear that the traditional methods of collection development and technical services must be modified in order to meet the information needs of Latinos. Even if you follow our tips, you will still find it frustrating at times. There are many questions, and no one has all the answers. You are to be commended for taking on this challenge.

NOTES

1. Luis Herrera and Albert J. Milo, "Managing Administrative Change for Ethnic Collection Development," in *Developing Library Collections for California's Emerging Majority: A Manual of Resources for Ethnic Collection Development*, ed. Katherine T.A. Scarborough. (Berkeley, Calif.: Bay Area Library and Information System, 1990), 18.
2. California Department of Education, *Recommended Readings in Spanish Literature: Kindergarten Through Grade Eight* (Sacramento, Calif.: California Department of Education, 1991).
3. Robert Haro, *Developing Library and Information Services for Americans of Hispanic Origin* (Metuchen, N.J.: Scarecrow Press, 1981), 112–119.
4. Adela Artola Allen, "Library Services for Hispanic Young Adults," *Library Trends* 37 (Summer 1988): 80–105.
5. There are several cataloging projects under way that are attempting to deal with the challenge of providing Spanish-language subject headings. Oakland Public Library and San Francisco Public Library have developed a list of over 1,500 Spanish headings; WLN (Washington Library Network) has Spanish headings in its online authority file; and a private publisher, Floricanto Press (see Appendix C for contact information), is developing a comprehensive list of Spanish-language subject headings. An excellent way to track developments in this area is to subscribe to the free REFORMANET electronic discussion group (see Chapter 11 for details).

APPENDIX A
LATINO BOOK DISTRIBUTORS

Adler's Foreign Books
8220 Christina Ave
Skokie, IL 60076
(800) 235–3771
(708) 676–9944
fax (708) 676–9909

AIMS International Books, Inc.
7709 Hamilton Ave
Cincinnati, OH 45231
(800) 733–2067
(513) 521–5590
fax (513) 521–5592

El Almacen de Libros de Nana
848 Heber Ave
Calexico, CA 92231
(800) 737–6262
fax (619) 357–4271

Astran, Inc.
591 SW 8th St
Miami, FL 33130
(305) 858–4300 fax (305) 858–0405

Bilingual Educational Services
2514 S Grand Ave
Los Angeles, CA 90007
(800) 448–6032
(213) 749–6213
fax (213) 749–1820

Bilingual Publications Co.
270 Lafayette St, Suite 705
New York, NY 10012
(212) 431–3500
fax (212) 431–3567

Bilingual Review Press/Editorial Bilingue
Box 872702
Hispanic Research Center
Arizona State University
Tempe, AZ 85287–2702
(602) 965–3867
fax (602) 965–8309

Chullain Publishing Corp.
28625 Kennedy Gulch Rd
Conifer, CO 80433
(303) 838–4375
fax (303) 838–4791

Continental Book Co., Inc.
Western Division
625 E 70 Ave, Suite 5
Denver, CO 80229
(303) 289–1761
fax (800) 279–1764

Continental Book Co.
80–00 Cooper Ave, Bldg. #29
Glendale, NY 11385
(718) 326–0560
fax (718) 326–4276

D.D.L. Books, Inc.
6521 NW 87 Ave
Miami, FL 33178
(800) 635–4276
(305) 592–5929
fax (305) 477–5632

Donars Spanish Books
653 Cressa Dr
Loveland, CO 80537
(800) 552–3316

(970) 663–2124
fax (970) 667–5337

Downtown Book Center, Inc.
School and Library Division
247 SE First St
Miami, FL 33131
(800) 599–8712
(305) 377–9939
fax (305) 371–5926

Ediciones Universal
P.O. Box 450353
Miami, FL 33245–0353
(305) 642–3234
fax (305) 642–7978

European Book Co., Inc.
925 Larkin St
San Francisco, CA 94109
(415) 474–0626
fax (415) 474–0630

Fiesta Book Company
591 SW Eighth St
Miami, FL 33130
(305) 858–4843
fax (305) 858–9934

Fondo de Cultura Economica USA
2293 Verus St
San Diego, CA 92154
(800) 532–3872
(619) 429–0455
fax (619) 429–0827

Bernard H. Hamel Spanish Books
10977 Santa Monica Blvd
Los Angeles, CA 90025
(310) 475–0453
fax (310) 473–6132

Hispanic Books Distributors
1665 W Grant Rd
Tucson, AZ 85745
(520) 882–9484
fax (520) 882–7696

Ideal Foreign Books, Inc.
132–10 Hillside Ave

Richmond Hill, NY 11418
(718) 297–7477
fax (718) 297–7645

Imported Books
P.O. Box 4414
Dallas, TX 75280
(214) 941–6497

Latin American Book Store, Ltd.
204 N Geneva St
Ithaca, NY 14850
(607) 273–2418
fax (607) 273–6003

Latin Trading Corp
539 W H St., Suite B
Chula Vista, CA 91910
(619) 427–7867
fax (619) 476–1817

Lectorum Publications, Inc.
137 W 14th St
New York, NY 10011
(800) 345–5946
(212) 929–2833
fax (212) 727–3035

Libros Centroamericanos
P.O. Box 2203
Redlands, CA 92373
(800) MI-LIBRO
(909) 798–1342
fax (909) 335–9945

Libros Latinos
P.O. Box 1103
Redlands, CA 92373
(800) MI-LIBRO
(909) 793–8423
fax (909) 335–9945

Libros Sin Fronteras
P.O. Box 2085
Olympia, WA 98507–2085
(206) 357–4332 (voice/fax)
(800) 454–2767 (orders)

Los Andes Publishing, Inc.
P.O. Box 2344

La Puente, CA 91746
(800) 532–8872
fax (562) 531-0799

Mariuccia Iaconi Book Imports
970 Tennessee St
San Francisco, CA 94107
(800) 955–9577
(415) 821–1216
fax (415) 821–1596

Milligan News Co., Inc.
150 N Autumn St
San Jose, CA 95110
(800) 873–2387
(408) 286–7604
fax (408) 286–3077

Multi-Cultural Books and Videos, Inc.
28880 Southfield Rd, Suite 183
Lathrop Village, MI 48076
(800) 567–2220
fax (810) 559-2465

National Textbook Company (NTC)
4255 W Touhy Ave

Lincolnwood, IL 60646
(800) 323–4900 (orders only)
(708) 679–5500
fax (708) 679–2494

Quality Books, Inc.
918 Sherwood Dr
Lake Bluff, IL 60044–2204
(800) 323–4241
(708) 295–2010
fax (708) 295–1556

Santillana Publishing
2043 NW 87th Ave
Miami, FL 33172
(800) 245–8584

Schoenhof's Foreign Books, Inc.
76A Mount Auburn St
Cambridge, MA 02138
(617) 547–8855
(617) 547–8551

T.R. Books
822 N Walnut Ave
New Braunfels, TX 78131–0279
(800) 659–4710
(210) 625–2665
fax (210) 620–0470

APPENDIX B LATINO AUDIO AND VIDEO DISTRIBUTORS

LATINO AUDIO DISTRIBUTORS

Audio Forum
96 Broad St
Guilford, CT 06437
(203) 453–9794

Doremi
2261 S Atlantic Blvd
Commerce, CA 90040
(213) 265–4678

Dove Audio, distributed
through Penguin USA
120 Woodbine St
Bergenfield, NJ 07621
(201) 387–0600

LATINO VIDEO DISTRIBUTORS

Aims
9710 DeSoto Ave
Chatsworth, CA 91311–4409
(800) 367–2467

Altschul Group Corporation
1560 Sherman Ave, Suite 100
Evanston, IL 60201
(800) 421–2363
(847) 328–6700
fax (847) 328–6706

East Texas Distributor
530 N Puente St
Brea, CA 92621
(800) 852–4542

Facets Video
1517 W Fullerton Ave
Chicago, IL 60614
(800) 331–6197

MacArthur Foundation Library Video Project
1807 W Sunnyside
Chicago, IL 60640
(800) 847–3671

Madera Cinevideo
525 E Yosemite Ave
Madera, CA 93638
(209) 661–6000
fax (209) 674–3650

Multi-Cultural Books and Videos, Inc.
28880 Southfield Rd, Suite 183
Lathrup Village, MI 48076
(800) 567–2220
fax (810) 559–2465

National Latino Communications Center
PO Box 39A60
Los Angeles, CA 90039
(213) 953-2928

APPENDIX C
LATINO PUBLISHERS

Ancient City Press
Box 5401
Santa Fe, NM 87502
(505) 982–8195 (voice/fax)

Arte Público Press
Affil of Univ of Houston
MO Anderson Library, Rm 2
Houston, TX 77204–2090
(800) 633–2783
(713) 743–2841
fax (713) 743–2847

Bilingual Review Press
Box 872702
Hispanic Research Center
Arizona State University
Tempe, AZ 85287–2702
(602) 965–3867
fax (602) 965–8309

Children's Book Press
246 First Street, Suite 101
San Francisco, CA 94105
(415) 995–2200
fax (415) 995–2222

Children's Press
Grolier Publishing
P.O. Box 1331
Danbury, CT 06813
(800) 621–1115
(203) 797–3500
fax (203) 797–3657

Chulainn Publishing Corp
28625 Kennedy Gulch Rd
Conifer, CO 80433
(303) 838–4375
fax (303) 838–4791

Corona Publishing Co
P.O. Drawer 12407
San Antonio, TX 78212
(210) 341–7525

Curbstone Press
321 Jackson St
Willimantic, CT 06226
(860) 423–5110
fax (860) 423–9242

Editorial Caribe
P.O. Box 141000
Nashville, TN 37214–1000
(615) 391–3937

Editorial Edil
P.O. Box 23088
Río Piedras, Puerto Rico 00931
(809) 763–2958
fax (809) 765–5065

Editorial Plaza Mayor, Inc.
Avenida Ponce de Leon 1527
Barrio el Cinco
Río Piedras, Puerto Rico 00927
(809) 764–0455
fax (809) 764–0465

Editorial Unilit
1360 NW 88 Ave
Miami, FL 33172
(800) 767–7726
(305) 592–6136
fax (305) 592–0087

Floricanto Press
16161 Ventura Blvd, Suite 830
Encino, CA 91436–2504
(818) 990–1879

Fondo de Cultura Economica USA
2293 Verus St
San Diego, CA 92154
(800) 532–3872
(619) 429–0455
fax (619) 429–0827

Latin American Literary Review Press
121 Edgewood Dr
Pittsburgh, PA 15218
(412) 371–9023
fax (412) 371-9025

Los Andes Publishing Inc.
P.O. Box 2344
La Puente, CA 91746
(800) LECTURA
fax (562) 531–0799

Santillana Publishing Co., Inc.
2043 NW 87th Ave
Miami, FL 33172
(800) 245–8584

TQS Publications
P.O. Box 9275
Berkeley, CA 94709
(510) 601–6938

10 OUTREACH AND MARKETING/PUBLIC RELATIONS

CHALLENGE

Judith: *I just attended a great program on outreach and marketing library services. I went thinking I could bring back some ideas we could adapt to reach out to our Latino community. My biggest concern is that the program was designed for libraries that already have the funds and personnel for effective outreach and marketing. We're not so lucky.*

Al: *Surely there are some ideas we can implement.*

Judith: *Actually, there are some ideas that wouldn't require additional staff or funds.*

Al: *Well, what are they? We need to start somewhere—something is better than nothing. Once we're ready to offer some programs for Latinos, we can work on a publicity plan.*

In order to meet the changing and growing needs of our communities, it is becoming a *basic service* to reach out beyond our walls and make library services not only *accessible* but also *relevant* to diverse populations. Library services must be shaped not just by our professional perceptions but by "customer-focused" planning. This means service that goes beyond the traditional realm of what we have offered in the past, and far beyond the clientele to whom we have offered it.[1]

This chapter focuses on two main areas. In the first area, we concentrate on how to do effective outreach to attract Latinos in your community. In the second area, we offer advice on planning effective marketing and public relations of library programs and services to the Latino community. We have included some examples of successful program flyers used by some of the libraries we visited.

EFFECTIVE OUTREACH

Marcia Trotta's *Managing Library Outreach Programs* is very helpful and highly recommended. Even though Trotta's book is designed for children's services outreach, it can very easily be adapted to help you in any type of outreach. She provides a wealth of information on outreach services and includes many necessary worksheets and forms for starting and maintaining a systematic outreach program. If your library is in a position to develop an ongoing comprehensive outreach service program with the appropriate library personnel—outreach coordinator, staff, and volunteers—to support that program, Trotta's in-depth book will get you started. It is not necessary for us to duplicate her work in our book.

Not to minimize the importance of Trotta's work, we want to deal with the realities of Latino library outreach that we witnessed in our visits around the country. Of all the libraries interviewed, only a few libraries (such as New York Public Library, Chicago Public Library, and Tucson-Pima Public Library) had systematic, fully funded outreach services programs.

Although the Partnership for Change (PFC) libraries we visited in California were able to develop outreach services during their funding period, most had to cut those specific personnel when the funds were gone. That was the bad news. The good news was that the PFC funds gave them the head start in developing outreach services, some of which they were able to continue, such as maintaining their programming partnerships with external organizations.

A couple of years ago, Denver Public Library (DPL) reactivated its outreach services program. In the 1970s, the library had an outreach librarian, but the position was eliminated soon thereafter. DPL currently has budgeted some of its own general fund moneys to create several bilingual outreach librarian positions. Funding these positions demonstrates DPL's real commitment to provide effective outreach to its Latino community.

LEVELS OF OUTREACH

Because of the range of outreach services provided by various public libraries, we have identified an outreach services continuum with three levels—maximum, intermediate, minimum. The most advanced level of outreach services (maximum) is evident at the New York Public Library (NYPL) which has an Office of Outreach Services that coordinates all outreach services throughout the many NYPL branches. This is a massive undertaking because of the complexities of one of the largest public library systems. Consequently, this undertaking is at the high end of the outreach continuum. NYPL has community specialists working in the various boroughs; their fieldwork programs consist of working in the Latino communities to determine their information needs/issues. The NYPL community specialists each have an Outreach Advisory Committee of 30–40 members from external groups who assist librarians on determining community needs.

At the intermediate level of the outreach continuum is the Tucson-Pima Public Library. Tucson-Pima has an Outreach Services Unit with a coordinator and four full-time librarians funded by the library's general fund which provides for systematic outreach services. Youth services and literacy services are the focus of the Tucson-Pima Library outreach efforts.

Denver Public Library falls just below the intermediate level of the outreach continuum because the library has no formal coordinating outreach services office or unit. However, using library general funds, it is aggressively developing its outreach program for its minority communities.

At the lowest level (minimum) of the continuum would be the small public library in rural Kansas that has no additional staff or funds to devote to outreach. However, this library realizes that some outreach is necessary to meet the information needs of a growing Latino community. In this chapter, we primarily address the outreach activities that fall between the minimum and intermediate levels.

REALITY BITES!

Most of you, at this time, do not have the funds to develop a comprehensive outreach services program, much less hire an outreach coordinator—although you can write a proposal for funds to develop an outreach program. What are you supposed to do? Our answer is *something is better than nothing*!

Let us revert to the challenges facing the librarian from the small community in Kansas. Why does she need to do some basic outreach? Many of the Latinos in her community have recently immigrated to the United States from various Latin American countries. In those countries, there are no public libraries as we know them. These immigrants do not know that American public libraries are available to them. Libraries in their countries are viewed more as academic libraries are viewed here in the United States (that is, their services are designed for a particular clientele). Immigrants are not accustomed to free library services, and the library needs to reinforce the concept of free services in its programming and marketing. These challenges are reasons for the Kansas librarian and others to do some outreach. Here are some other challenges for you to consider:

- the language barrier
- cost factors (for example, fines, lost books)

- distrust of another white institution
- undocumented immigrant status[2]

Dealing with all these challenges at once may seem overwhelming to you. Remember, however, that you need to take the overall challenge of reaching out and serving Latino residents step by step. Approach this challenge by attending first to those outreach efforts that are doable and within your current staffing and funding levels.

OUTREACH STRATEGIES FOR YOUR LATINO COMMUNITY

Realizing that you and your current staff are it, here are some strategies to consider when reaching out to your Latino community:

1. You need to know as much as possible about the Latino community that you plan to serve.
2. You need to learn about the Latino culture (and any possible subcultures) in your community.
3. You and your staff need to demonstrate a sensitivity toward Latinos regardless of their socioeconomic background.
4. You need to discover and contact the formal and informal Latino leaders who can serve as resource people in this effort.
5. You need to identify the organizations, agencies, and individuals with whom you can form partnerships in your outreach efforts.
6. You need to do effective public relations and marketing of your services to Latinos in your community.
7. You need to know where to promote your programs and services efficiently and effectively.
8. You need to be able to develop and provide specialized Spanish-language resources for the Latino community.
9. You need to be able to communicate with Latinos of all ages.[3]

Items 1–7 are doable with your current staffing; the main challenge here is the time. Items 8 and 9 are more problematic and are a definite challenge. As we mentioned in Chapter 7, there are ways to meet this challenge, such as writing a proposal for external funds for bilingual staff or engaging bilingual volunteers for specific bilingual hours in the library and/or for assistance in selecting and acquiring bilingual or Spanish-language library materials.

OUTREACH *A LA MINIMUM*

Okay, so you don't have funds to hire an outreach librarian or to develop and implement an in-depth outreach services plan. Don't let that stop you. Three areas of outreach *a la minimum* that are doable include

- creating partnerships in the community

- offering library programs and services designed particularly for the Latino community
- marketing those programs outside the library and in the Latino community.

OUTREACH AND PARTNERSHIPS

Because outreach and partnerships go hand in hand, the best thing you can do is to develop partnerships with organizations, agencies, and individuals who can provide personnel, program expertise, facilities, and public relations resources (see Chapter 8).

Let us review those possible partners. Your partners could include social services agencies, civic organizations/clubs, churches and religious groups, government agencies, local government departments (such as police, fire, parks and recreation), educational institutions, and daycare centers.

Once your partnerships are established and your joint programs and services are identified, you can determine which ones are achievable given your staff and funding constraints. Concentrate on providing those programs. Leave the more costly ones until you find external funds or until you can integrate them into your library's general programs and services. Remember, some action is better than no action.

PROGRAMS AND SERVICES

Chapter 5 provides great detail concerning ideas for programs and services for your Latino community. What needs to be mentioned here is that nothing can be done in terms of outreach and marketing until your library has reviewed and designed programs and services that will attract Latinos. You need to have something to promote to them that is a result of some type of Latino community analysis (see Chapter 4). After your analysis of Latino community information needs, you can proceed with program planning.

Remember that your library already has programs and services in place that can be of interest to Latinos. Probably, however, there is no systematic outreach and marketing to attract them to your library for some of the basic services already provided. You can start at this basic level while you develop some specialized programs to interest them.

MARKETING AND PUBLIC RELATIONS FOR THE LATINO COMMUNITY

Once you have developed some programs and/or services for the Latino community based on the results of the community analysis, you must market those programs to your specific audience. A very good, in-depth manual, *Marketing: A How-to-Do-It Manual for Librarians* by Suzanne Walters, covers this area in depth.[4] We do not want to replicate Walters's manual; however, we want to include some basic tips and examples of how to market specifically to your Latino community. For our purposes, we use marketing and public relations (PR) interchangeably. Here are some effective tips on handling your PR.

TIP 1: PLAN WELL

Almost everything we suggest that you do has a planning component. Outreach and PR are no different. Make sure to have a mini-PR plan for each of your programs/services. Let's take the HomeworkHELP Center project example mentioned in previous chapters. Simultaneously with the planning and implementation of this new program, you and your staff need to have your PR plan in place. This plan should include the following components:

- identifying your target audience (in our scenario, it would be Latino children and young adults in school)
- identifying the most effective PR/marketing mechanism to be used for the effort (flyers describing the HomeworkHELP Center distributed in schools and in the community, PSAs on the radio and TV stations, presentations before the school administrators and school board)
- identifying the most effective places to reach that audience (for example, schools, homes, popular young adult hangouts, churches, malls)

TIP 2: USE PROMOTIONAL FLYERS

Promotional flyers are usually the least expensive way to advertise a program or event. They can be disseminated in many different ways such as by hand and/or as posters on bulletin boards. Production costs can be very low depending on the final product. We recommend that the flyers be printed on bright-colored paper.

TIP 3: USE BILINGUAL PR

All your PR pieces must be bilingual; if you cannot offer bilingual or Spanish programs because you lack bilingual staff, volunteers, or partners to present them, you should still promote your English language programs on bilingual flyers. This allows monolingual (Spanish-language) Latinos to understand what kind of programming the library does offer. They can still share that information with others—family, friends, coworkers.

If you have a computer with a graphics package, it is very easy to create attractive flyers. If not, you can use clip art or draw basic pictures.

Figures 10–1a to 10–9b are some examples of bilingual flyers used for programming PR. Again, we selected actual flyers used by various public libraries we visited. We chose to include these examples because we wanted to recognize these libraries for the excellent work they have done in marketing to and serving their Latino communities.

Some flyers are fancier than others. However, we wanted to show you the range of PR flyers from homemade, low-budget flyers to professionally produced flyers. Such resources as equipment, personnel, and time will probably determine how fancy any of your PR flyers can be.

Figures 10–1a to 10–6b are examples of library PR flyers for children and young adult programming. Figures 10–1a and 10–1b represent a basic bilingual flyer (front and back) advertising bilingual story hours.

Figures 10–2a and 10–2b publicize another program. This two-sided, bilingual flyer also includes an example of a programming partnership with an external agency.

Figure 10–3 to 10–5b are examples of bilingual flyers with the Spanish and English text both appearing on one side. Figures 10–6a and 10–6b represent a two-sided bilingual flyer for a young adult library program.

Figures 10–7a to 10–9b are examples of bilingual flyers for adult library programs. Figures 10–7a to 10–8b are two-sided bilingual flyers which indicate that they should be posted on the Spanish language side. The two-sided bilingual flyer represented in Figures 10–8a and 8b also shows a programming partnership with two external organizations.

Figures 10–9a and 10–9b are an adaptation of a two-sided, bilingual flyer with a spot for the author's photo. Obviously, the original flyer was professionally designed and produced. Remember that you can raise money to do such a piece or request that the piece be a donation from the printing company. If you do that, make sure that the company is listed as a partner on the flyer or given credit on the flyer for its donation.

Figures 10–10a to 10–11b are not program flyers; they are bilingual, promotional materials that provide basic library information. Figures 10–10a and 10–10b show a two-sided, bilingual bookmark that provides basic information on loan periods and library hours.

Figures 10–11a and 10–11b are examples of a two-sided, bilingual welcome note that describes basic library regulations.

TIP 4: EMPHASIZE THAT LIBRARY PROGRAMS AND SERVICES ARE FREE

It's important to emphasize in all your promotional pieces that library programs and services are free. Of the flyer examples we provided, very few mentioned that their programs were free (10–2a/b; 10–5a/b; 10–7a/b; 10–8a/b). This omission would be fine if the libraries were only trying to attract present library users. Latinos who are new to the community or new to the country, however, need to know that public library programs and services are free.

TIP 5: WRITE EFFECTIVE PRESS RELEASES

Writing press releases about your library programs is another effective PR method. If you have a local or area newspaper, submit a write-up of the program. If there is a Spanish-language newspaper in your community or if the local newspaper has a Spanish-language section, submit the write-up in Spanish also.

A press release includes a heading that says "Immediate Press Release" or "Please Release on (date)." It should also include:

- the name of the organization submitting the press release
- the date of the press release
- the contact person and his/her telephone number
- a catchy headline/title
- the five "Ws"—who, what, when, where, and why
- # # # (to signify the end of the press release)

Figures 10–12a and 10–12b show a two-sided press release, with English and Spanish versions, for the library event advertised in Figures 10–9a and 10–9b—Isabel Allende Day at Santa Ana Public Library.

TIP 6: DON'T FORGET ABOUT PSAs

Remember to use the media for public service announcements (PSAs). The only cost here is the time to write the PSA and submit it to the appropriate media (radio and/or television). If your local or area radio station has a Spanish-language listening segment, you can also submit the PSA in Spanish. Figure 10–13 is an example of the PSAs for the Isabel Allende Day event. Public service announcements should include the following:

- average length of 30 seconds (:30)
- prescribed format as shown in Figure 10–13
- telephone number for further information

TIP 7: GIVE EFFECTIVE PRESENTATIONS IN THE COMMUNITY

Most library administrators are excellent at presentation and persuasion. These skills are essential, especially during budget hearings. Remember to use these skills in your PR efforts. You can set up presentations and/or interviews with radio and television stations as well as with schools, civic organizations, or community groups.

TIP 8: DEVELOP A DISTRIBUTION LIST

For future PR purposes, we suggest that you develop a PR distribution list. This list would include all the different organizations (partners) who have assisted the library in its PR efforts within the Latino community.[5] This list will be handy each time you are ready to market a particular program or service to Latinos. The list should include the categories listed below.

- Flyer distributions—Include all the organizations, agencies, and individuals who are willing to distribute library flyers and other PR information to the Latino community (at no charge). If at all possible, include the number of flyers they are willing to distribute each time.
- Flyer and poster postings—Include all the organizations, agencies, and businesses that have agreed to post PR materials on their bulletin boards and windows for the Latino community.
- Publications distribution—Include all publications in your local community and region that are willing to provide free news releases and/or PSAs of your special programs designed to attract the Latino audience. This list should be subdivided by categories such as newspapers, magazines, organization newsletters, church bulletins, and radio and television stations.
- Unable to help—List organizations that have been unable to help. Make sure to include the last date they were contacted. The list is important because it helps prevent any embarrassment to the library and irritation for the organization. However, it does not hurt to call them once in a while. Sometimes the leader or manager changes, and with that personnel change may come a positive philosophical change toward helping organizations like the public library.
- Freebies—Although this category is not directly related to PR, we suggest you still include it. List retail businesses that will consider providing donations of food, gifts or gift certificates, books,

facilities, and other services (such as printing, daycare, or transportation). Figures 8–3a and 8–3b show the form to use for the freebies list.

TIP 9: INCLUDE ESSENTIAL INFORMATION IN THE DISTRIBUTION LIST

Essential information for the distribution list includes:

- contact person
- address
- telephone and fax numbers
- e-mail address
- a checklist of what the organization is willing to do
- number of copies for distribution
- requirement to call ahead
- last date of list compilation.

Figure 10–14 is a sample form to use or adapt for compiling this list. You may find some of the same organizations, agencies, or businesses are listed on your partnerships form (see Figure 8–2). Remember that your PR list can be printed and/or entered into a database to allow for easy and continuous updating.

CONCLUSION

Programming, partnerships, outreach, and marketing/public relations are all interrelated. When developing programs and services for your underserved Latino community, it is difficult to consider one of these components without considering the others. That is, in fact, the beauty and the challenge of trying to serve any community. However, remember that you already have a lot of experience in all of these components. The challenge for you now is to apply those marketing/PR experiences designed for your general library users and then to design programs and services for a new and growing clientele—the Latinos in your community.

You must reach out to let the Latino community know you are determined and excited to serve them and meet their information needs. You need to attract the Latino community to your library, and that is your challenge. Outreach not only includes the development of programs designed to interest this underserved community but also includes your marketing efforts to reach out and get them to attend library programs—at the library or at other partnership sites.

We hope that the ideas that we have obtained from public libraries throughout the country will be helpful as you begin to reach out to the Latino community. You have to start somewhere and sometime; remember that sooner is better than later and something *is* better than nothing. As you begin to meet this service challenge, it should only get easier with more experience under your belt. Success, whether big or little, is important to recognize when trying to reach out to a relatively new constituency. Celebrate your successes!

NOTES

1. Marcia Trotta, *Managing Library Outreach Programs: A How-To-Do-It Manual for Librarians* (New York: Neal-Schuman Publishers, 1993), vii.
2. Hispanic Services Committee, *Hispanic Services: A Practical Manual for the Public Librarian* (Chicago: Chicago Public Library, 1990), 9.
3. Marsha Abanira, "Outreach Services to the Spanish-Speaking Community," (paper presented at the First Binational Conference of Librarians in California and Baja California, Tijuana, Baja California, Mexico, January 13–14, 1984, ERIC ED 264 870), 19.
4. Suzanne Walters, *Marketing: A How-To-Do-It Manual for Librarians* (New York: Neal-Schuman Publishers, 1992).
5. We want to thank the Oxnard Public Library, Oxnard, Calif., for this idea.

Figure 10–1a. Sample Bilingual Flyer—English Side

October

Story Hour
In
Spanish/English

10/8/92
3:30 P.M.
South Chula Vista
Public Library
389 Orange Avenue
585-5771

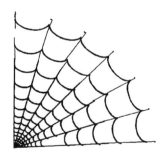

Permission to adapt and reproduce granted by South Chula Vista Public Library.

Figure 10–1b. Sample Bilingual Flyer—Spanish Side

October
Octubre

hora de Cuentos
en
Español/Inglés

10/8/92
3:30 P.M.
Biblioteca de South
Chula Vista
389 Orange Avenue
585-5771

Permission to adapt and reproduce granted by South Chula Vista Public Library.

Figure 10–2a. Sample Bilingual Flyer—English Side

Partnerships For Change

presents:

THE SAN DIEGO HUMANE SOCIETY
&
S.P.C.A.

Free Admission

Wednesday
January 26th., 1994
3:30 p.m.

Learn to take care of your pets.

Fill out an application
for your library card

at

THE LOGAN HEIGHTS BRANCH LIBRARY
811 SOUTH 28th STREET, SAN DIEGO, CA 92113
(619) 533-3968

Figure 10–2b. Sample Bilingual Flyer—Spanish Side

Compañeros Para un Buen Cambio

presentan:

LA SOCIEDAD HUMANITARIA DE SAN DIEGO
&
S.P.C.A.

Entrada Gratis

Miércoles
26 de enero de 1994
3:30 p.m.

Aprende a cuidar
tus mascotas

Llena una solicitud para
tu tarjeta de la biblioteca

en la

SUCURSAL BIBLIOTECARIA DE LOGAN HEIGHTS
811 SUR CALLE 28, SAN DIEGO, CA 92113
(619) 533-3968

Figure 10–3. Sample Bilingual Flyer—English/Spanish

FIESTA DE NAVIDAD

Santa Monica Public Library

A bilingual Christmas celebration with stories, music, and refreshments

Una celebración bilingue con cuentos, música y refrescos

El martes, 22 de diciembre a las 7 p.m.
Tuesday, December 22, at 7 p.m.

FAIRVIEW BRANCH LIBRARY - SUCURSAL
FAIRVIEW
2101 Ocean Park Boulevard
Santa Monica

(301) 450-0443
Sylvia Anderle

****

Persons with disabilities please call Sylvia Anderle
at 458-8637 for special arrangements.

Personas con impedimentos físicos favor contactar
a Sylvia Anderle por el 458-8637 para hacer los
arreglos que competa.

Figure 10–4. Sample Bilingual Flyer—English/Spanish

STORYTIME

——————reunion——————

Celebración infantil

JUNE/JUNIO

JOIN US
FOR
STORIES, SONGS, GAMES
FOR
YOU AND YOUR BABY

WHEN: Monday, June 5, 1995
          at 10:00 a.m.

WHERE: EAST LOS ANGELES LIBRARY
          4801 E. 3rd ST.
          LOS ANGELES, CA.

VENGA Y DISFRUTE
DE LOS
CUENTOS, CANCIONES, JUEGOS
PARA
USTED Y SU BEBE

CUANDO: Lunes, 5 de Junio de 1995
          a las 10:00 a.m.

DONDE: BIBLIOTECA DEL ESTE DE L.A.
          4801 E. 3RD ST.
          LOS ANGELES, CA.

"Begin at the Beginning with Books" is funded by the California
State Library under the Library & Services & Construction Act.

Permission to adapt and reproduce granted by County of Los Angeles Public Library.

Figure 10–5a. Sample Bilingual Flyer—English/Spanish

Trilogía De Payasos

Pieza teatral de pantomima en tres actos.

Personajes: Dos payasos

Duración: 60 minutos

... La Biblioteca Pública

Del

Este De Los Angeles

Localizada en el

4801 E. 3rd Street en el
Este De Los Angeles

a las
11:00 De La Mañana

el sábado
Dia 22 De Enero de 1983

Entrada Gratis

Clown Trilogy

Theatrical piece in pantomime in three acts.

Characters: Two Clowns

Length: 60 minutes.

... The East Los Angeles Public Library

located at

4801 E. 3rd Street
East Los Angeles

at
11:00 in the morning
on

Saturday January 22, 1983

Entrance Free

Para más información llamar a la biblioteca
al (213) 264-0155.

Figure 10–5b. Sample Bilingual Flyer—English/Spanish (cont.)

"La Rueda" es un grupo de teatro de tiempo completo integrado por Judith García y Eduardo Sánchez. Ha participado en diversos festivales teatrales entre ellos: el 7° Festival de Teatro Chicano en Los Angeles, en 1976; 3° Festival Latino Americano de Teatro México, 1977; 1° Festival Internacional de Teatro de Expresión Ibérica, Porto Portugal, 1978; 1° Festival Internacional de Pantomima en Guanajuato, México, 1979; y 1° Festival "The Gathering" en Minnesota, Estados Unidos, en 1981.

Su experiencia abarca a audiencias de todas edades y lenguas así mismo como presentaciones en los más variadados escenarios: parques, escuelas, teatros, fiestas, y ferias.

La Rueda
Teatro y Pantomima
2337 Ocean View Avenue, #6
Los Angeles, California 90057
(213) 389-8854

"La Rueda" is a full time theater and mime duet, whose members consist of Judith García and Eduardo Sánchez. La Rueda has been invited to participate in many theater festivals. Some of the more prominent of these being: 7th Annual Chicano Theater Festival, Los Angeles in 1976; 1st Festival Internacional de Expresión Ibérica, Porto Portugal, 1978; 3rd Festival Latinoamericano de Teatro Mexico, 1977; 1st Festival Internacional de Pantomima, Guanajuato, Mexico, 1979; and The Gathering Theatre Festival in Minnesota in 1981.

Both children and adult audiences have been captivated by the delightfully stimulating Teatro La Rueda.

As a group, La Rueda's objective is to interact with our audience on such a provocative basis as to entice the spectator into a participant and thereby bringing us closer to our public with each turn or revolution of the wheel....

Este programa fue co-patrocinado por Los Amigos de la Biblioteca Pública del Este de Los Angeles (East Los Angeles Friends of the Library).

Los Angeles County Public Library
12/82

Figure 10–6a. Sample Bilingual Flyer—English Side

PAINT MURALS!   SCULPT!

DRAW!   MAKE FURNITURE!

YOU CAN MAKE ART!!

THURSDAYS   VIRGINIA PARK
NOVEMBER 3 - DECEMBER 9   2200 VIRGINIA AVENUE
2:00 - 4:00 PM   SANTA MONICA

COURSES TAUGHT IN SPANISH BY:
MARGOT DEL VALLE
MARCIAL GODOY

LATINO OUTREACH PROGRAM
(310) 450-0443

Figure 10–6b. Sample Bilingual Flyer—Spanish Side

PINTA MURALES!   ¡ESCULPE!

RETRATA!   ¡HAZ MUEBLES!

¡¡TU PUEDES HACER ARTE!!

JUEVES   VIRGINIA PARK
NOVIEMBRE 3 - DICIEMBRE 9   2200 VIRGINIA AVENUE
2:00 a 4:00 PM   SANTA MONICA

CURSOS SE CONDUCIRÁN EN ESPAÑOL POR:
MARGOT DEL VALLE
MARCIAL GODOY

PROGRAMA CONTACTO LATINO
(310) 450-0443

Figure 10–7a. Sample Bilingual Flyer—English Side

QUEENS BOROUGH PUBLIC LIBRARY
NEW AMERICANS PROGRAM

| PROGRAMA EN ESPAÑOL |
| Program in Spanish |

presents

A WORKSHOP FOR SPANISH-SPEAKING NEWCOMERS
HOW TO SUCCEED IN THE USA
LEARN HOW TO PURSUE YOUR OWN AMERICAN DREAM

LEARN HOW TO:
- Set your goals

- Develop a work plan

- Remain focused

- Overcome obstacles

SPEAKER:
CAMILO F. CRUZ, PhD
EDUCATOR, AUTHOR of
"IN SEARCH OF THE AMERICAN DREAM
-A GUIDE FOR SUCCESS IN THE UNITED STATES"

TUESDAY
DECEMBER 14
6:00-8:00 p.m.

| ADMISSION IS FREE |
| For reservation |
| call: 718/990-0883 |

JACKSON HEIGHTS BRANCH LIBRARY
35-51 81 STREET
QUEENS
BY BUS: 33, 89   BY TRAIN: #7 to 82 STREET

| Branch Hours |
| Mon./Wed. 10-8 |
| Tues.1-8 |
| Thurs./Fri. 10-6 |
| Sat. 10-5 |
| Sun. 12-5 |

-PLEASE POST ON SPANISH SIDE-

Figure 10–7b. Sample Bilingual Flyer—Spanish Side

BIBLIOTECA PÚBLICA DE QUEENS
PROGRAMA NUEVOS AMERICANOS

PROGRAM IN SPANISH
PROGRAMA EN ESPAÑOL

Presenta

UN TALLER PARA HISPANO-PARLANTES RECIEN LLEGADOS

COMO TRIUNFAR

en los ESTADOS UNIDOS
APRENDA COMO CONSEGUIR SU PROPIO "*SUEÑO AMERICANO*"

TEMAS A DESARROLLAR:

- Fijar sus metas

- Desarrollar un plan de trabajo

- Mantenerse enfocado

- Sob eponerse a los obstáculos

FACILITADOR:
CAMILO F. CRUZ, PhD
Educador, Autor de
"En busca del sueño americano
-Guía para triunfar en los Estados Unidos"

MARTES
14 de DICIEMBRE
6:00 - 8:00 p.m.

ENTRADA GRATUITA
Para reservación
718/990-0883

BIBLIOTECA PÚBLICA de JACKSON HEIGHTS
35-51 81 STREET
QUEENS
POR BUS: 33, 89   POR TREN: #7 HASTA 82 STREET

Horario de la Biblioteca
Lunes 10-8
Martes/Mierc. 1-8
Jueves/Vier. 10-6
Sab. 10-5
Dom. cerrada

Figure 10–8a. Sample Bilingual Flyer—English Side

Queens Borough Public Library
New Americans Program

| Program in Spanish |
| Programa en Español |

presents

AIDS and Your Family
a basic orientation <u>in Spanish</u>

Presentation includes:
- What is AIDS?
- How is AIDS contracted?
- Can families protect themselves?
- Where can one get help?

Speaker: Luz Santiago
Hispanic AIDS Forum
Latino Families Program

Admission is free. For more information, call (718) 990-0883 NAP.

Wednesday, May 19, 5:30-7:30 p.m.

Jackson Heights Branch
35-51 81 Street
Queens

By train: #7 to 82 Street
By bus: Q19B, Q29, Q32,Q33

-PLEASE POST ON SPANISH SIDE-

Permission to adapt and reproduce granted by Queens Borough Public Library.

Figure 10–8b. Sample Bilingual Flyer—Spanish Side

Queens Borough Public Library
Programa Nuevos Americans

| Program in Spanish |
| Programa en Español |

presenta

EL SIDA y su FAMILIA
una orientación básica en español

La sesión incluye:
- ¿Qué es SIDA?
- ¿Cómo se contrae?
- ¿Cómo se protege la familia?
- ¿Dónde se encuentra ayuda?

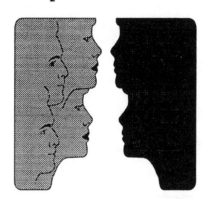

Facilitadora: Luz Santiago
Foro Hispano sobre el SIDA
Proyecto de Familias Latinas

Entrada gratuita. Para más información (718) 990-0883.

Miércoles, 19 de Mayo 5:30-7:30 p.m.

Biblioteca Pública de Jackson Heights
35-51 81 Street
Queens

Por tren: #7 hasta la calle 82
Por bus: Q19B, Q29, Q32,Q33

Figure 10–9a. Sample Bilingual Flyer—English Side

KNOWLEDGE IS POWER...PEOPLE WHO READ SUCCEED
**FEATURING THE INTERNATIONALLY KNOWN AUTHOR
OF <u>THE HOUSE OF THE SPIRITS</u>**

ISABEL ALLENDE
WEDNESDAY, APRIL 19, 1995

➤ CELEBRATION THROUGHOUT THE DAY:
   10:30AM – 7:30PM

➤ CHILDREN'S ACTIVITIES   (INSERT PHOTO)

➤ COMMUNITY/CITY
   ORGANIZATION EXHIBITS

➤ SOUTH AMERICAN MUSIC

➤ *KNOWLEDGE LINK*
   PRESENTATION

➤ LIVE ENTERTAINMENT

➤ FOOD

➤ STORYTIMES

➤ LIBRARY TOURS

➤ MUCH, MUCH MORE!!

ISABEL ALLENDE
Author of *PAULA*, published by HarperCollins Publishers
in May, 1995. Photo Credit: Jerry Bauer.

*I AM NOT THE SAME WOMAN, MY DAUGHTER
HAS GIVEN ME THE OPPORTUNITY TO LOOK
INSIDE MYSELF AND DISCOVER INTERIOR
SPACES...EMPTY, DARK, STRANGELY PEACEFUL...
I HAD NEVER EXPLORED BEFORE.
FROM HER BOOK <u>PAULA</u>*

READING AND BOOK SIGNING:
TIME: 6:00 PM ● PLACE: ROOMS A & B

AT

SANTA ANA PUBLIC LIBRARY
26 CIVIC CENTER PLAZA ● SANTA ANA, CA 92701
(714) 647-5267
CO-SPONSORED BY MARTINEZ BOOKS & ART
220 West Third Street, Santa Ana, CA 92701, (714) 973-7900

FREE VALIDATED TWO-HOUR PARKING NEXT TO THE LIBRARY

Figure 10–9b. Sample Bilingual Flyer—Spanish Side

LEER ES PODER:... LOS QUE LEEN TRIUNFAN
PRESENTANDO A LA MUNDIALMENTE CONOCIDA
AUTORA DE <u>LA CASA DE LOS ESPIRITUS</u>

ISABEL ALLENDE
MIÉRCOLES, ABRIL 19, 1995

➤ CELEBRACIONES DURANTE TODO EL DÍA:
  10:30AM – 7:30PM

➤ ACTIVIDADES PARA NIÑOS

➤ EXHIBICIONES DE ORGANIZACIONES DE LA
  COMUNIDAD/MUNICIPALES

➤ MÚSICA DE SUDAMERICA

➤ PRESENTACION DE
  "KNOWLEDGE LINK"

(INSERT PHOTO)

➤ ENTRETENIMIENTO EN VIVO

➤ COMIDA

➤ CUENTOS

➤ RECORRIDOS CON GUÍA
  DE LA BIBLIOTECA

➤ Y MUCHO, MUCHO MÁS

ISABEL ALLENDE
Autora de *PAULA*, publicado por HarperCollins Publishers
en mayo, 1995. Foto de: Jerry Bauer.

LECTURA Y FIRMA DE SUS LIBROS:
HORA: 6:00 PM ● LUGAR: SALAS A/B

EN LA

BIBLIOTECA PÚBLICA DE SANTA ANA
26 CIVIC CENTER PLAZA ● SANTA ANA, CA 92701
(714) 647-5267

CO-PATROCINIO DE MARTINEZ BOOKS & ART
220 West Third Street, Santa Ana, CA 92701, (714) 973-7900

REVALIDAMOS DOS HORAS DE ESTACIONAMIENTO GRATIS ENSEGUIDA DE LA BIBLIOTECA

Figure 10–10a. Sample Bilingual Bookmark—English Side

South Chula Vista
Library
389 Orange Ave.

Loan Periods

28 Days:
Books/Magazines

14 Days:
Audiocassettes
Books on Tape
Compact Discs
New Books

3 Days:
Videocassettes

7 Days:
Non-Fiction Videos

The Hours Are:

MONDAY	12-8 PM
TUESDAY	12-8 PM
WEDNESDAY	10-6 PM
THURSDAY	10-6 PM
FRIDAY	12-6 PM
SATURDAY	10-4 PM
SUNDAY	1-5 PM

Tel 585-5755

Figure 10–10b. Sample Bilingual Bookmark—Spanish Side

South Chula Vista
Library
389 Orange Ave.

Plazos de Préstamo

28 Días:
Libros/Periódicos

14 Días:
Audiocassettes
Libros en Cassettes
Discos Compactos
Libros Recientes

3 Días:
Videocassettes

7 Días:
Videos Educativos

Horario:

LUNES	12-8 PM
MARTES	12-8 PM
MIÉRCOLES	10-6 PM
JUEVES	10-6 PM
VIERNES	12-6 PM
SABADO	10-4 PM
DOMINGO	1-5 PM

Tel 585-5755

Permission to adapt and reproduce granted by South Chula Vista Public Library.

Figure 10–11a. Sample Bilingual Welcome Note—English Side

WELCOME TO THE SANTA BARBARA PUBLIC LIBRARY SYSTEM

Enclosed is your new library card, which may be used for library services at branches of the Santa Barbara Public Library as well as at the Black Gold Cooperative member libraries listed on the back of your card.

Your new card is valid as soon as you add your signature in ink. While using your library services, please be aware of these regulations:

- you are responsible for all material checked out on your card;

- a charge will be made for lost or damaged items and material returned overdue;

- library cards are not transferable;

- you must present your card in order to borrow materials;

- a fee will be charged for lost, stolen, or damaged cards;

- notify the library promptly of change of name or address;

- notify the library immediately if your card is lost or stolen in order to prevent improper use.

USE YOUR LIBRARY CARD OFTEN!

Figure 10–11b. Sample Bilingual Welcome Note—Spanish Side

BIENVENIDOS A LA BIBLIOTECA PÚBLICA DE SANTA BARBARA

Adjunto encontrará su nueva tarjeta de la biblioteca, la cual puede ser utilizada en cualquiera de las sucursales de la Biblioteca Pública de Santa Bárbara así como en cualquiera de las bibliotecas del Sistema "Black Gold" que aparecen indicadas en la parte de atrás de su tarjeta.

Su nueva tarjeta es válida tan pronto como le coloque su firma autógrafa en tinta. Al utilizar los servicios de la biblioteca tenga presente lo siguiente:

- usted se hace responsable por todos los materiales que hayan sido prestados con su tarjeta;

- se le cobrará una multa por materiales extraviados o dañados y también por materiales devueltos pasada la fecha de devolución;

- las tarjetas de la biblioteca no son transferibles;

- debe presentar su tarjeta para solicitar materiales en préstamo;

- un recargo se cobrará por reemplazo de tarjetas extraviadas;

- notifíquenos en caso de extravío de su tarjeta;

- notifíquenos en caso de cambio de dirección o de nombre.

Figure 10–12a. Sample Bilingual Press Release—English Side

FOR IMMEDIATE PRESS RELEASE

FROM: SANTA ANA PUBLIC LIBRARY   DATE: 4 APRIL 1995
         26 Civic Center Plaza
         Santa Ana, CA 92701

CONTACT: MAGGIE OWENS   PHONE: 714/647-5287

CITY WILL DECLARE APRIL 19
"ISABEL ALLENDE DAY"
AT SANTA ANA PUBLIC LIBRARY

A proclamation by the Santa Ana City Council will declare April 9, 1995 as "Isabel Allende Day" to honor world-renowned author Isabel Allende of Chile, and to welcome her to Santa Ana. Ms. Allende is the author of such best sellers as *Of Love and Shadows, Eva Luna, The Stories of Eva Luna, The Infinite Plan*, and *The House of the Spirits*, which was made into a movie in 1993. Following the Proclamation and welcome to the City a news conference will be held at 3:00 p.m. at the Santa Ana Public Library.

A variety of events will be held throughout the day at the library, including tours of the library, storytimes and crafts for children, and an open house of the Santa Ana History Room, the student Homework Center, and the Gift Shop.

From 4:00 to 7:30 p.m., City agencies and community groups will join in for an evening of festivities featuring music, folkloric dance, food sampling, special displays and exhibits.

At 6:00 p.m., Ms. Allende will be promoting and autographing her new book, *Paula,* and giving a reading from the book, which is a memoir of the fatal illness of her 28-year-old daughter. The author hopes to reach youth to encourage them to read and to obtain and use a library card. She sincerely believes in the theme "Knowledge is Power...People Who Read Succeed."

The meeting and reading will be held in Assembly Room A on the Mezzanine of the Santa Ana Public Library, located at Ross and Civic Center Drive. The public is invited.

Ms. Allende's appearance is co-sponsored by Martinez Books & Art, 220 West 3rd Street in Santa Ana. For additional information call the Santa Ana Public Library at 714/647-5264.

Figure 10–12b. Sample Bilingual Press Release—Spanish Side

PARA SU PUBLICACION INMEDIATA

DE: BIBLIOTECA PÚBLICA DE SANTA ANA   FECHA: 4 DE ABRIL DE 1995
         26 Civic Center Plaza
         Santa Ana, CA 92701

CONTACTO: MARTHA GARCÍA ALMARZOUK   TELÉFONO: 714/647-5279

LA CIUDAD DECLARA EL 19 DE ABRIL
"EL DÍA DE ISABEL ALLENDE"
EN
LA BIBLIOTECA PÚBLICA DE SANTA ANA

El Consejo de la Ciudad de Santa Ana proclamará el 19 de abril de 1995 como "El Día de Isabel Allende" en honor de la mundialmente conocida autora Chilena Isabel Allende y le dará la bienvenida a Santa Ana. Allende es la autora de los libros titulados *De Amor y de Sombra, Eva Luna, Cuentos de Eva Luna, El Plan Infinito,* y *La Casa de los Espíritus.* Todos de gran éxito de venta y el último llevado a la pantalla grande en 1993. Después de la Proclamación y bienvenida a nuestra ciudad, una conferencia de prensa tendrá lugar en la Biblioteca Pública de Santa Ana a las 3:00 p.m.

Una gran variedad de eventos tendrán lugar durante el día en la biblioteca los que incluirán: recorridos con guía de la biblioteca, cuentos, actividades de artesanía y piñata para niños, muestra al público del "Salón de Historia de Santa Ana" del "Centro de Tareas" y del "Bazar."

De las 4:00 a las 7:30 de la tarde, las agencias de la Ciudad y grupos de la comunidad estarán presentes para celebrar y disfrutar la música, danza folklórica, comida y exhibiciones especiales.

A las 6:00 de la tarde, Isabel Allende promoverá, firmará autógrafos y leerá extractos de su más reciente libro *Paula* en el cual relata el fatal padecimiento de su hija de sólo 28 años. La conocida autora espera acercarse a los jóvenes con su mensaje para fomentar en ellos la lectura y el que obtengan una tarjeta de la biblioteca. Isabel Allende cree sinceramente en el lema de "Leer es Poder...Los que Leen Triunfan".

Esta reunión será en el Salón de Asambleas ubicado en la Mezzanine de la Biblioteca Pública de Santa Ana, en la esquina de Civic Center Drive y Ross. Se invita al público en general.

Esta presentación de Isabel Allende es co-patriocinada por Martinez Books & Art, 220 West 3rd Street en Santa Ana. Para obtener más información, llame a la Biblioteca Pública de Santa Ana al 714/647-5264.

Figure 10–13. Sample Bilingual PSA—English/Spanish

:30   **"ISABEL ALLENDE DAY"**

:30

                PUBLIC SERVICE ANNOUNCEMENT:

The Santa Ana City Council will declare April 19, 1995, as "Isabel Allende Day" to honor world renown author Isabel Allende of Chile, and to welcome her to Santa Ana. Ms. Allende wrote *"The House of the Spirits."* Numerous events will be held throughout the day at the library. At 6:00 p.m., Ms. Allende will be giving a reading from her most recent book, *"Paula,"* which is a memoir of the fatal illness of her daughter and will be signing autographs. The public is invited. The library is located at Ross & Civic Center Drive. For additional information call 714/647-5267.

:30   **PSA RADIO-"DÍA DE ISABEL ALLENDE"**
:30

          ANUNCIO DE SERVICIO PÚBLICO:

La Ciudad de Santa Ana proclamará el 19 de abril como el "Día de Isabel Allende" en honor de la visita que la conocida autora hará a la Biblioteca Pública de Santa Ana. Allende escribió **"La Casa de los Espíritus."** Un sinúmero de eventos tendrán lugar durante todo el día en la Biblioteca. A las 6:00 de la tarde la autora leerá extractos de su más reciente libro *"Paula,"* en el que relata el padecimiento fatal de su hija y firmará autógrafos. Se invita al público en general. La Biblioteca está ubicada entre las calles Ross y Civic Center Drive en Santa Ana. Para obtener más información llame al 714/647-5267.

Permission to adapt and reproduce granted by Santa Ana Public Library.

Figure 10–14. Publications Distribution Form

1. Organization/ _____

   Agency Name _____

2. Contact Person _____

3. Address _____

   _____

   _____

4. Telephone _____ Fax _____

5. E-mail Address _____

6. We are willing to help the library accordingly (please check *all* that apply):

   _____ Post flyers

   _____ Hand out flyers

   _____ Deliver flyers door-to-door

   _____ Mail flyers

   _____ Publish news release

   _____ Announce PSAs

   _____ Sorry, unable to help

7. Please send us _____ (number of) copies.

8. _____ Yes _____ No   Please call us before you bring materials over for distribution.

11 RESOURCE DIRECTORY

This chapter includes selected publications, library organizations and committees, and Internet resources that could be helpful when you are developing your Latino library services, programs, and collections. For those of you planning to start your core collection, especially in children's and young adult materials, the section "Resources Listing Recommended Materials for Latinos—Children/Young Adults" should be most helpful.

PUBLICATIONS

GENERAL

Burlingame, Dwight F., ed. *Library Fundraising: Models for Success.* Chicago: American Library Association, 1995.

Cassell, Kay Ann. *Knowing Your Community and Its Needs.* Small Libraries Publications, no. 14. Chicago: American Library Association, 1988.

Cassell, Kay Ann, and Elizabeth Futas. *Developing Public Library Collections, Policies and Procedures.* How-to-Do-It Manuals for Libraries, no. 12. New York: Neal-Schuman Publishers, 1991.

Cuesta, Yolanda. "From Survival to Sophistication: Hispanic Needs=Library Needs." *Library Journal* 115 (May 15, 1990): 22–28.

Cura, Federico. "Latin American Goes On-Line." *Hispanic* (April 1996): 46–49.

Dame, Melvina Azar. *Serving Linguistically and Culturally Diverse Students: Strategies for the School Library Media Specialist.* New York: Neal-Schuman Publishers, 1993.

DuMont, Rosemary Ruhig, and others. *Multiculturalism in Libraries.* Contributions in Librarianship and Information Science, no. 83. Westport, Conn: Greenwood Press, 1994.

Evans, G. Edward. "Needs Analysis and Collection Development Policies for Culturally Diverse Populations." *Collection Building* 11, no. 4 (1992): 16–27.

Garza, Jose P. *Hispanic Library Programs: A Planning Manual.* Chicago: Chicago Public Library, 1989.

Gonzales, Enrique. "Getting Wired: The Explosion of the Internet Translates into Opportunities for Hispanics." *Hispanic* (March, 1996): 24–32.

Granados, Joseph N. *Spanish for Librarians* (cassette and booklet). Oak View, Calif.: Granados School of Languages, 1992.

Kravitz, Rhonda Rios, and others. "Serving the Emerging Majority: Documenting Their Voices." *Library Administration and Management* 5 (Fall 1991): 184–188.

Latrobe, Kathy Howard, and Mildred Knight Laughlin, comps. *Multicultural Aspects of Library Media Programs.* Englewood, Colo.: Libraries Unlimited, 1992.

Line, Maurice. *Library Surveys: An Introduction to Their Use, Planning, Procedure and Presentation.* 2nd ed. Revised by Sue Stone. London: Bingley, 1982.

Lodge, Sally. "Spanish-Language Publishing for Kids in the U.S. Picks Up Speed." *Publishers Weekly* 244 (August 25, 1997 Special Supplement: Books Across the Border): S48–S49.

Metoyer-Duran, Cheryl. *Gatekeepers in Ethnolinguistic Communities.* Norwood, N.J.: Ablex, 1992.

Moran, Barbara B. "Construction of the Questionnaire in Survey Research." *Public Libraries* 24 (Summer 1985): 75–76.

Nauratil, Marcia J. *Public Libaries and Nontraditional Clienteles: The Politics of Special Services.* Westport, Conn.: Greenwood Press, 1985.

Ocón, Ben, and William Archuleta. *Spanish Practice and Review.* Salt Lake City, Utah: Salt Lake City Public Library, 1995.

Parrish, Karen, and Bill Katz, eds. *Multicultural Acquisitions.* New York: Haworth Press, 1993.

Pilger, Mary Anne. *Multicultural Projects Index: Things to Make and Do to Celebrate Festivals, Cultures, and Holidays Around the World.* Englewood, Colo.: Libraries Unlimited, 1991.

Promis, Patricia. *¿Habla Español?: No, But I Can Try to Help You: Practical Spanish for the Reference Desk.* Chicago: Reference and Adult Services Division, American Library Association, 1991.

Rand Corporation. *Public Libraries Face California's Ethnic and Racial Diversity.* Santa Monica, Calif.: Rand Corporation, 1988.

Taylor, Sally. "In Search of the Spanish Market." *Publishers Weekly* 244 (August 25, 1997 Special Supplement: Books Across the Border): S36–S47.

Taylor, Sally. "The Latin Touch." *Publishers Weekly* 244 (August 25, 1997 Special Supplement: Books Across the Border): S4–S34.

Zambrana, Ruth E. *Understanding Latino Families: Scholarship, Policy, and Practice.* Thousand Oaks, Calif.: Sage Publications, 1995.

Zielinska, Marie F., and Francis T. Kirkwood, eds. *Multicultural Librarianship: An International Handbook.* New York: K. G. Saur, 1992.

LIBRARY SERVICES AND COLLECTION DEVELOPMENT FOR LATINOS

Allen, Adela Artola, ed. *Library Services for Hispanic Children: A Guide for Public and School Librarians.* Phoenix, Ariz.: Oryx Press, 1987.

———. "Library Services for Hispanic Young Adults." *Library Trends* 37 (Summer 1988): 80–105.

American Library Association. Reference and Adult Services Division. Committee on Library Services to the Spanish Speaking. *Directory of Resources on Library Services to the Spanish Speaking.* Chicago: American Library Association, 1993.

Ayala, Reynaldo, and Marta Stiefel Ayala. *Report Card on Public Library Services to the Latino Community: Final Report.* Sponsored by REFORMA (National Association to Promote Library Services to the Spanish-Speaking) and funded by a grant from the W. K. Kellogg Foundation. Calexico, Calif.: REFORMA, 1994.

Bielke, Patrica F., and Frank J. Sciara. *Selecting Materials for and About Hispanic and East Asian Children and Young People.* Hamden, Conn.: Library Professional Publications, 1986.

Cuesta, Yolanda, and Patricia Tarín. "Guidelines for Library Service to the Spanish-Speaking." *Library Journal* 103 (July 1978): 1350–1355.

Freiband, Susan J. "Developing Collections for the Spanish Speaking." *RQ* 35 No. 3 (Spring 1996): 330–342.

Hoffert, Barbara. "¡Se Lea Español Aquí!/Spanish Is Read Here." *Library Journal* 117 (July 1992): 34–37.

Josey, E.J., and Marva L. DeLoach. *Ethnic Collections in Libraries.* New York: Neal-Schuman Publishers, 1983.

Scarborough, Katharine. "Collections for the Emerging Majority." *Library Journal* 116 (June 15, 1991): 44–47.

Scarborough, Katharine T. A., ed. *Developing Library Collections for California's Emerging Majority: A Manual of Resources for Ethnic Collection Development.* Berkeley, Calif.: Bay Area Library and Information System, 1990.

Tarín, Patricia A. "Books for the Spanish-Speaking: Sí se Puede." *Library Journal* 112 (July 1987): 25–28.

Zwick, Louise Yarian, and Oralia Garza de Cortes. "Library Programs for Hispanic Children." *Texas Libraries* 50 (Spring 1989): 12–16.

RECENT ENGLISH-LANGUAGE REFERENCE BOOKS ABOUT LATINOS

Annuario Hispano/Hispanic Yearbook. McLean, Va.: T.I.Y.M. Publishing Company, Inc., Annual.

Castillo-Speed, Lillian, ed. *Chicana Studies Index: Twenty Years of Gender Research, 1971–1991.* Berkeley, Calif.: Chicano Studies Library Publications Unit, University of California at Berkeley, 1992.

Chabrán, Richard, and Rafael Chabrán eds. *Latino Encyclopedia*. 6 vols. New York, London, Toronto: Marshall Cavendish, 1996.

Chicano Database (computer file). Berkeley, Calif.: Chicano Studies Library Publications Unit, University of California at Berkeley, 1989–.

Graham, Jose S., comp. *Hispanic-American Material Culture: An Annotated Directory of Collections, Sites, Archives, and Festivals in the United States*. Westport, Conn.: Greenwood Press, 1989.

Hispanic Americans Information Directory. 4th ed. Detroit: Gale Research, forthcoming.

Hispanic Databook of U.S. Cities and Counties. Milpitas, Calif.: Toucan Valley Publications, 1994.

Kanellos, Nicolas, ed. *The Hispanic Almanac: From Columbus to Corporate America*. Detroit: Visible Ink Press, 1994.

———. *Hispanic-American Almanac: A Reference Work on Hispanics in the United States*. Detroit: Gale Research, 1993.

Kanellos, Nicolas, and Claudio Esteva-Fabregat, eds. *Handbook of Hispanic Cultures in the United States*. 4 vols. Houston: Arte Publico Press, 1993–. The four volumes are: History, Anthropology, Sociology, Literature and Art.

Kanellos, Nicolas, and Cristela Perez, eds. *Chronology of Hispanic-American History: From Pre-Columbian Times to the Present*. New York: Gale Research, 1995.

Novas, Himilce. *The Hispanic 100: A Ranking of the Latino Men and Women Who Have Most Influenced American Thought and Culture*. New York: Carol Publishing Group, 1996.

Reddy, Marlita A., ed. *Statistical Record of Hispanic Americans*. Detroit: Gale Research, 1993.

Reyes, Luis, and Peter Rubie. *Hispanics in Hollywood: An Encyclopedia of Film and Television*. New York: Garland, 1994.

Schick, Frank L., and Renee Schick. *Statistical Handbook on U.S. Hispanics*. Phoenix, Ariz.: Oryx Press, 1991.

Schon, Isabel, and Lourdes Gavaldón de Barreto, eds.; translation from the Spanish by Jason Douglas White. *Contemporary Spanish-Speaking Writers and Illustrators for Children and Young Adults: a Biographical Dictionary*. Westport, Conn.: Greenwood Press, 1994.

Schorr, Alan E. *Hispanic Resource Directory, 1992–94: A Comprehensive Guide to Over 6,000 National, State, and Local Organizations, Agencies, Programs and Media Concerned with Hispanic Americans,* Westport, Conn. Juneau, Alaska: Denali Press, 1994.

Tardiff, Joseph C., and L. Mpho Mabunda, eds. *Dictionary of Hispanic Biography*. New York: Gale Research, 1996.

Telgen, Diane, and Jim Kamp, eds. *¡Latinas!: Women of Achievement*. Detroit, New York, and Toronto: Visible Ink, 1996.

Telgen, Diane, and Jim Kamp, eds. *Notable Hispanic American Women*. Detroit, Washington, London: Gale Research, 1993.

RESOURCES LISTING RECOMMENDED MATERIALS FOR LATINOS—GENERAL

Augenbraum, Harold. *Latinos in English: A Selected Bibliography of Latino Fiction Writers of the United States.* New York: Mercantile Library of New York, 1992.

Bibliotecas para la Gente. *Spanish-Language Reference Books: An Annotated Bibliography.* Berkeley, Calif.: University of California, Chicano Studies Publications Unit, 1989. "Bibliotecas para la Gente" means "Libraries for the People."

Clayton, Larry, ed. *The Hispanic Experience in North America: Sources for Study in the U.S.* Columbus, Ohio: Ohio State University, 1992.

Gonzalez, Ray, ed. *After Aztlán: Latino Poets of the Nineties.* Boston: Godine, 1992.

Gutierrez, David G., and Roberto G. Trujillo. *The Chicano Public Catalog: A Collection Guide for Public Libraries.* Berkeley, Calif.: Floricanto Press, 1987.

Josslin, Daniel, comp. "Spanish-Language Books: A Source List." *Library Journal* 113 (April 15, 1988): 48–51.

Kanellos, Nicholas. *Biographical Dictionary of Hispanic Literature in the United States: The Literature of Puerto Ricans, Cuban Americans, and Other Hispanic Writers.* Westport, Conn.: Greenwood Press, 1989.

Katz, Bill, and Linda Sternberg Katz, eds. *Magazines for Libraries.* 9th ed. New Providence, N.J.: R. R. Bowker, 1997. (See the chapter by Joseph R. Diaz, and others, on "Latin America" that focuses on Latin America, Spain, Portugal, and Latinos in the United States.)

Marting, Diane E. Spanish American Women Writers: *A Bio-Bibliographical Source Book.* Westport, Conn.: Greenwood Press, 1990.

Matos, Antonio, ed. *A Guide to Reviews of Books from and about Hispanic America.* Reference Library of the Humanities Series. Ponce, Puerto Rico: AMM Editions, 1989.

Pearson, John C. "Sources of Spanish-Language Materials." *Library Journal* 115 (May 15, 1990): 29–33.

Restrepo, Fabio, ed. *Spanish-Language Books for Public Libraries.* Chicago: American Library Association, 1986.

Ryan, Bryan, ed. *Hispanic Writers: A Selection of Sketches from Contemporary Authors.* Detroit: Gale Research, 1991.

RESOURCES LISTING RECOMMENDED MATERIALS FOR LATINOS—CHILDREN/YOUNG ADULTS

Duran, Daniel. *Latino Materials: A Multimedia Guide for Children and Young Adults.* New York: Neal-Schuman Publishers, 1979.

Hayden, Carla D., ed. *Venture into Cultures: A Resource Book of Multicultural Materials and Programs.* Chicago: American Library Association, 1992.

Helbig, Alethea K., and Agnes Regan Perkins. *This Land Is Our Land: A Guide to Multicultural Literature for Children and Young Adults.* Westport, Conn.: Greenwood Press, 1994.

Johnson, Lauri, and Sally Smith. *Dealing with Diversity Through Multicultural Fiction: Library-Classroom Partnerships.* Chicago: American Library Association, 1993.

Kruse, Ginny Moore, and Kathleen T. Horning. *Multicultural Children's and Young Adult Literature: A Selected Listing from CCBC Choices.* 3rd edition. Madison, Wis.: Cooperative Children's Book Center, University of Wisconsin-Madison, 1988.

Libros en Español para los Pequeños. New York: New York Public Library, 1990.

Miller-Lachmann, Lyn. *Our Family, Our Friends, Our World: An Annotated Guide to Significant Multicultural Books for Children and Teenagers.* New Providence, N.J.: R. R. Bowker, 1992.

Rochman, Hazel. *Against Borders: Promoting Books for a Multicultural World.* Chicago: American Library Association, 1993.

Schon, Isabel. *Basic Collection of Children's Books in Spanish.* Metuchen, N.J.: Scarecrow Press, 1986.

———. *The Best of the Latino Heritage: A Guide to the Best Juvenile Books about Latino People and Cultures.* Lanham, MD and London: Scarecrow Press, 1997.

———. *A Bicultural Heritage: Themes for the Exploration of Mexican and Mexican-American Culture in Books for Children and Adolescents.* Metuchen, N.J.: Scarecrow Press, 1978.

———. *Books in Spanish for Children and Young Adults: An Annotated Guide.* Series I (1978), Series II (1983), Series III (1985), Series IV (1987), Series V (1989). Metuchen, N.J.: Scarecrow Press.

———. "Books in Spanish Published in the U.S." *Booklist* 92 (January 1, and January 15, 1996): 852–854.

———. *A Hispanic Heritage: A Guide to Juvenile Books About Hispanic People and Cultures.* Series II. Metuchen, N.J.: Scarecrow Press, 1985.

———. *A Hispanic Heritage: A Guide to Juvenile Books About Hispanic People and Cultures.* Series III. Metuchen, N.J.: Scarecrow Press, 1988.

———. *A Latino Heritage: A Guide to Juvenile Books About Latino People and Cultures.* Metuchen, N.J.: Scarecrow Press, 1995.

(Isabel Schon is a regularly featured book review columnist for *Booklist.* She is also a frequent book review contributor to *Multicultural Review, Science and Children, Journal of Youth Services in Libraries,* and *Horn Book Magazine.*)

Schon, Isabel, ed. *Contemporary Spanish-Speaking Writers and Illustrators for Children and Young Adults: A Biographical Dictionary.* With the collaboration of Lourdes Gavaldón de Barreto; translation from the Spanish by Jason Douglas White. Westport, Conn.: Greenwood Press, 1994.

Zwick, Louise Yarian. "Cuentos y Canciones Infantiles: Recordings in Spanish for Children." *School Library Journal* 35 (February 1989): 23–26.

LIBRARY ORGANIZATIONS AND COMMITTEES

REFORMA

REFORMA (National Association to Promote Library Services to the Spanish-Speaking) was founded in 1971. This affiliate of the American Library Association is committed to the improvement of the full spectrum of library and information services for Latinos. The association encourages membership from both individuals and institutions. There are 16 REFORMA chapters in cities across the country. REFORMA publishes a quarterly newsletter, *REFORMA Newsletter*; sponsors REFORMANET, an electronic discussion group; and has a home page (see Internet Resources below).

Contact: Since there is a change in REFORMA's presidency each year, contact the American Library Association's Office for Literacy and Outreach Services to get the names and addresses of the current REFORMA leadership.

REFORMA
c/o American Library Association
Office for Literacy and Outreach Services
50 E Huron St
Chicago, IL 60611
(800) 545–2433, ext. 4223

AMERICAN LIBRARY ASSOCIATION (ALA)

Association for Library Service to Children, Committee on Selection of Children's Books and Materials from Various Cultures

This committee encourages libraries and librarians to meet the variety of language and cultural needs of children.

Contact:
ALSC Committee on Selection of Children's Books and Materials from Various Cultures

c/o American Library Association
50 E Huron St
Chicago, IL 60611
(800) 545–2433, ext. 2163

Association for Library Service to Children/REFORMA, Pura Belpré Award Selection Committee

This joint ALSC/REFORMA committee annually honors and recognizes a Latino writer and illustrator whose work best portrays, affirms and celebrates the Latino cultural experience in an outstanding work of literature for children and youth.

Contact:
ALSC-REFORMA, Pura Belpré Award Selection Committee
c/o American Library Association
50 E Huron St
Chicago, IL 60611
(800) 545–2433, ext. 2163

Council Committee on Minority Concerns and Cultural Diversity

This ALA Council committee is responsible for promoting and advancing ethnic and cultural diversity within ALA as well as addressing concerns of ALA's minority membership.

Contact:
Council Committee on Minority and Cultural Diversity
ALA Office for Literacy and Outreach Services (OLOS)
50 E Huron St
Chicago, IL 60611
(800) 545–2433, ext. 4294

Ethnic Materials and Information Exchange Round Table (EMIERT)

This ALA round table serves as a source of information on ethnic collections, programs, and services. It develops and offers programs that deal with the many aspects of ethnicity and librarianship at the ALA annual conference. It has recently instituted an electronic discussion group (see Internet Resources below).

Contact:
Ethnic Materials and Information Exchange Round Table
c/o American Library Association
50 E Huron St
Chicago, IL 60611
(800) 545–2433, ext. 4294

Fundraising Resource Center (ALA)

Contact:

American Library Association
50 E Huron St
Chicago, IL 60611
(800) 545–2433, ext. 5050

Library Administration and Management Association (LAMA), Cultural Diversity Committee

This committee promotes increased membership and participation in LAMA, recommends efforts LAMA should make to lead libraries in improving services to culturally diverse populations, and in general works to foster the development of a culturally diverse workforce in libraries.

Contact:

LAMA, Cultural Diversity Committee
c/o American Library Association
50 E Huron St
Chicago, IL 60611
(800) 545–2433, ext. 5038

Office for Literacy and Outreach Services (OLOS)

This ALA committee issues reports and promotes activities that improve library services to the poor and to ethnic minority groups.

Contact:

ALA, Office for Literacy and Outreach Services
50 E Huron St
Chicago, IL 60611
(800) 545–2433, ext. 4294

Reference and User Services Association, Management and Operation of Public Services Section, Library Services to the Spanish-Speaking Committee

This RUSA committee works to improve library services for Latinos at both the local and national levels.

Contact:

RUSA Library Services to the Spanish-Speaking Committee
c/o American Library Association
50 E Huron St
Chicago, IL 60611
(800) 545–2433, ext. 4398

Young Adult Library Services Association, Outreach Committee

This YALSA committee addresses the needs of young adults who face barriers of access to libraries because of economic, social, cultural, or legal reasons.

Contact:

YALSA Outreach Committee
c/o American Library Association
50 E Huron St
Chicago, IL 60611
(800) 545–2433, ext. 4390

CENTER FOR THE STUDY OF BOOKS IN SPANISH FOR CHILDREN AND ADOLESCENTS

The center is a resource center of books in Spanish and in English about Latinos, for children and young adults. The center's director, Isabel Schon, is a leading authority on the subject, with many books, articles, and book reviews to her credit. The center publishes bibliographies and proceedings of its annual conferences. It also offers workshops each summer, and has a home page (see Internet Resources below).

Contact:

Isabel Schon, Director
Center for the Study of Books in Spanish for Children and Adolescents
California State University, San Marcos
San Marcos, CA 92096–0001
(619) 750–4070

GUADALAJARA INTERNATIONAL BOOK FAIR/FERIA INTERNACIONAL DEL LIBRO (FIL)

This annual book fair in Guadalajara, Jalisco, Mexico (usually held in late November and early December) brings together over 9,000 professionals and representatives from over 900 Spanish-language publishing houses, distributors and booksellers from all over the world. The American Library Association organizes a delegation of American librarians to attend FIL and provides significant financial support.

Contact:

David Unger, U.S. Coordinator
FIL/New York
Division of Humanities NAC6293
City College of New York
New York, NY 10031
(212) 650-7925

SEMINAR ON THE ACQUISITION OF LATIN AMERICAN LIBRARY MATERIALS (SALALM)

SALALM is an international organization concerned with the control and dissemination of bibliographic information about Latin American publications, the development of library collections of Latin Americana to support educational research, and the development of library materials for the Spanish- and Portuguese-speaking populations of the United States.

Contact:

Laura Gutiérrez, Executive Secretary
SALALM Secretariat
Benson Latin American Collection
Sid Richardson Hall 1.109
University of Texas
Austin, TX 78713

INTERNET RESOURCES

There are so many resources on the Internet pertaining to Latinos that it is impossible to list all of them. Following is a selected list of the most useful electronic discussion groups, World Wide Web home pages of organizations, and World Wide Web link sites that are of particular interest to Latinos, and to those developing Latino library services.

ELECTRONIC DISCUSSION GROUPS

REFORMANET

REFORMANET is an electronic discussion group sponsored by REFORMA (National Association to Promote Library Services to the Spanish-Speaking). It is open to anyone (one does not have to be a REFORMA member to join or to contribute) with an interest in promoting Latino library services.

To subscribe to REFORMANET:
Address: listproc@lmrinet.gse.ucsb.edu
Subject: leave blank
Message: subscribe reformanet firstname lastname

EQUILIBR

EQUILIBR is an electronic discussion group open to anyone with an interest in diversity in libraries.

To subscribe to EQUILIBR:
Address: listserv@cmsa.berkeley.edu

Subject: leave blank
Message: subscribe equilibr firstname lastname

EMIE-L

EMIE-L is an electronic discussion group sponsored by the Ethnic Materials and Information Exchange Round Table of the American Library Association. EMIE-L is a forum for the exchange of information related to multicultural information services.

To subscribe to EMIE-L:
Address: requests@lists.gseis.ucla.edu
Subject: subscribe emie-l
Message: leave this field blank

WORLD WIDE WEB HOME PAGES

REFORMA (National Association to Promote Library Services to the Spanish-Speaking)

REFORMA's home page is devoted to the general topic of developing library services to Latinos. Here you can find information on the organization, its mission, and selected resources. The home page is in English.

Home page address:
http://latino.sscnet.ucla.edu/library/reforma/index.htm

Center for the Study of Books in Spanish for Children and Adolescents

The center's home page is bilingual. There is a variety of information on the center, its publications, and its conferences and workshops. The center has plans to provide a database of recommended books in Spanish at this Web site.

Home page address:
http://www.csusm.edu/campus_centers/csb

WORLD WIDE WEB LATINO LINK SITES

CLNet

CLNet is a joint project of the Chicano Studies Research Center at the University of California, Los Angeles, and the Linguistic Minority Research Institute at the University of California, Santa Barbara. It has an impressive list of links to Web sites that serve all segments of the Latino community, not just Chicanos.

Home page address:
http://latino.sscnet.ucla.edu

Felipe's Things Latino Page

Hundreds of links to webzines, newspapers, journals, usenet groups, and organizations.
Home page address:
http://edb518ea.edb.utexas.edu/latinos.html

Hispanic Pages in the USA

An extensive list of links to a wide variety of home pages in the United States.
Home page address:
http://coloquio.com/index.html

LatinoLink

LatinoLink collects articles from a wide variety of English-language sources on a wide variety of topics including current news, business, travel, art, music, and politics. Good coverage of both domestic and foreign sources.
Home page address:
http://www.latinolink.com

LatinoWeb

LatinoWeb's mission "is to empower the Latino by providing a gateway on the Internet where private, non-profit and public sectors can exchange information." It has numerous links to Latino agencies.
Home page address:
http://www.latinoweb.com

MUNDO LATINO

MUNDO LATINO links hundreds of Spanish-language Web sources from many Spanish-speaking countries.
Home page address:
http://www.mundolatino.org

MundoNet

MundoNet, Inc.'s aim is to provide the most comprehensive directory of Latino sources on the Internet. This site is bilingual.
Home page address:
http://www.mundonet.com

BIBLIOGRAPHY

Allen, Adela Artola. *Library Services for Hispanic Children: A Guide for Public and School Librarians.* Phoenix, Ariz.: Oryx Press, 1987.

Allen, Adela Artola. "Library Services for Hispanic Young Adults." *Library Trends* 37 (Summer 1988): 80–105.

California Department of Education. *Recommended Readings in Spanish Literature: Kindergarten through Grade Eight.* Sacramento, Calif.: California Department of Education, 1991.

California State Library. *Helping California Libraries Respond to Change.* A brochure prepared by the California State Library. Sacramento, Calif.: California State Library, n.d.

Constantino, Rebecca. "It's Like a Lot of Things in America: Linguistic Minority Parents Use of Libraries." *School Library Media Quarterly* 22 (Winter 1994): 87–89.

Güereña, Salvador. "Community Analysis and Needs Assessment." In *Latino Librarianship: A Handbook for Professionals.* Jefferson, N.C.: McFarland & Company, 1990.

Haro, Robert. *Developing Library and Information Services for Americans of Hispanic Origin.* Metuchen, N.J.: Scarecrow Press, 1981.

Herrera, Luis, and Albert J. Milo. "Managing Administrative Change for Ethnic Collection Development." In *Developing Library Collections for California's Emerging Majority: A Manual of Resources for Ethnic Collection Development,* edited by Katherine T.A. Scarborough. Berkeley, Calif.: Bay Area Library and Information System, 1990.

Hispanic Services Committee. *Hispanic Services: A Practical Manual for the Public Librarian.* Chicago: Chicago Public Library, 1990.

Kirsch, Irwin, and others. *Adult Literacy in America: A First Look at the Results of the National Adult Literacy Survey.* A special study commissioned at the request of the National Center for Education Statistics. Washington, D.C.: U.S. Government Printing Office, 1993.

Minudri, Regina (panelist). "Managing Diversity: Library Directors Speak Out." Annual Conference of the California Library Association, Oakland, Calif., Nov. 14, 1993.

National Commission on Library and Information Services. *Report of the Task Force on Library and Information Services to Cultural Minorities.* Washington, D.C.: U.S. Government Printing Office, 1983.

Perez-Peña, Richard. "Big Cities Win Appeals Ruling on '90 Census." *New York Times,* 9 August 1994, sec. A1.

Peterson, Ray E. *Recruitment and Retention of Minority Personnel and Trustees in Public Libraries.* Denver, Colo.: Colorado Department of Education, Office of State Library and Adult Education, 1996.

Pisano, Vivian H., and Margaret Skidmore. "Community Survey—Why Not Take an Eclectic Approach?" *Wilson Library Bulletin* 53 (November 1978): 250–253.

Rodriquez, Jill, and Maria Tejeda. "Serving Hispanics Through Family Literacy: One Family at a Time." *Illinois Libraries* 77 (Fall 1996): 331–335.

Salazar, Ramiro. "The Bottom Line: Saving Youth Means Saving Our Future." In *Library Services for Children and Youth: Dollars and Sense*. New York: Neal-Schuman Publishers, 1994.

Stavans, Ilan. *The Hispanic Condition: Reflections of Culture and Identity in America*. New York: Harper Collins, 1995.

Talbot, Christine. "What Is a Multicultural Library Service?" *Library Association Record* 92 (July 1990): 501–503.

U.S. Bureau of the Census. Census *of Population: General Population Characteristics, 1990*. Series CP-1. Prepared by the Economics and Statistics Administration, Department of Commerce. Washington, D.C.: U.S. Government Printing Office, 1992.

U.S. Bureau of the Census. *Census of Population: Persons of Hispanic Origin in the United States*. Prepared by the Economics and Statistics Administration, Department of Commerce. Washington, D.C.: U.S. Government Printing Office, 1993.

U.S. Bureau of the Census. *Census of Population: Social and Economic Characteristics, 1990*. Series CP-2. Prepared by the Economics and Statistics Administration, Department of Commerce. Washington, D.C.: U.S. Government Printing Office, 1993.

U.S. Bureau of the Census. *County and City Data Book 1994: A Statistical Abstract Supplement*. 12th edition. Prepared by the Economics and Statistics Administration, Department of Commerce. Washington, D.C.: U.S. Government Printing Office, 1994.

U.S. Bureau of the Census. *Current Population Reports: Population Projections of the United States by Age, Sex, Race, and Hispanic Origin: 1995 to 2050*. Prepared by the Economics and Statistics Administration, Department of Commerce. Washington, D.C.: U.S. Government Printing Office, 1996.

U.S. Bureau of the Census. *We, the American Hispanics*. Prepared by Ethnic and Hispanic Statistics Branch, Population Division, Bureau of the Census. Washington, D.C.: U.S. Government Printing Office, 1993.

Zwick, Louise Y. "Cuentos y Canciones Infantiles: Recordings in Spanish for Children." *School Library Journal* 35 (February 1989): 23–26.

Zwick, Louise Y., and Oralia Garza de Cortes. "Library Programs for Hispanic Children." *Texas Libraries* 50 (Spring 1989): 12–15.

INDEX

ABOUT THE AUTHORS

Camila A. Alire is the dean of libraries at Colorado State University, Fort Collins, Colorado. She has lectured with the co-author on library services to Latinos throughout the country. She is past-president of national REFORMA (National Association to Promote Library Services to the Spanish-Speaking), an affiliate of the American Library Association.

Orlando Archibeque is the social science bibliographer at the Auraria Library, University of Colorado at Denver. Previously, he worked as local documents librarian at the Pikes Peak (Colorado Springs, CO) Library District and as business/economics librarian at the University of Colorado at Colorado Springs. He has lectured with the co-author on providing library services to Latinos. He is past-president of the Colorado Chapter of REFORMA.